Never Fall for Your Back-Up Guy

A romantic comedy

It's Complicated
Book 1

Kate O'Keeffe

Wild Lime Books

Wild Lime
Books

For my dad, who I miss every day.

About This Book

Three things I've learned this week:
  1) Never fall for a client
  2) Never fall for your best friend
  3) And most importantly, never fall for your back-up guy
  ...especially if they're all the same person.

  I'm the queen of dating disasters—I've had more rotten dates than you can shake a long stemmed rose at. After years of one disappointment after another, I'm beginning to feel like I'll never say "I do."

  So after being dumped one too many times I do something stupid:

  I make a pact with my best friend Asher. If neither of us are married by 35, we tie the knot. That's five full years of searching for The One.

  I've got to meet Mr. Right by then, don't I?

  But when I take a job redecorating Asher's bachelor pad, I realise he's a lot different from the guy I thought he was. Against all odds, I find myself falling for my best friend. Maybe my back-up guy could be The One after all?

Except there's only one problem...
My back-up guy has a secret that could ruin everything.

Also by Kate O'Keeffe

It's Complicated Series:
Never Fall for Your Back-Up Guy
Never Fall for Your Enemy
Never Fall for Your Fake Fiancé
Never Fall for Your One that Got Away

Love Manor Romantic Comedy Series:
Dating Mr. Darcy
Marrying Mr. Darcy
Falling for Another Darcy
Falling for Mr. Bingley (spin-off novella)

High Tea Series:
No More Bad Dates
No More Terrible Dates
No More Horrible Dates

Cozy Cottage Café Series:
One Last First Date
Two Last First Dates
Three Last First Dates
Four Last First Dates

Wellywood Romantic Comedy Series:

Styling Wellywood

Miss Perfect Meets Her Match

Falling for Grace

Standalone title:

One Way Ticket

Writing as Lacey Sinclair:

Manhattan Cinderella

The Right Guy

Prologue

"It's not you, it's me."

My full glass is raised mid-way to my lips, and I blink in disbelief across the sticky wooden Soho pub table at Zack, the guy I've been seeing for almost two months (well, six weeks and five days, but let's not get pedantic here). "What did you say?" I squeak, my voice piercing the hum of chatter and music—some 80s ballad about never giving up on love we'd been laughing about only moments ago.

It feels a touch ironic now.

Zack runs his fingers through his mop of sandy blonde hair, his lips pulled into a thin line. "You see the thing is, Zara, you're at this place in your life that is really great and everything, and I think you're great. Totally great."

So far so...*great*.

"It's just I'm not in that place. Even though one day I'm sure I will be. But not now. Or any time soon, really. I'm in a different place altogether. You know?"

Uh, no?

"What are you talking about exactly? You lost me

1

several places ago." I smile, making light of the conversation, despite being pretty sure what's about to come next.

"Okay. I'll get it straight for you. You're here," he cups his hands as they hover over the table, "And I'm over here." He moves his hands to the opposite side. "See all this space in between us? That's the gulf between our respective places, and neither of us can cross that gulf because, well, there are man-eating crocodiles between us. Got it?"

"Man-eating crocodiles?" I arch my brows. "So, I should be fine, what with not being a man and all."

"Ha! You're funny. I forgot about that."

I refocus the conversation. "You know when you said, 'it's not you, it's me,' it sounded a lot like you were breaking up with me." I let out a high-pitched laugh to show him exactly how ridiculous the notion is that we're breaking up. We're Zara and Zack. Zack and Zara. We're not breaking up. When we first got together, I loved the way our names sounded like we were a pop duo from the 70s. And I thought we had something.

Zack, it would seem, doesn't agree.

His face doesn't crack. "I definitely want you in my life." His brows are pulled together in concern as he reaches for my hand.

I let out a relieved—and frankly surprised—puff of air. "Good to know. You really had me going there for a bit."

"It's just—"

Right. He hasn't finished.

"—you're in this place over here where you want like, *commitment*, and I'm in this place over here—" He begins gesturing about his dang places once more.

I burst out with an irritated, "Enough with the places!"

People at the neighbouring tables tilt their heads in our direction. I ignore them. Instead, I force myself to calm down before I shoot him a tense smile. "I'm not sure that visual works for me."

"Really? Because it works for me."

Clearly.

I lay my hands on the sticky table, think better of it, lift them back up, and say, "Are you breaking up with me?"

He scrunches up his nose and replies, "In a manner of speaking...yeah."

Hope shrivels up inside of me. "I see."

"But I still want you in my life, you know, as more than a friend. Like, a hot friend. You know?"

"A hot friend?"

What did I ever see in this guy?

"Just because we're not together doesn't mean we can't...you know. Whenever we want to."

My eyebrows ping up to meet my hairline. "Are you seriously telling me you're breaking up with me and you want me to be your booty call?"

"Would that be so bad?" he questions.

I rise to my feet suddenly, surprising even myself. My chair falls crashing to the ground, and I know half the pub is now gawking at me. "Yes, Zack, it would be bad. Very, very bad."

He shrugs. "Your call, Zara, but you know it makes sense."

I grab my handbag from the back of the fallen chair, and am forced to wrestle with it when it tangles up. Heat bursts across my cheeks. "No, it doesn't make sense," I reply, trying to reclaim some control in the situation, even though I have less than none. "No sense at all. You can stay in your 'place,' and I'll happily stay in mine. I just hope the man-eating crocodiles don't work out they can crawl over to you."

"Don't be like that. You haven't even finished your

drink."

I eye the untouched glass of wine on the table. My hand twitches. It would be so easy to pick it up and throw it in his face like a *Real Housewife* right now. I resist the urge. I may have been dumped, but I still have my dignity.

So instead, I say, "See you later," without meaning to see him ever again, then turn on my heel and storm out of the pub, my cheeks aflame with humiliation. Once outside, I take a gulping breath of the cool evening air.

How could he do this to me? Didn't we have something? We were Zara and Zack. We were *good* together.

Weren't we?

I storm down the busy street toward the Tube stop with anger, humiliation, and regret duking it out for pole position in my head.

Anger wins, but only by a fraction.

As I round the corner, I begin to slow my pace.

If I'm totally honest with myself, Zack wasn't that great a boyfriend. Not really. He was pretty self-absorbed and we didn't have a whole lot in common. I mean, I tried to like his taste in music, but listening to someone screech at the top of their lungs into a mic about how they feel about pirates—seriously, it's a thing—just isn't my scene, no matter how long he spent trying to convince me.

I reach the Tube stop, flash my Oyster card as I sail through the turnstiles, and step onto the downward escalator.

Normally, I wouldn't take a breakup with a guy I've known a couple of months quite so hard. I mean, it's not like we'd been dating for years and talked about having a future together or anything. In fact, up until this time last year I approached life with an attitude that screamed *live in the moment*. I was all about doing what I wanted and having fun with it. Getting serious with a guy—especially one into pirate rock—wasn't even a passing thought.

And then something happened.

I got old.

Okay, not *old* old. I'm not ninety-five or anything. I turned twenty-nine, that joke age, the last year of being officially young. People told me it could happen, I could change. And I did.

I got serious.

I grew up.

I know, right? Me, carefree, happy, confident Zara Huntington-Ross. Fun loving, never thinking about tomorrow. Just living my life one enjoyment-filled day at a time.

And then suddenly, I began to focus on things like my interior design career and went into partnership with my friend Scarlett, the most driven person I know. Going to parties with my besties, Tabitha, Lottie, Kennedy, and Asher, became less important. Heck, I even stayed in some Saturday nights, choosing instead to go to my childhood home and hang out with the family. Me, voted *most likely to have a good time* in high school—okay only by my friends. But still.

And dating? Dating became less of a sport and more of a search for The One.

Which led me to Zack and his pirate music.

I arrive on the platform and a train swooshes into the station. Stepping on board, I find a seat and plonk myself down heavily in it. A guy in a kilt, who looks like a poor imitation of Jamie from *Outlander,* checks me out across the aisle. I shoot him a *thanks but no thanks* smile, and stare out the window at the blackness as the train whizzes through underground tunnels.

Now, at almost thirty, it feels like my time is running

out. I'm not a kid anymore. If I want it all—career, husband, tribe of kids, a couple of dogs and a chicken coop out the back—I need to meet someone. The problem is, I keep meeting jerks like Zack who aren't in the same "place" as me, guys who have the luxury of not having a biological clock ticking like a bongo drum in their head.

As I sit, I do what I always do when I need someone to talk to. I pull out my phone and start to tap out an email. I need to think this through, I need to find a solution.

I need my dad.

Dear Dad, I begin.

You know how I dated a bunch of guys you didn't approve of? Remember you always said they were only up for a laugh, not the kind of guys you wanted to see your daughter with? Well, I hate to say it, but you were right.

But don't go gloating or anything.

For the first time in my life, I want something more than they can offer me. I want to meet a man who will sweep me off my feet, like you did with Mum.

How do I find the right guy?

How do I find a man like you?

I could really do with your help.

Miss you. Love you.

Your Za-Za xoxo

I stare at the screen for a moment before I hit send, then I lean against the back of the vinyl seat. The wannabe *Outlander* Jamie shoots me another look, so I close my eyes and work on the basis that if I can't see him, he can't see me.

Mature, I know.

Searching for The One is *hard*. Like really, really hard.

If only there was a way to know that if I fail in my attempt to find love, I could still get what I want. I'm talking the marriage, the kids, the dogs and chickens. Definitely the dogs and chickens.

What I need is a safety net, someone to fall back on in case my quest to find The One fails.

And then it hits me like a punch to the solar plexus. I need a back-up guy. Yes! That's what I need. I need a guy I can rely on to be there for me when all else fails. I need someone to catch me if I fall, someone I like, someone I know, someone who I could imagine having all the stuff I want with, even when there's no romantic love.

The train comes to a screeching, lurching halt, and I glance out the window. Fulham Broadway. My stop.

I step off the train and join the line of people making their way up to the footpath, lost in thought. Up on the street, I pass by a restaurant I see every day and the delicious aroma of garlic naan bread and Indian spices hits my nostrils. My belly rumbles in the hopes of being fed. With my date with Zack cut short, I'd totally skipped dinner.

I look up at the sign and read the name, Bollywood Star. I make a snap decision. A chicken tikka masala and garlic naan bread will definitely go some way to healing my heart. Or at least filling my stomach.

As I head towards the entryway, I glance in the window and do a double take. Asher McMillan, one of my closest friends, is sitting at a table. At over six feet tall with creamy olive skin, a square jaw, and thick dark hair, he's hard to miss. My sister-in-law, Emma, always says he looks like Taylor Lautner in *Twilight*, only with his shirt on. And she's right (about his looks *and* his shirt). His five o'clock shadow accentuates his jawline, and his deep brown eyes are always full of mischief. Right now, they're trained on his date, a cheerleader type with bouncy blonde hair and eyelashes so thick and long they must be giving her eyelids a decent workout with each and every flutter.

And she sure is fluttering them at him right now.

But my mind's on other things.

Asher is the perfect back-up guy for me. Not only is he one of my BFFs and a whole heap of fun to be around, he's not looking for anything serious right now—although he wants to settle down at some stage in the future. I know, because he's told me himself. But for now, he's playing the field, enjoying being a young, hot American guy in London and all that it brings.

What's more, he's a great guy. He gets me. He'll know it's just a safety net thing, nothing serious. He'll know I'm looking for The One.

I lift my hand to wave and as his gaze locks with mine, his eyebrows shoot up before his handsome face morphs into a grin. I make a gesture that tells him I'm coming in to crash his date, then enter the restaurant and make my way through the tables to where he's sitting.

He stands to greet me with a quick hug and a broad grin on his face. "I told you to stop stalking me, Zee. Seriously, this is getting weird."

My giggle ends in a snort. "As if I'd ever bother to stalk *you*."

"Well, you're meant to be on your own date with Zeke or Zane or whatever his name is right now, and yet here you are crashing mine."

"It's Zack, and we broke up."

"Should I be sad about that?"

I press my lips together and shake my head.

"Good, because I hated the guy."

"No, you didn't."

"Uh, yeah, I did. He was an idiot."

"Ash, you only met him that one time."

"And he spent the entire time looking at himself in the mirror."

I cast my mind back to when I introduced Zack to my friends. It was at my local pub where the walls are lined with mirrors. "He thought he had something caught in his beard," I protest.

"The whole night?" Asher questions.

"Ahem."

In sync, we both turn to look at Asher's date, who is gazing up at us from her seat at the table with a look of annoyance on her pretty face.

"Hi there. Remember me?" she says sweetly—with an edge.

"Sorry," Asher replies. "This is my friend, Zara. Zara this is—" He pauses mid-sentence, and I know he's searching for the poor girl's name. After too long he lands on, "Caroline," and lets out a relieved puff of air. "Zara, this is Caroline, my date for the evening."

Her features pinched, she cocks an eyebrow in his direction. "It's Caro*lyn*, not Caro*line*."

"Gosh, I'm so sorry. It must be my accent. American."

Her features soften as her lips spread into a smile. "That's okay. Your accent is so cute."

He dazzles her with his smile and inside I roll my eyes. Okay, I roll them on the outside, too, because this is so typically Asher. He's handsome and charming enough to get away with forgetting his date's name. Whereas I remember every last detail about my date and *still* get dumped.

The world is not a fair place.

"Aw, thanks," Asher replies, and they share a look that

makes me want to vomit.

"Carolyn, would you mind if I borrowed Asher for a sec? I just need to ask him a quick question and then he's all yours. I promise."

Her eyes dart between Asher and me, clearly deciding whether to let us go. In the end she must decide I'm no threat. She nods and says, "Yeah, but don't hog him for too long."

"I won't." I tug on Asher's arm and lead him over towards the exit.

"Are you making me abandon my date?" he asks as I push through the door to the street. "Because it was going pretty well."

Out on the footpath, I turn to face him. "If only you could remember her name. I'm sure you've never pronounced Carol*lyn* as Caro*line* in your life."

He shrugs. "I thought I did well to get her name in the ballpark." He lets out a light laugh before he says, "As much as I love to be dragged out of restaurants by beautiful women, can you tell me what this is all about? I am meant to be on a date with a very attractive woman whose name may or may not be Caroline."

I cut right to the chase. There's no need to beat about the bush with this. "Asher, I need you to be my back-up guy."

His eyes widen into dinner plates. "I'm sorry, your what now?"

"My back-up guy. You know, if neither of us are married by a certain age, we'll get married."

He erupts into laughter, showing his perfect rows of pearly whites as he throws his head back. "Zara, are you drunk?" he questions.

I cross my arms. This is not the reaction I was hoping

for. "No."

"Are you high?"

"No!"

"What's going on with you then? I mean, it's not every day a girl drags you away from your date and proposes marriage."

I let out an exasperated breath. "I'm not proposing marriage."

"Kinda sounds like it to me."

"All I'm saying is that we should be each other's back-up person. That way, if neither of us find The One, we can still have kids and marriage and all that stuff."

"Wow, Zara, I had no idea you felt this way about me."

I bat him on the arm. "Could you drop the jokes for one second please and listen to me?"

"Okay. Fire away, girl who wants to marry me." He pulls his lips into a line so as to stifle his smile. It doesn't work.

I shoot him a pointed look. "Just so we're clear, I'm not proposing. You would be a back-up, nothing more. If I can't find the love of my life, we'll get married as an absolute last resort."

"You sure know how to sweet talk a guy."

"You see that's the thing. I don't need to sweet talk you because I only want you as a kind of safety net. I'm not in love with you, I don't want to shag you, or marry you, or have your babies."

He makes a knife through the heart gesture. "Ouch. That hurts."

"You're not in love with me and you don't want to shag me, either, so let's not go getting all dramatic here. Let me tell you what I want."

"What you really, really want?" he teases, quoting my

11

favourite 90s girl band, the Spice Girls.

I ignore his joke as I begin to pace up and down the footpath, excitement mounting over the genius of my plan. "You see, I want to fall in love with someone. *Deeply* in love. I want the kind of love I've never had, the kind that sweeps you off your feet. The kind of love that eats up everything in your head and your heart."

"You want your Big Love."

"Yes! The problem is, I've been looking for a year now and I've not found it."

"A year isn't that long."

"I know, but it's my birthday next week and —"

"And you're freaking out," he finishes for me, and I give a reluctant nod. "Thirty ain't so bad, Zara. Believe me, it's not. I think you'll survive it, just like I did. With or without me as your back-up guy."

"It's different for a woman, Asher. We've got these biological clocks ticking away that get louder and louder every day."

"Can't you invest in some earplugs?"

My laugh is full of exasperation. What I love about Asher—his fun nature, his ability to make light of things—is making this so much harder than I thought it would be right now. "Can you please be serious for just a minute?"

His smile drops. "Sure. Go ahead."

"I'd give it, I don't know, five years? Yeah, that feels right. By then I'll be turning thirty-five and that's plenty of time to find the man of my dreams, and still be able to have a bunch of kids and dogs and chickens before it's too late."

He arches his brows. "Chickens? In *Fulham*?"

"I'll move to the country," I reply with a wave of my hand. "So, what do you say?" I regard him through hopeful eyes. He's *got* to say yes.

"That's five years and one week."

"Yup."

"And you'll actively search for your Big Love."

"Yup."

"And we both date whomever we want between now and then."

"That's right."

He studies my face for a beat as I hold my breath, then extends his hand. "Deal."

Happiness bubbles up and bursts out of me as I fling my arms around his neck and pepper his cheeks with kisses. "Thank you, thank you, thank you!"

He laughs as he darts a look through the window at his date and then peels my hands from around his neck. "Maybe a little less with the public displays until we're married. Okay, wifey?"

I let out an excited giggle. "You won't have to marry me, you know."

His lips stretch into a smile. "A guy can only hope."

I give him another quick hug before I say goodbye and throw a contented smile through the window at Carolyn. As he returns to his table, I purchase my takeaways, and then trip on light feet down the street to my flat.

Lying on my bed in my PJs an hour later, I tap out another email before I switch the light off and fall asleep.

Dear Dad,

Ignore my last email. I've got a fix. I've got my safety net. And soon, I just know I'll have my Big Love.

Miss you. Love you.

Your Za-Za xoxo

Chapter One

"We're losing. Badly. You need to pull out the big guns, birthday girl." Asher brandishes his pool cue at me, a smile teasing the edges of his mouth.

I take a sip of my drink, push my long dark hair behind my ears, and shoot Asher my best smile. "I'm on it. Keep your hair on."

He knits his brows together as he pats the thick thatch of dark hair on top of his head. "Keep my hair on? I think you'll find it's pretty well attached to my head."

"It's an expression, Ash. Quite common here in England." I shoot him a look as I collect the pool cue from his hands and examine the table to find the best angle to take my shot. "And anyway, you're thirty years old. The days may be numbered for those luxurious locks of yours."

"Never. Gonna. Happen. There's no way I'm losing my hair."

I throw him an appraising look. Even if he did lose his hair, he'd still be a major heartbreaker. "I can so see you as a slap head."

"A slap head?" he guffaws. "Not cool, wifey. Not cool."

We've been calling each other "wifey" and "hubby" ever since we became one another's back-up person a week ago. It's harmless banter because we both know we're never going to actually go through with it.

"My dad is in his late fifties and he has a super thick head of hair," he continues, obviously still hung up on my comment. "So did his dad, and his before him. Really, we've got a long line of thick, manly hair in the McMillan family."

My lips lift into a smile. "Is that so?"

"Oh, yeah." He runs his fingers through his hair, which is, I'll admit, thick. "These babies are here to stay."

I plant the end of my pool cue on the ground and lean against it. "You know what I think? I think the man doth protest too much."

"Come on, Zara. Leave the poor guy alone," my friend, Kennedy, says with a laugh from her spot at the bar leaner. Her perfect teeth smile and long tresses made her a fan favourite on the Dating Mr. Darcy reality TV show. I inherited Kennedy from my sister-in-law, Emma, who was on the show with her. As Kennedy put it, being a single girl in a new city, there's only so much time she can spend with married people—particularly Emma and my brother, Sebastian, who are deeply in love and spend way too much time canoodling with one another.

She needed to be with the city's single population.

"Thank you," Asher says to her. "Us Americans need to stick together."

"Totally," Kennedy agrees, flashing that smile.

"U.S.A! U.S.A!" Asher chants with his fist in the air like he's at a sports stadium.

My friends Lottie, Tabitha, and I do a collective, British eyeroll.

"I'm embarrassed for you, Asher," Tabitha says, as she drains her drink. "We need another round." Tabitha is my wild friend from school, who is very much a *live in the moment* kind of girl. Like I used to be. She's been known to end a night out being stuck up a tree—or in a prison cell for drunk and disorderly behaviour.

She's a lot of fun.

"You always need another round, babe," Lottie, the sweetest of my friends, and also my flatmate, observes with a wry smile.

"Your point?" Tabitha questions her.

Lottie raises her hands in the surrender sign. "I'm just saying."

"You know what? It's hard to be an American in London sometimes," Kennedy says, deflecting attention from Tabitha. "Right, Asher?"

"So true," he replies. "Understanding what the heck you're all saying is the first hurdle. Like 'keep your hair on.' What does that even mean? Is my hair gonna float off my head in some freak accident?"

"No one could accuse you of being obsessed with your hair," I say with a laugh. "The expression means relax. And you know, we're not the ones pretending it's our accent difference when we get the name of our date wrong."

"You did that, Asher?" Kennedy asks, her eyes wide.

"Asher doesn't exactly find it hard to be an American in London if all the British girls lining up to date him is anything to go by. Do you, Asher?" Lottie asks in her sweet way—with an edge. Lottie might be the gentlest of our friend group, but she's tough in her own way.

"They don't line up," he protests. "Well, not in any formal way, at least. It's more of a random scattering. Maybe

I should suggest they form a line? It would make things a lot simpler for me."

"See?" I say with a shake of my head. "He's doing just fine."

"Take your shot, Zee," he says to me.

I position myself, line up my shot, and tap the white ball into the number thirteen, which slips safely into the side pocket.

"Great work, wifey," Asher says and we high-five.

"You two are hilarious," Tabitha says from her spot, where she's propping up the table. "You become one another's back-ups and suddenly you're all *wifey this*, and *hubby that*."

"Maybe Asher could be everyone's back-up guy?" Lottie suggests, and then adds, "No, wait. That wouldn't work, not unless they change the British marriage laws."

I cock an eyebrow. "That's the reason why it wouldn't work? Because polygamy is against the law?"

"Are you telling me you don't want to be my sister wife?" Kennedy asks. "I'm offended."

"Yeah, me too," Tabitha adds with a giggle.

"Ladies, ladies," Asher says. "There's no need to fight over me."

The three of us burst into laughter, and he offers us a mock offended look.

"Asher's ego is clearly alive and kicking," Tabitha observes.

"And you girls know we're not actually going to get married, right? We're just a safety net for one another. Five years is stacks of time to find Mr. Right," I explain.

"I don't want to find Mr. Right," Asher tells us with a wry smile, and I shake my head at him.

"No, you just want a constant stream of Miss Right-For-

Nows," Kennedy says. "Are you gonna take your shot, Zee, or should you just declare Lottie and me the winners right now."

I walk around the table, working out which shot to take next. It's not an easy decision, with no clear gimme in sight.

"You're not gonna find an easy shot," Kennedy says as I stop to assess the table. "In fact, I'd say now's about the time you'll lose to me and Lottie. *Again.*"

I throw her a look that says *bring it on*, position my cue over my hand, and pop! I tap my cue against the white and it hurtles across the table, aiming for the number 15 ball. It hits its target, sending the ball racing right into the number 8, forcing it into the pocket. "No!" I call out in dismay.

"Oh, too bad," Kennedy says as she gleefully high-fives Lottie.

Wasting no time, Kennedy hops off her stool and places her hand on my shoulder. "Time to get us our next round of drinks, I think, Zee."

I jut out my lower lip. "It was a tough shot. I don't even think you would've been able to get that one."

"You're probably right," she replies with a smile, "but I'll take that drink all the same."

"Is that fair on me, the almost-birthday girl?" I ask.

"Yes," both she and Lottie reply with conviction.

I take the drink orders from them and together Asher and I make our way through the busy London pub, with its high wooden ceiling and long leadlight windows. "Sorry. I totally messed that game up."

"It was a tricky shot," Asher replies.

"I guess. There is one thing though. At least we didn't lose to my brother. I hate that even more."

"And they say you're competitive. I think I've been there for all of your pool losses to Sebastian. It ain't pretty."

19

I shake my head. "I'm talking since birth."

"You played pool as a baby?" He widens his eyes in mock surprise. "Wow, advanced."

I nudge my friend with my elbow. "You're hilarious. Actually, now that I think of it, I wonder if they make baby pool cues? That would be totally cute."

He chuckles. "Cute and dangerous. Have you seen many coordinated babies?"

"Good point. What do you want to drink?" I get the bartender's attention.

"I'll order. I've been working on something."

"Really."

"Watch."

A bartender asks, "What can I get you?" He's wearing a nametag that reads *Priscilla*.

"Alright, geezer," Asher begins, and I turn to him in surprise. "I'll have a pint of Newky an' all, fanks, mate."

I narrow my eyes at him. "Are you trying to sound like you've got a serious speech impediment or is that your approximation of a cockney accent?"

"Hey! I thought it was pretty good."

"It wasn't."

"She's right," Priscilla, the bartender says. "It was terrible, mate, and I'm from Australia."

Asher feigns offence. "I thought it was great. I was aiming for David Beckham."

"It was a lot more Dick Van Dyke in *Mary Poppins* than David Beckham, hubby," I reply. "Sorry."

"Yeah, that's what he sounded like!" Priscilla comments. "Dick Van Dyke with that bloody terrible fake cockney accent."

"How about you get me that pint, buddy, and I'll keep working on it," Asher says with a laugh.

Priscilla gives him a supercilious look. "No worries, Mr. Van Dyke. I'm on it. Anything else?"

We run through our list and pay for our drinks. Together, we carry them back through the pub to where our friends are perched on bar stools.

"How's your business going? Had any more interesting clients lately?" Kennedy asks me as I take a sip of my glass of red wine.

"Oh, Scarlett handles a lot of the new clients. She's much more experienced than me. She's been a designer for years and had some amazing clients. You know, celebrities and the super-rich. People you see in the news."

"Like serial killers?" Asher says.

"No, Ash. Not like serial killers. Actual famous people."

"Exciting! Anyone we'd know?" Kennedy asks.

"I'm not meant to say."

Tabitha raises her eyebrows. "Is client confidentiality a big thing in interior design these days?"

"For some people it is," I reply. I glance around the pub before I lean in closer and all four of them follow suit. It's not like anyone will overhear us in this busy pub, but you can't be too careful, can you? Walls and ears and all that stuff. "There's this one client that Scarlett handled on her own because it was pretty sensitive."

"And?" Kennedy leads.

"And... let's just say the word 'royalty' might apply to this person."

"Royalty?" Kennedy says way too loudly, and I shush her right away as my eyes dart around the room. "Which one? Harry and Meghan have left the country, so it won't be them. Is it Kate and Wills? Oh, I say it's Kate and Wills."

I lean back on my stool and raise my palms. "I've said enough," I reply, as though I've hinted at a state secret and not that Scarlett redesigned a very, *very* minor royal's new London flat a month or two ago.

Kennedy's face is bright. "Babe, that is so cool. Royalty."

"If you believe it," Asher comments.

"What? Why wouldn't we believe it?" I question. A platinum blonde-haired vision heading our way catches my attention. "You can ask her yourself."

Scarlett Lamington, business partner and friend, comes waltzing over to our table. She's always immaculately dressed, and tonight is no exception. She's in a figure-hugging dress that hits just above the knee, with her platinum hair falling in soft curls down her back and her freshly manicured nails painted a perfect red. With her made up face and killer heels, she looks like she belongs somewhere much more glamorous than our local pub.

"I'm so happy you came," I say to her, as she pulls me in for a hug. I get a lungful of her expensive perfume.

"I wouldn't miss it for the world. You don't turn thirty every day of the week." She pulls a face. "Thank goodness." She greets everyone with a warm smile. "How are you all? It's nice to see you again."

"Zara was just telling us that you did some interior design for a member of royalty, Scarlett, but she won't tell us who," Kennedy says as Scarlett perches her pert little butt on the edge of a stool.

"Oh, I couldn't possibly tell. Some people prefer to be discreet," she says with a mysterious air. "Now, who do I have to sleep with to get a drink around here?" She shoots Asher a flirtatious smile.

"I'll get you a drink," I offer, hopping to my feet. "I got the last round for everyone else, so it's only fair. What will you have?"

"I'll have a gin and tonic. Artisanal gin, please. Something like boysenberry or grapefruit. Surprise me."

"Got it." I feel a hand on my arm.

"You stay put and enjoy yourself, almost-birthday girl," Asher instructs. "I'll go get your drink, Scarlett."

"Thanks," she replies.

He shoots me a smile before he leaves for the bar.

"Isn't he sweet? I think we should all have an Asher," Scarlett says, and we both look over at him. He's leaning on the bar as he puts in his order with Priscilla, and I wonder if he's trying out his terrible cockney accent once more. I hope for Priscilla's sake he isn't.

As Kennedy, Tabitha, and Lottie chat among themselves, I ask her, "Did you hear from Josie Smith this afternoon?"

She scrunches up her pretty face. "She's going with Karina for the design. Can you believe it? Another client lost to them."

The interior design chain, Karina Design moved into a large shop on the high street around the corner from our little shop about three months ago and we've been losing clients ever since. We're the definite David of the David and Goliath combo, and it does not feel good.

My belly tightens. "Seriously? That's the fourth client this month to bail on us for the shiny new shop on the high street. What are we going to do?"

"I know," she replies with a sigh. "All we can do is keep on trying to win new business. Do a new window design? Maybe drop our prices? Throw some marketing money at some more ads?"

"We've got to do all of it, and fast, or else ScarZar might become an ancient relic."

"Don't talk like that," Scarlett sniffs. "It's a bad omen."

Asher returns and places a drink in front of Scarlett. "What's a bad omen?"

"Talking negatively about ScarZar," she replies. She takes a sip of her drink. "Ooh, that's delicious. I can taste the juniper berries, of course, but there's something else in there, isn't there? What is it? Black currant? Rose? Oh, I know, indigo."

"Indigo?" I ask with a chortle "How can you taste indigo? It's a colour, isn't it?"

"It's a rainbow colour, right? Although I strongly suspect no one really knows what colour it actually is," Asher comments as he takes a seat next to us. "I mean, if it's purple, why not say it's purple?"

"That's why *we're* the interior designers," I tease him.

He leans in closer to us and asks, "Did I hear that you're losing clients?"

"We'll be fine," Scarlett replies.

"Do you want to decorate my new place?" he asks.

I laugh. "I've told you before, you can't afford us."

He lifts his brows. "Do I have to beg?"

"Are you serious?" I narrow my gaze.

"Is Kelly Slater the greatest surfer of all time?" he asks.

I flick my eyes to Scarlett and we both giggle. I don't understand Asher when he starts to talk surfing. Being from San Diego, he virtually grew up at the beach, and it's obvious he misses it.

"I don't know who this Kelly Slater chick is, so I can't answer that," Scarlett replies.

"*He* is a world surfing record holder, eleven times over, and *he* has set up this amazing surf ranch in the California desert where you can ride a manufactured wave. It's not the beach, but it's pretty awesome."

24

Scarlett shoots him a condescending look. "You're never going to convince me to take up surfing, Asher."

He cocks an eyebrow in her direction. "Not my intention. Believe me."

"Asher, you don't have to get us to decorate your place," I say. "Although it's kind of you, we don't need friends and family offering us charity. We'll find clients."

"Look, you saw my new place, Zee. It's super bland and boring right now. It could totally do with some design."

"We have real clients, you know. Real, *paying* clients," Scarlett says pointedly.

"I'm a real, paying client, and I want Zara to design my entire flat."

I flick my eyes to Scarlett's. After a beat she says, "He seems genuine."

I beam at my friend. "I'd love to do it. Thanks, Ash."

His lips lift into a smile that lights up his whole face. "Awesome. Swing by next week and we'll get things rolling."

Tabitha drapes her arm around Asher's shoulder. "Where are you swinging by next week?" Her voice is slurred from a little too much booze.

"I'm going to redesign Asher's new flat," I tell her, and Kennedy and Lottie join the conversation.

"Oh, your place totally needs that," Kennedy tells him. "If it wasn't for your surfboards, there'd be no colour anywhere."

"Don't forget the blokey black leather sofas," Lottie says.

"Can black be considered a colour?" Kennedy asks.

"Black is black, baby," Tabitha declares, still leaning on Asher. "Hey, can we toast the almost-birthday girl?"

"Oh, yes. Let's," Scarlett says.

Everyone collects their glasses from the table and raises them.

"To Zara, our very best friend, who is sadly falling prey to the ravages of time," Tabitha says before she hiccups loudly and grins at us all.

"How about this?" Kennedy says. "To Zara, the best friend a girl can have—oh, and an Asher."

"Thank you for remembering me," he replies.

"To the best friend a girl and an Asher can have," Lottie, Tabitha, and Scarlett repeat as we all clink glasses and take a sip.

"That makes me sound like I'm my very own gender," Asher complains.

"You are. You're Asher," I reply.

"I need another drink," Tabitha announces once she's drained her glass.

"I don't think you do, babe." Lottie hops to her feet. "Come on, let's get you home. It's a weeknight and the elderly members of our group need their beauty sleep. Isn't that right, Asher and Zee?"

"Thanks a lot. You'll all be thirty before you know it, and anyway, I've got three more days left of my twenties."

"I'm desperately holding onto my final few months," Kennedy says.

Lottie lets out a sigh. "Yeah, me too."

"You might be thirty on Saturday, Zee, but you don't look a day over thirty-one to me," Asher says and he wins a punch to the arm from me.

"Don't listen to him, babe. You're gorgeous and we all adore you," Tabitha declares. "And I'm not just saying that because I had two lovely drinks really rather quickly and they've made my head the teensiest bit squiffy."

"She's right. You are gorgeous and we do all adore you," Lottie agrees as Asher and Scarlett and Kennedy nod.

"Aw, thanks you guys." I beam at them. ScarZar may be struggling right now and I might be about to turn the dreaded thirty, but I've got my friends, my London family.

Chapter Two

Monday morning rolls around, and I exit the Tube Stop at Kensington High Street and take my daily walk to our design shop. At first, we had a bunch of clients. After taking night school classes in interior design together, we'd given up our jobs to start the business—Scarlett as a marketing assistant for a tech company and me as a graphic designer. We were incredibly grateful to have made a splash in the London interior design scene, even if it was just a tiny one.

I find my pace slowing as it always does when I reach Karina Design. Although we love our charming bijou shop down the cobblestoned mews, it can't compete with the big, flashy, in-your-face shop.

We're the epitome of the little guy, up against the big, corporate design chain with its big budgets and gang of designers. We're just like Meg Ryan to Tom Hanks in *You've Got Mail*—although I'm fairly certain neither Scarlett nor I are having an online love affair with Karina's owner, not least of all because the owner is a woman in her 80s.

Today, Karina has a new display. It's got a group of canary yellow chairs suspended on a rope from the ceiling, with a sea of scatter cushions in bright hues beneath. It's eye catching and ingenious, and I can't help but feel a twinge of jealousy that our window is only a quarter the size and, because our shop is so small, suspending chairs from our ceiling would be a health and safety violation.

With the spring well and truly gone from my step, I make my way further along the busy street. I come to a stop in front of one of my favourite shops, a pet store called Penelope's Pooches that always has a puppy or two in the window, and today is no exception. Really, it's impossible to pass without stopping to look. I've wanted a dog since forever, but it's never seemed the right time.

Today, as I come to a stop in front of their picture window with its pale blue trim and clouds hanging from the ceiling on string, the most adorable little face gazes back at me.

My heart skips a beat.

That's my dog.

Yeah, I hear it. It's probably not the most rational thought I've had today. But I'm running with it.

I gaze at the puppy and take a step closer, all but pressing my face up against the cool glass. The puppy bounces out of its bed, its tail wagging so hard its little body can barely keep up. Its face is calling out to me *Buy me! Buy me! I'm yours!* with every bounce of its little body. Although it's small, it looks to be a few months old.

"Hello, little Jack Russell," I say through the glass.

The puppy's response is to tilt its head to the side, its ears pricked up. My heart might be beating normally right now, but it's begun to melt all over the pavement for the little creature so eager to see me.

I decide to go in *just* to have a look. I know, I know. No one ever *just looks* at a puppy they're thinking of getting and walks away. In fact, it's probably an impossible human feat. But who knows? I may be that person with an ironclad resolve.

Then again, maybe not.

I push at the door, but it doesn't budge. I peer inside and see a couple of people in pale blue boilersuits stacking shelves. One look at the sign tells me the shop is closed.

I turn back to the puppy and its tail begins to wag violently once more. "I'll be back later, okay? Just make sure no one else takes you."

It's only response is to gaze back at me.

With a final glance, I reluctantly continue my walk to the shop.

Five minutes later, I make my way through the door into our shop. Scarlett is on the phone.

"I'm very sorry that you've chosen to go in another direction, Janice. Is there anything we can do to change your mind?" Scarlett says from behind the desk.

I glance at her tense features and my heart sinks to my toes. I mouth "Janice Cromwell?" and when Scarlett gives me a grim nod, I know we've likely lost one of our biggest new clients.

"No, I understand. They do have a good reputation, you're totally right," she continues as I turn the sign from closed to open. "We might be a lot smaller, but we do have that personal touch so many clients love, and we—"

She pauses mid-sentence and I bite my lip.

"Yes, thank you, Janice...okay...if you ever change your mind, you know where we are... Yes, I understand." She hangs up and lifts her eyes to mine. "Janice Cromwell and her 5-bedroom townhouse off Sloane Square no longer feels she can continue our working relationship." She slumps her shoulders as she lets out a defeated puff of air.

"Don't tell me. Karina?"

"Yup. Another paycheque in the shredder."

"Oh, Scarlett. That's terrible. We'd already done so much work on the design."

"I know we had, but it was all a waste of time. Janice Cromwell has abandoned ship and gone to the Dark Side."

I watch as she pulls up the work calendar we share to keep track of when we each have appointments so that at least one of us is in the shop at all times. She deletes Janice's entry, and in an instant our week looks dismally empty.

"Don't give up hope," I say, trying to remain buoyant.

She pastes on a smile. "You're right. There will be other Janice Cromwells, with her huge budget and expensive taste."

"Well, at least we've got Asher," I say with a grin.

She harrumphs. "Friends doing us favours isn't exactly going to buy us an island, babe."

"I know, but it's a start."

Scarlett's phone rings again. She picks it up and says hello as she wanders out to the storeroom and mini kitchenette at the back of the shop.

Left alone, I smooth out my ponytail as I survey the shop. We had a delivery of the most stunning, luxurious, deep green velvet sofa last week, which I staged with a collection of jewel tone cushions and a brass floor lamp. It's the kind of sofa you could imagine supermodels sinking into, looking awfully glam, and I smile whenever I look at it.

I notice a book on landscape gardening off centre on the brass and glass coffee table, so straighten it up.

I peer out the window, hoping to see a gang of potential new clients rushing the door, but the quiet mews is empty but for a tortoise shell cat, sauntering down the cobblestones.

"Okay, babe. I'd better dash. Kisses. *Ciao ciao ciao.*" Scarlett gives her characteristic farewell as she hangs up her phone. I've never once known her to say a simple *bye*. She's not even Italian. She's from Solihull, but you'd never know it from her accent.

"Last night was fun," I say to change the subject from the dreary topic of before.

"It's not every day one of my besties turns such a shockingly old age," she teases.

"Three more days, remember? And besides, you'll be thirty at the end of summer, you know."

She puts her fingers in her ears and trills, "La la la la la. If I can't hear you, it's not going to happen."

I grin at her. "Denial isn't just a river in Egypt, I see."

"At least you get a big party at Martinston," she says, naming my family's house in the country where all of my family but me still live. "I bought the most gorgeous dress to wear on Saturday. I want to look good for Harry."

"You still dating Harry Honeydew?"

"Oh, yes. He's a total catch. There's no way I'm giving up on him."

"Because you like him. Right?"

"Oh, that too," she replies with a wave of her hand. "We'll both be there to commiserate with you."

"I'll be thirty, not dead. And you know what? I'm not bothered about turning thirty. In fact, I think it's going to be pretty wonderful."

She raises an eyebrow. "'Wonderful' might be taking it a bit far, babe. It's one step closer to the grave, or worse: wrinkles." She gives a dramatic shudder.

I roll my eyes. "You're *such* a drama queen."

"Wrinkles are a real and present danger at our age, Zara. You need to take them seriously." She shoots me a meaningful look and I self-consciously scrutinize my face in the gilded mirror.

"You know turning thirty is no big deal. I've made my peace with it"

"You have?"

Although I've told my closest friends—Tabitha, Kennedy, and Lottie—about Asher being my back-up guy, I haven't mentioned it to Scarlett yet. My best friends know it's just a safety net, that I won't actually end up *marrying* the guy. Something tells me Scarlett might not understand it like they do.

"I've got a plan."

"You're having Botox!" she declares in excitement.

"No. Not a *wrinkle* plan, Scarlett. More of a life plan."

She rolls her liner-rimmed grey eyes. "Don't tell me you've become one of those life coach devotees who can't do anything that's not in her grand plan. Who are you seeing? Not Delilah Sorbonne? She told me that I needed to work with sea urchins. I mean, what is *that* about? Can you even get a job working with sea urchins?" She shudders. "Ugh."

"No sea urchins. I've got a plan to get what I want, that's all."

"What do you want?"

"What do I really, really want?" I say, repeating Asher's 90's girl band line.

Scarlett regards me as though I've lost my mind. "You're quoting The Spice Girls to me now?"

"It's a joke."

"Not your best work, babe. I'll ask again: what have you worked out that you want?"

33

"You know what it's like out there in the dating jungle. It's scary and unpredictable."

"That's an understatement."

"So, I've got myself a back-up guy in case things go pear shaped for me in the love stakes. He's my safety net. If I don't meet the man of my dreams in the next five years, I'll marry the guy."

"You'll *marry* him? Zara, you really have gone insane." She throws her hands up in the air. "That's it. ScarZar is dead. You'll be carted away by the men in white coats before the day's done and I'll be left on my own, battling Karina."

"Might I refer you to my earlier comment about you being a drama queen?"

"Babe, you've got to admit that going through with marrying some back-up guy definitely falls into the less sane side of the ledger."

"It's a practical plan."

"Who is this back-up guy of yours, anyway?"

"Asher."

Her jaw drops. Literally. "Asher? *He's* your back-up guy and...and he agreed to marry you?"

"Well, yes, but not for five years. And it's not going to happen, anyway. It's a back-up plan. Nothing more."

She regards me through wondering eyes. "But he's gorgeous."

I'm mildly offended.

She pulls her lips into a line. "I think that's the most bizarre thing I've heard in my entire life: you marrying Asher. What about love? What about soul mates? Don't you want all of that?"

"Oh, don't get me wrong. I'm still looking for my soul mate. Only this way I can take my time doing it, knowing that if I don't find him, I can still get married and have a family. It's the perfect plan, and five years is loads of time to find him, fall in love, and get married."

Scarlett looks anything but convinced. "I suppose so."

"I'm also thinking of getting a dog."

She shakes her head as though I've loaded too much information into it and she's trying to make room in her brain. "You are?"

"You know I've wanted a dog for ages. On my way in today, I saw the one I want in the window of Penelope's Pooches." I grin as I think of the cute dog in the window.

"What kind?"

"The best kind. A Jack Russell."

"Cute! Wow, Zara. Dog ownership, a back-up guy. Are you having a mid-life crisis or something?"

"I'm turning thirty, not fifty."

"Tell me more about the dog. Ooh, he could come here and be our shop dog! People would love it."

"I know! That's exactly what I was thinking. You know that dress boutique off the King's Road with the little black miniature poodle?"

"I love going in that shop."

"And you know why?"

"You're going to tell me it's because of the dog and not the gorgeous dresses."

"It *is* the dog. And the dresses. But mainly the dog. That dog makes the place friendlier, more relaxed. It gives it a personality all of its own. That's what my dog will do for this place."

"I like it. We can have photos done of our interiors with the dog in them, sitting there looking all cute and Jack Russell-y. It could be our signature, a shorthand to show prospective clients who we are and what our philosophy is."

I giggle, excitement bubbling over. "That's a lot for one small dog to do, but I love it."

She smiles. "You know what? I think a shop dog might be just what we need. Can I come with you when you go to get it?"

"Of course you can!" I throw my arms around her and give her a quick squeeze. "You are not going to regret this."

"As long as the dog doesn't smell."

I beam at her. "It'll smell like roses. Promise."

The bell above the door tinkles and a mother and daughter walk in. The mother is wearing what I like to call the Kensington Uniform: a knee-length shift dress under a smart tailored coat and a row of pearls. Always a row of pearls. The daughter on the other hand is a goth. Long black hair, white face foundation with black-rimmed eyes, and every piece of clothing she's wearing is black, black, black.

"Hello, ladies, and welcome to ScarZar Interiors. How can I help you?"

"My daughter has moved into a new flat and the décor is simply hideous," Mrs. Kensington Uniform says.

"M*uuuuu*m," the daughter complains, looking mortified. She's probably only eighteen or nineteen and still deeply embarrassed by her mother. "It's not that bad."

"Oh, darling, it is. It's simply awful. Wallpaper has peeled off the walls and you and your friends all sit on beanbags instead of chairs. I think I even spotted a beer crate in the corner. A beer crate!"

"It's called rustic, Mum," the daughter replies with a roll of her eyes and a flash of her tongue piercing.

"No, darling, it's simply no style at all, that's what it is." She looks back at me. "My daughter needs design rehab."

I offer them a smile. "Well, I'm sure we can help with

that. What were you looking for exactly? Some chairs and a sofa, I assume? Some new wall treatments, and perhaps a coffee table to replace the beer crate?"

"I want the whole lot done. Living room, bedroom, dining. Do you do outdoor spaces too?" she asks.

Scarlett materializes at my side. "Did I hear you say you want to redecorate the whole flat? Hi, I'm Scarlett. Zara and I own ScarZar."

"Victoria Hamilton, and this is my daughter, Chloe."

We all shake hands, the daughter as though it's the most uncomfortable thing she's had to do in her entire life.

"Lovely to meet you, Victoria and Chloe," Scarlett says with a smile. "What style direction are you interested in taking?"

The tall, lanky daughter shrugs. "I dunno."

"And that's the problem," her mother chastises as she rolls her eyes at us.

"I always say that if you stand for nothing, you'll fall for everything," Scarlett says, trying to sound like some sort of wise style guru—although I know she's only quoting a Katy Perry song. "So, how about I tell you what we can do for you?"

Victoria beams. "That sounds amazing. Doesn't that sound amazing, Chloe?"

"I suppose," is her wildly enthusiastic reply.

"We can accommodate it all: modern, Hollywood glam, farmhouse, rustic farmhouse, modern farmhouse. All the farmhouse styles. Then there's ultra-modern, loft style, Hamptons, of course, the blue and white classic. And let's not forget there's..."

I watch as the customers' eyes glaze over. Well, to be fair, Chloe's eyes were already glazed over way before Scarlett began, but now her mother looks like a deer in headlights, too. Scarlett has a habit of throwing way too much info at people. Sure, she knows her stuff, but she doesn't need to prove it with every person who walks through the door.

Karina stealing our business has a lot to answer for.

"I'm getting a moody vibe from you, Chloe, dark with ornate accents," I interject and win a surprised look from Scarlett. "Am I right?"

"Maybe?" She's not giving me a lot here.

"How about I show you some examples of what I'm talking about?"

Her face brightens for the first time since she walked into the room. "Sure."

I take her and her mum over to the computer, where I pull up examples of the gothic style. "See the darker tones but still with light walls and natural light to create a contrast? Does that look like what you're interested in?"

Chloe's eyes dart to her mother. "Do you like that?"

"I think it looks dreadful, but if you like it, darling, then I'm happy to pay for it. As long as there's none of that," Victoria exclaims as she points at an image of a dungeon-like room with walls covered in swords.

"I can understand that perfectly," I reply with a smile. "A room can have too many swords on the walls."

"I don't want swords, but I do like the style," the daughter says.

"How about I go out to back and get some fabric samples and we can use them as a springboard for working out a style plan?"

"Marvellous," Victoria replies.

"Take a seat," I say, gesturing at the green velvet sofa. "I'll be right back."

As I'm rifling through our extensive material samples,

Scarlett slinks over to me. "I'm sorry, I went overboard again, didn't I?"

"It's fine. Just maybe don't throw the book at them when they walk into the shop. People can get freaked out. And then there's the fact that it was pretty obvious the daughter was going to go in the goth direction, what with looking like the walking dead and all. The navy and white Hamptons palette was hardly going to cut it."

"Good point. I'll tone it down. I panicked. Losing so much business to Karina lately has totally got inside my head."

"I get it. I do it, too. But this is a real opportunity, so let's grab it, okay?"

Her pinched expression morphs into a tentative smile. "We need this."

"We do."

"Hey, don't you have that meeting with your future husband shortly?"

"My future husband?" I question. "Oh, right. You mean Asher." I glance at the mock Baroque wall clock. I'm meeting him at his flat over in Notting Hill in just over half an hour.

She takes the samples from my hands. "You go and do what you have to do. I'll take over and I absolutely promise not to blind anyone with my extensive knowledge."

I giggle. "Your problem is that you know too much."

She grins at me. "It's tough being so expert. Now go and see your husband."

I collect my handbag, slot my tablet into its case, and say, "Back-up only, Scarlett."

She grins at me. "You just keep telling yourself that."

Chapter Three

I arrive at Asher's building one minute early for our appointment. Since I had a few extra minutes to spare, I stopped off at Starbucks and picked up a couple of coffees for us. Got to keep the clients happy, you know, especially when they're one of your besties.

Although I've been to Asher's new place once before, it was only to watch a baseball game a few weeks ago, and other than noticing that the place felt empty, I didn't pay a whole lot of attention to it.

"Hello?" comes his voice over the intercom.

I grin at the camera and hold up one of the coffee cups. "One double shot cappuccino with full fat milk, extra froth, and chocolate."

"If it was just you without the coffee I might not let you in," is his reply as the intercom buzzes and the door clicks open.

"You're a comedian."

I take the three flights of stairs to his floor, and he greets me in the hallway with a grin, his phone held to his ear.

"That sounds good. I'll check in with Chris and let you

know... Uh-huh... Yeah, okay. Hey look, Geoff, I've gotta go. I've got my future wife standing in front of me with a takeout coffee in her hand."

I arch an eyebrow.

"I'll explain some other time. See you in the office later." He ends his call and slots his phone into the back pocket of his pants. "Personally delivered coffee. A guy could get used to this treatment."

"Don't. It's a one-off, even if you do tell your colleagues I'm your future wife." I hand him his coffee. "Which I'm not, by the way."

"Well, you are until you find Mr. Right."

He's got a point.

He stands back for me to enter his flat. "Come on in."

I walk into his large, spacious living room. I run my designer's eye over the space. I'd noticed its size when we watched the game together a couple of weeks ago, but I hadn't fully appreciated the gorgeous parquet flooring, the exposed brick on one of the walls, or the custom mouldings in the high ceilings. With its bare walls, curtain-less windows, oversized television above the fireplace, and black leather sofas designed for comfort rather than style, it screams *bachelor pad* with a strong, masculine voice.

"You know, Asher, I love what you've done with the place. You have a real eye," I say with a sardonic smile.

"Do you treat all your clients with this level of disdain, or do you reserve it for the devilishly handsome ones?"

I giggle. "Only the devilishly handsome ones. Seriously, though, this is such a great flat. It has so much potential." I wander around the open-plan living room and kitchen. I point at his collection of three surf boards in the corner by the window. "Surf boards are so useful in London. You must use them...*never*."

"They remind me of home."

"And Kelly Slater."

"At least someone was listening to me last night."

"It's cute the way you're into a guy called Kelly."

"For the last time, he's big news."

I grin at him. "You are so easy to wind up, hubby." I point at an empty spot by one of the large windows. "No dining table yet, huh?"

"I thought I'd better have my designer's advice on it before I go splashing the cash. Mmmm, good coffee."

I walk over to the edge of the room and turn to survey it. With the windows behind me, the place is flooded with sun, and although it's bereft of furniture, I can see how amazing it could be. "First up, before I go making suggestions and getting all excited about this project, are you seriously going to get me to decorate this place?"

"I'm not just being nice, if that's what you're asking."

"I thought I'd check."

He opens his arms wide. "Can't you see I need your help?"

"This place is so empty, it would be the perfect spot for some yodelling."

He cups his hands around his mouth. "Echo, echo, echo!"

"More like yodel-ee-hee-hoo," I sing.

He shakes his head, his lips quirking. "Zee? Don't ever do that again."

"What? Why? I played Liesl in my school production of *The Sound of Music*, I'll have you know."

"Liesl didn't yodel."

"Oh, now that's where you're wrong. She did yodel, in the song about the goatherd."

He cocks an eyebrow. "How do you know that?"

I tap the side of my head. "There's a lot of info in this brain of mine, you know." I pull out my tablet, and we both sit down on his—admittedly extremely comfortable—ugly sofa. "What style are you thinking?"

"I dunno. Comfortable? Is that a style?"

"It can be."

I flick on the tablet and immediately an image of the most exquisite opaque and clear striped glass perfume bottle with an ornate silver stopper pops up on the screen.

"What's that?" Asher asks.

"My fantasy perfume bottle. One day."

"You've got a whole Pinterest board dedicated to perfume bottles?"

"It's my thing," I reply, defensive.

"Huh."

I glance at him out of the corner of my eye. "What does that mean?"

"Nothing. It's just that I didn't know perfume bottle porn was a thing."

"You're hilarious."

"Do you collect them or something? Because I can give you an empty bottle of my cologne, if you like. Or my deodorant, if that's your thing, too."

"That would be a hard no. Perfume bottles are beautiful works of art. Some of them can be pricey, though. This one in particular is an antique made of Murano glass."

"It's pretty."

"You're just saying that because my secret's out. You know I've got a thing for little glass bottles now."

"No. I mean it. I've learned something new about Zara Huntington-Ross today, and I kinda like it."

I slide my eyes to his, not sure if he's being sarcastic.

The look on his face tells me he's genuine. "Shall we move on to your place?"

"Sure."

I tap the screen to pull up the mood board I've compiled for him.

"Tell me what you like best out of these images." I pull up a board I'd put together for him before I went to the shop this morning. "I've tried to think 'stylish bachelor pad' for you. Nothing too fussy. Simple, clean lines."

He surveys the screen. "I like this one," he says, pointing at a room done in a darker palette with a tan leather L-shaped sofa, cream floor rug, and modern chandelier that stands out against the exposed brick. "I like the ceiling light thing-y."

"It's called a chandelier, Asher."

"That makes it sound girly to me, and I'm deeply masculine, as you know." He has a glint in his eye as the edges of his mouth twitch.

"That's what comes to mind when I think of you: deeply, deeply masculine. What about this ceiling?" I point at another image. "Can you see how they've used rows of lighting to highlight the mouldings? Doesn't it look amazing? We could totally do that here."

We both look up at the ceiling.

"That would be cool. Before I forget, there's one thing in here that's non-negotiable."

I eye the TV over the fireplace. "Let me guess. Your TV."

"You got it."

"That's so you can sit at home watching replays of *Days of Our Lives* because you're tragic and you have no friends?" I ask with a mock innocent look on my face.

"Yeah. That's right. I'm a guy who watches reruns of

daytime soaps," he deadpans. "I'm serious. You are not doing anything to my TV. Tonya stays right where she is."

"Tonya? *Seriously*? You named your TV 'Tonya.'"

"Only because she totally looks like a 'Tonya.' Don't you think?"

I flick my gaze back to his TV. "Ah, no? *It* looks like a television to me."

He sucks in air in mock outrage. "How dare you insult my Tonya."

I snort giggle. "Well, there is one good thing about you having an appliance you think is a woman: you've managed to keep a relationship going for longer than a month."

"Burn! I'll have you know, I've had relationships for longer than a month."

"Oh, yeah? Who?"

"Does high school count?"

"You graduated from high school well over a decade ago?" I ask and he nods. "So no, high school doesn't count."

"Dang it! Hmm, let me think. There was Jessy Sainsbury. I dated her in college for at least a year. Or was it six months? I forget."

"See? I've never known you to have a relationship with a woman for more than a month or two."

"You got me."

"So the TV stays, what about—"

"Tonya. Tonya stays."

"Asher, I'm not calling your TV by a woman's name, especially one named after that ice skater Tonya Harding."

"She isn't named after Tonya Harding," he protests. "My Tonya would never be accused of knee-capping another ice skater."

I giggle. "Because your Tonya is a *television*."

"I guess I could find myself another interior decorator."

"Oh, ha ha." I point at the image he'd liked, trying to refocus the conversation on something besides his weird relationship with an appliance. "Are you happy for me to come up with a design like this for the living room?"

"Sure thing. What about the kitchen?"

"I love your kitchen. The veined marble is gorgeous, and it's classic white."

"Not boring?"

I shake my head. "Not boring."

"Okay. Living room done. This is easy." He pushes himself up. "I'm taking you to the bedroom now, wifey."

"Okay. Lead the way."

We wander across the parquet flooring and down a carpeted hallway, past what looks to be his office and a bathroom, and into the large master bedroom. The walls are still white, there are no curtains, and the bed is large and made up in simple white bedding. Just like the living room, it's plain and sparsely decorated.

I'm not going to deny it. It's weird looking around a guy friend's bedroom. I mean, I know Asher pretty well. We've been friends since he first moved to London two years ago and we met at one of Tabitha's legendary parties. We hit it off straight away, and we've been the best of friends since. But unlike with my girlfriends, who I've had sleepovers with and hung out doing make-up and hair for nights out, up until this point I'd been nowhere near Asher's bedroom.

"The room's a good size, but you need curtains. In high summer it'll be light by four thirty in the morning."

"That's where you come in, Zee."

"This room definitely needs some work."

"I don't like to look at my bedroom as a place for work, if you know what I mean." He waggles his eyebrows at me suggestively and I shake my head.

"Your business, Ash. Not mine." I eye a used coffee cup on the floor by the bed. "You don't even have bedside tables."

He follows my line of sight. "You mean nightstands? Yeah, I guess I need some of those."

I wander past the bed and into the walk-in wardrobe. Unlike the bedroom, it's full to the brim of boxes and clothes and shoes and tubs, stacked right to the ceiling. "So this is where you keep *everything*."

He leans his shoulder against the doorframe. "I guess I've got a bunch of stuff I don't know what to do with."

"Ash, it's so full of stuff in here, you can barely swing a cat."

"And you know how much I love to swing cats around the place."

I laugh. "It's a weird expression."

"Right? These shelves need replacing, too." He clasps onto a shelf at chest level—his, not mine, since he's got a good five inches on me—and wobbles it. "See? Crappy construction."

"We can get that replaced for you. I know some wardrobe designers."

"It's a closet."

"Only in America. Here it's a wardrobe." I brush past him and head to the ensuite. Just like the kitchen, it's totally white, from the bath and basin to the floor and wall tiles. The only colour in the room is from Asher's shaving foam and assorted bottles of shampoo and lotion.

"This is a nice ensuite," I pronounce as Asher arrives at my side. The room isn't huge, and his large, manly frame seems to fill all the available space.

"It's all white, which is boring. Isn't it?"

"It's classic. And it means you've got to keep it clean."

"My housekeeper does that for me." When I shoot him a supercilious look he says, "What? I'm a busy man. I don't have time to clean."

"Sure you don't."

"What would you do with this room?"

"Nothing. It's gorgeous. But you've got to be happy with it."

"It's fine. It's just boring."

"We'll get you some accessories in your favourite colour. Unless you want to go to the expense of having it all ripped out and replaced? Which personally, I think would be a crime against bathrooms."

"I wouldn't want to commit a crime against a bathroom."

"Tonya would miss you if you had to go to jail."

"See? You get me. That's why I want you to be my decorator."

I laugh. "So you'll leave the bathroom as is?"

"I'll leave the bathroom as is."

"Good."

"I prepared a few ideas for your bedroom, too. Let's sit back down and I'll show you."

We return to the living room where I take him through a couple of bedroom concepts I think he'll like.

"I like that one," he says, pointing at a grey panelled room with a low king size bed and modern wooden furniture.

"Me too. It's cool and sophisticated yet comfy and welcoming."

He looks at me blankly. "If you say so."

I flick the tablet cover over the screen. "Okay. I've got a good idea of what you're looking for. And you want all new furniture except for your ridiculously oversize bed, right?"

"I bought that ridiculously oversize bed, as you call it, when I moved here from the States. I am not parting with it. Besides, it took four guys and a crane to get it up here to the third floor. That baby's staying."

"You don't do things by halves, do you? In terms of budget, what are you thinking? Redecorating can be costly. And before you answer, you don't have to go spending a whole load of cash just because it's Scarlett and me. If all you want me to do is get some scatter cushions, a new floor rug, and some 'nightstands,' that's totally fine."

"No, I want to go big. The whole shebang. As you say, this place could be amazing, and I like amazing. So, go for it. Weave your Zara magic."

"Seriously? " I ask, exhilarated at the prospect of transforming this place. "You want me to do the full Monty?"

"Isn't the full Monty that movie with a bunch of men getting naked? Because a) I'm not interested at all in seeing that, and b) you'll need to wait until we're married."

"It's an expression meaning go all the way."

He waggles his eyebrows at me suggestively. "Well, that means something else altogether where I'm from."

"Enough with the innuendo. I'd better get going. I'll pull some ideas together and get you the budget ballpark." I pull out my phone and look at my depressingly empty calendar. "Shall we get together in about a week?"

"For sure." He walks me to the door. "Back to work, huh?"

"Actually, I'm thinking of following through on one of my life goals today."

"Bungee jumping in a bear costume off the London Eye?"

"Can you even do that?"

He lets out a laugh. "Are you telling me you'd consider it if it was a thing?"

"Of course not. I'm going to do something much cooler than that. I'm going to go see a woman about a dog. Penelope, actually, about a Jack Russell at Penelope's Pooches."

His brows ping up toward his hairline. "You're doing what now?"

"I walk past that shop every day, and every day I think, I want one of those dogs. On my way to the shop today, this gorgeous little Jack Russell pup was in the window, and I tell you Asher, that dog is meant to be mine. I'm going there now."

"You're gonna go get a puppy you saw in a store window?"

I beam at him as excitement fills my belly. "I am."

"Did you hear this tune when you were gazing at this dog that's supposedly meant to be yours?" He begins to hum and after a few seconds I work out the song.

"*How Much is That Doggie in the Window*? Really?"

"Come on! It's the perfect soundtrack to that moment. You've got to admit it."

I chortle. "Sure."

He pulls the door open to his flat and holds it for me. "Are you sure you should be getting a dog, wifey?"

"Absolutely," I say with conviction. "I've never been more sure of anything in my life."

"You know you'll have to walk it and feed it. All that stuff."

"I'm perfectly capable of walking and feeding a dog," I reply pointedly. "I grew up with dogs. My dad had a bunch, and I used to play with them loads."

"What will you do with this dog of yours during the day while you're at work?"

"Jack Russells are small enough to take to work. She'll be our shop dog. We'll be known as the interiors shop with the adorable dog. Scarlett's already on board with it and people will love it. Believe me."

"Uh-huh."

I shoot him a sideways look. "Have you got something against dogs or something? Because you're sounding a bit like a canine curmudgeon right now."

"What's a canine curmudgeon?"

"Someone who doesn't like dogs. Clearly."

"I like dogs. Heck, I *love* dogs. I'm just not sure you've thought this through."

"Well, it's just as well you're not my husband then, isn't it? Because my dog is in the window at Penelope's Pooches just waiting for me to become her new mummy."

He shakes his head, his lips curved in a smile. "You've got your mind made up."

I give a single, firm nod of my head. "I have."

"Well, in that case, I cannot wait to meet this new puppy of yours."

"Do you want to come with me? I'm heading there right now to meet Scarlett."

"As much as I'd love to, I've got to get back to work. Thanks for everything, including the coffee."

"You're welcome. I'm excited to decorate this place for you."

"And I'm excited for you to get your dog."

I narrow my gaze. "No, you're not. You think I'm being rash and impulsive."

"Does it matter what I think?"

"No, actually. It doesn't." I flash him my grin and say "TTFN," before I waltz down the hallway toward the stairs.

"Remind me what 'TTFN' means?"

"Ta ta for now," I call out over my shoulder. "Really, Asher. You've lived in Old Blighty for over two years now. Get with the lingo, will you?"

"See you later," he says with a laugh as he closes the door.

A moment later, I'm back on the street, full of ideas for how to decorate Asher's flat.

But those ideas need to wait. Right now, I've got a date with destiny—dog destiny, to be precise.

Chapter Four

Dear Dad,

You know how much I loved Kelly and Hannah growing up? Well, I've made a decision. No more putting it off. No more 'one day' thinking, because that day has come. And it's today.

I'm going to get my dog.

Miss you. Love you.

Your Za-Za xoxo

I hit send and slot my phone back into my purse. Dad will get it. He'll love that I'm getting my own dog. With rising anticipation, I tuck my tablet under my arm, button up my coat against the cool London air, and take the short walk from the Tube stop to Penelope's Pooches.

Once I reach the shop, I look in the window. With a start, I notice there's no sign of the puppy from this morning. It's been replaced with a small ball of fluff who happily yaps at me as I peer in at it.

The little Jack Russell *can't* be gone.

Why didn't I drop everything this morning and get it? Could it have already been sold?

I look up and read the sign instructing people to come inside and "talk pooches with Penelope." Well, that's exactly what I'm going to do.

"Sorry, sorry!" Scarlett comes rushing down the street toward me, her hair streaming behind her as she clutches onto her unbuttoned coat. "I got held up. We might have a new client!"

"Hey, that's great. Who is it?"

"A woman called Delilah Smith." She catches her breath, her cheeks pink from the exercise.

"She sounds familiar. How would I know her?"

"Footballer's wife. Married to a guy called Tony Smith who plays for Chelsea."

We both pull a face. Neither of us know much about football, let alone knowing who the players are.

"Anyway, she wants us to come and look at their new London pad. They want a total redesign." She clutches onto my arm. "Zara, it's an eight-bedroom, four-living room house with a pool."

I blink at her. "Seriously? And she wants us to design the whole place."

She presses her lips together and nods, her blue eyes bright. "Can you believe it? If we get this, we could be in *Hello* magazine someday. We will be on the map, girl."

"We'll *own* the map."

"Oh, yeah. We'll make that map our *beeeyotch*."

"Speaking of..." I nod at the entrance to the pet shop. "Let's go get me a puppy—if it's still here. It's not in the window anymore."

She points at the white fluff ball. "What about that one? It's cute."

"It's not the one I want." I push the door open to a tinkling bell, step inside, and look around the shop. The moment my feet hit the floor, I feel like I'm in another world. There's a huge colourful portrait of a West Highland Terrier on the wall, shelves filled with dog beds and treats, and racks of dog accessories, from hats to booties and clothes. The floor itself is soft and springy, and each step I take I bounce along like I'm on an oversized balloon.

"This is freaky," Scarlett says as she bounces next to me.

"Welcome to Penelope's Pooches," a soft and feminine voice says behind us.

We turn to see a woman in her 30s, her hair in pigtails, making her look more than a touch like Pippi Longstocking, wearing a pale blue boilersuit with the word *Penelope* embossed in bright pink lettering on her chest. She's got a friendly smile on her plump, make-up-free face.

I glance from her nametag up to her face. "Hi, Penelope." I say. When she offers me an uncertain look, I say, "You are Penelope, aren't you?"

Her smile broadens. "Not exactly."

I glance around the store. There are two other staff members nearby, both busy stocking shelves, one holding a clipboard in her hand. They're dressed the same as the woman beside me, right down to the boilersuit and pigtails. "Which one is Penelope?"

"Oh, let me explain. You're obviously new to our dog-cept."

"Dog-cept?" Scarlett questions.

"It's a melding of the words 'dog' and 'concept.' Dog-cept."

Scarlett's eyes flash to mine. "Ok*aaay*."

"Our dog-cept states that we are *all* Penelope."

I raise my eyebrows in question. "Really?" A door at the

back of the shop swings open and a man comes breezing in. He too is dressed in the exact same boilersuit, although he's not sporting the same hairstyle. "Even the guys?"

"Even the guys," she confirms.

I cast my mind back to "Priscilla," the opinionated Australian bartender on Friday night. "Is that, like, a new London trend or something? Calling guys by women's names?"

"Penelope is more of a way of being, a way of looking at the world, a way of experiencing life, than an actual person."

R*iiii*ght.

"How does that work exactly?" Scarlett asks.

"A Penelope is a pooch lover, a life giver and keeper, a person with canine sensibilities and a deep understanding of the natural environment. A Penelope is not a person or a group of people, more it's you and it's me. Or it can be."

Well that cleared it up.

"Does that mean we're Penelopes?" I gesture between Scarlett and myself.

She sizes us up. "You could be."

"Babe, I think you've got to buy a dog in order to become a Penelope," Scarlett says.

The woman recoils from us with a shocked expression on her face, as though she's been prodded with a hot poker. "You don't *buy* a dog."

"You don't?" I question.

Penelope shakes her head vehemently. "Oh, no. You become part of its pack."

Scarlett's eyes slide to mine. I know what she's thinking. And I'm thinking it, too.

"Sorry. I think what my friend meant to say is that we really want to become part of one of your dogs' packs."

"Oh, you want to be the *leader* of a dog's pack, Zara," Scarlett corrects, and I nod in agreement.

"True," I confirm. "So, the dog I'm interested in is the one you had—"

Penelope cuts me off with a stern, "We choose not to use the 'l' word here at Penelope's Pooches."

"We do?" I question.

"We embrace an egalitarian conceptualisation of the canine pack. It's part of our dog-cept."

This place feels increasingly more like a cult than a pet store. And haven't they got the whole canine pack hierarchy thing totally wrong?

Scarlett elbows me in the ribs and I do my best to keep a straight face. "Okay. Not an 'l' word, and not *buying* a dog. What I mean is can I please...*meet* the Jack Russell you had in the window earlier today?" I hold my breath and hope I've said the right thing. Surely "meet" is acceptable in the dog-cept? If that's even a thing, which I strongly suspect it's not.

The Penelope's features relax. "You can absolutely meet our little Jack Russell. Glass of champagne?"

I almost get whiplash from the turnabout.

"We'd love to, but we've got to go back to work after this," I explain. "I'm dying to meet her. I mean, I assume she's a her. She looks like a her." I pause and add, "Or are you non-binary here, too? You know, as part of your dog-cept?"

The Penelope bursts into peals of laughter, ending in a loud snort. "Oh, you're so funny. That would be *absurd* for a dog to be non-binary. Fancy that!"

"Oh, totally absurd," I reply with a fake laugh because of course *none* of this is weird in the least. I refocus her on the task at hand. "So, that dog from the window this morning. Is she still here?"

"Oh, yes. We don't keep a dog in the window for more than a short period of time. They get peer fatigued, you know, which is when too many people peer at them."

Scarlett's nose makes an odd sound as she suppresses a laugh. I shoot her a look.

"Of course," I say.

"What we do is, after a certain period of time in the window, we ask the dogs if they'd like to leave the window and instead return to their den. Today, Steve decided to do just that. We like to give our dogs agency. It's part of our—"

"Dog-cept," Scarlett finishes for her. "Yeah, we've got it."

"Her name is Steve?" I ask, confused. "Weird name for a girl. Weird but cute."

And I can always change it...

"Her full name is Stevedore Clemence Norwich."

"Stevedore Clemence Norwich. That's quite a name. Isn't a Stevedore a port worker? 'Cos she didn't look much like one of those." I let out a light laugh but immediately clam up when I take in the unamused expression on Penelope's face. ·

"We believe Stevedore is a very proud dog name. It has a long, illustrious history here at Penelope's Pooches."

A long, illustrious history? Hasn't the shop only been open for a year?

I rearrange my features to look serious and avoid looking at Scarlett, who's still snorting with barely suppressed laughter at my side. "Of course it is. It's a very proud name, I'm sure. I didn't meant to be disrespectful to, err, Stevedore."

"I'll need some details about you both first." She pulls a tablet from her boilersuit pocket. "

Scarlett's hands shoot up. "I'm not the one, errr, joining the dog's pack. That's Zara. I'm just here for the ride." She adds under her breath, "Plus, I'm a human."

"What's your full name?" Penelope asks me.

"Zara Huntington-Ross."

"Do you live in a flat or a house with a yard?"

"I'm in a flat, which I share with my friend, Lottie. She also adores dogs and will be wonderful with Stevie, I'm sure."

She gives me a stern look. "We'll need to meet her, too."

"Of course."

"And see your flat."

She goes on to ask me a few more standard questions, noting my replies down on her tablet as Scarlett wanders around the shop looking at their merchandise.

Then things take a turn for the weird. Not that things hadn't been weird from the moment we stepped inside this shop, of course. But they definitely get weirder.

"Tell me, Zara, if you were a cowboy in a small American town in the late-1800s and the sheriff was calling up men to form a posse to catch a couple of bandits who'd robbed the local bank, would you join him?"

I blink at her, my mouth dropped wide enough to catch flies. Or a small bird. "I'm sorry?"

"If you were a cowboy in a small town in the late-1800s and the sheriff—" she repeats.

"I meant...why? Why do you need to know something like that?"

Penelope—now I'm beginning to wonder if they get serial numbers when they start working here, like Penelope-0-1-2 and Penelope-0-1-3—gives me a stern look. "Ms.

Huntington-Ross, we take this process very seriously at Penelope's Pooches. Please don't interrupt it."

"With all due respect, what's a posse and a bunch of cowboys got to do with me buying—"

She sucks in air.

"—I mean *becoming a part of a pack* with Steve?"

"We need to know so we can match you to the right dog," she replies as though I've asked the most obvious question of all time. "We can't have a posse member with a dog who would prefer to curl up in front of a fire. Likewise, we can't have a blue crayon with a yellow one, but then that goes without saying as I'm sure you'd agree."

We're onto crayons now? There has got to be an easier way to get a puppy.

"We can't?"

"No. Anyone who knows the colour wheel knows that blue and yellow are opposites, and in the canine-human relationship that will not work."

"Right. Got it," I reply, not getting it in the least.

"And on that point, if you could be a new colour of crayon, what would you be?"

"Err, can I choose one of the existing colours? Or do I have to make one up?"

She raises her eyebrows at me before she taps something on her tablet.

"Wait. Did I fail that one?"

She ignores my reply, instead peppering me with more random and seemingly irrelevant questions. Once she's determined that yes, I would join the posse, no I wouldn't want to walk across hot coals as part of a tribal initiation process, and on a scale of one to ten I rate the colour turquoise as a solid seven, she finally, *finally*, tells me I've passed the test to be considered for Steve.

How I managed that, I'll never know.

"Do you have something that smells of you that I could take to Steve? Your scarf, perhaps."

"You're going to give her my scarf to sniff?"

"Not just sniff. I want her to inhale your essence, really learn about you before she makes up her mind whether or not to meet you."

I went through all that and I still might not get to meet the dog?

I pull my silk scarf from around my neck and hand it to her.

"Why don't you take a seat in the pen and I'll ask Steve if she'd like to meet you." She indicates an area on the green carpet that's ringed by a low picket fence. "If she gives the go ahead, I'll be back shortly with her. See you soon!"

As she exits the shop via the back door, I blow out a puff of air. This whole thing is beyond weird, but I've got my heart set on Steve, so I've got to play ball.

I step over the little white picket fence and into the pen. There's a selection of chew toys and a couple of beanbags in the pen, so I choose one and sink into it.

"You do know Steve is a totally weird name for a dog, right?" Scarlett asks me from the other side of the pen.

"Yeah, it is, but it's also quite cute."

"Cute is 'Buddy' or 'Teddy' or 'Comet'. Not 'Steve.'"

I say in a hushed voice, "I bet Penelope would have something to say if I changed her name."

"Who cares?" she replies with a shrug. "I'm going to go and check out the doggie outfits."

As Scarlett moves to the other side of the shop, I sit and I wait. And wait. I watch as another customer enters the store and is immediately greeted by one of the Penelopes.

All he wants is some dog food, so he's finished and gone while I'm still waiting.

I pull out my phone and start to research furniture for Asher's flat. I'd may as well make use of my time. I find some gorgeous panels that would fit the look he told me he'd like for his bedroom, and a tan leather living room suite that he could comfortably lounge on in front of "Tonya."

"Steve said she'd love to meet you."

I look up to see my Penelope holding Steve in her arms. The puppy's looking at me, her skinny white tail wagging like a pair of windscreen wipers in a downpour, as she wriggles to be put down on the ground.

I spring out of the beanbag, which is no small feat, and gush, "Oh, she's absolutely darling! Can I hold her?" Warmth fills my chest.

"You'll need to ask her that," Penelope replies.

"Hi, Steve. I'm Zara. You sniffed my scarf. Can we have a cuddle?"

Her tail wagging moves into overdrive, which seems to be enough of a signal to Penelope that yes, indeed, Steve would like a cuddle.

I take her squirmy, warm, soft little body in my arms and she immediately climbs my chest and begins to lick and nibble on my earlobe. It tickles and I let out a giggle, which only makes her wriggle in excitement all the more.

"Oh, Steve. Who's a gorgeous girl, then? You are, that's who," I coo. I receive another set of licks in response.

Penelope claps her hands together and I look at her in surprise. "It's a match!" she declares, and instantly the other staff in their light blue boilersuits and pigtails begin to applaud, moving through the shop to join us. Someone hits play on a stereo somewhere and cheesy violin music, like you hear in old movies, fills the room as everyone gathers around me, an amused Scarlett watching in wonderment.

I feel like I should be holding Steve up above my head as Sir Elton declares that this is the circle of life to an audience of excited African wildlife who simultaneously bow to Steve's future "queen of the jungle" status.

I don't. That would be even weirder than this whole experience.

And that's saying something.

"Zara Huntington-Ross, Stevedore Clemence Norwich has chosen you to be a part of her pack," my Penelope states as the others nod and smile their agreement.

I gaze down at Steve. Her big dark brown eyes gaze back up at me, her ears standing to attention, and her little pink tongue locked and loaded, ready to attack my earlobe once more. It's love at first sight, pure and simple.

"I would love to join Steve's pack," I tell the assembled group, and they burst into spontaneous applause once more. Scarlett and a cluster of customers look on in bemused silence.

Half an hour and a lot of paperwork later, I've agreed to have my Penelope visit my flat on Saturday afternoon—their earliest "future dog den visitation" slot available—to ensure it's a suitable home for Stevie, and I bid my new little dog goodbye. Together, Scarlett and I head back to ScarZar, excited that I'm mere days away from become a mum to my own little Steve.

Chapter Five

Dear Dad
            I'm thirty! Can you believe it? The big 3-0.
            My 20s are over, kaput, gone. Your little girl is all grown up and it feels... weird. Wrong. Like I should be somewhere I haven't reached yet.? Somewhere waaay more grown up. Does that make sense?
     Let's just say I'm working on it.
     I'm thinking of you so much today.
     Miss you. Love you.
     Your Za-Za xoxo

The next few days are dominated by two things: work and my thirtieth birthday party in the country at my family's home, Martinston. I would have been more than happy to avoid the whole family celebration, but Mum and Granny insisted I mark the passing of time with a big party. The deal was clinched when Mum offered to pay for the whole thing, including buying all the booze, and with some of my friends, that's a pretty darn huge expense—I'm looking at you, Tabitha.

"Zara, the caterers will be here at six, the band arrives at six thirty and we've still got all the seating to get sorted out in the ballroom," Emma, my sister-in-law says, standing in the doorway to my childhood bedroom where I've been holed up, getting ready for the party. "But before all that, I've gotta say that you look totally gorgeous!"

"Do you think?" I smooth my dress down self-consciously. The party theme is "Black and White," and I've chosen to wear a white figure-hugging dress that reaches the floor, with a slit up the side and a halter-neck. Teamed with a pair of hot pink high heeled sandals and my hair in silky waves, I feel like a siren of the silver screen.

"Duh," she replies with a grin. "Your doppelgänger has got nothing on you tonight, girl."

Emma loves to tell me how much I look like Bond girl Gemma Arterton, but personally, I don't see it. She's a million times more gorgeous than me—and a Bond girl. *Hello?!*

I plant a kiss on Emma's cheek and immediately wipe off the lipstick mark I created. "You're a total suck up. You know that?" I say with a grin.

"Just stating the facts."

My brother, Sebastian, appears around the door. Placing his hands on his wife's waist, she looks up at him lovingly and he says, "My beautiful wife," before he promptly kisses her. In my doorway!

"Ahem," I say. "Haven't you got your own room to carry on in? You don't need to do all that kissy-kissy business in mine, do you?"

"Actually, I came to see you, but got side-tracked by my

hot Texan wife," Sebastian replies. "You can hardly blame me. Look at this mother of my child."

Emma beams up at him. "You're the best."

I roll my eyes, but secretly I'm happy for them that they've got one another. Although really, do they need to get so lovey-dovey in front of me all the time? The answer to that question is a definite no. And the fact they've got what I want has nothing to do with it. Honestly.

"All right. Enough of this carrying on. Emma, you wanted to tell me about the caterers and the band?"

She drags her adoring eyes from my brother's for long enough to reply, "We need to get the rest of the seating into the ballroom before the caterers arrive."

"Actually, don't worry yourselves with that," Sebastian says. "I've got some blokes on the job."

"What blokes?" I question.

"Johnny's texted to say he'll be here in about five minutes," he says, naming his best friend, "and Charlie's already downstairs."

"Charlie Cavendish?" I ask.

"The very same. I'd better get down there. You two keep doing whatever it is women do before parties."

Sebastian kisses Emma on the lips once more—chastely, thank goodness, because there's a limit to how much of that carrying on a sister needs to witness in her lifetime—and then leaves us.

"Charlie Cavendish, huh?" I say as I apply another layer of lipstick.

"You like Charlie?" Emma asks.

"No. I was thinking about Kennedy and the fact she and Charlie hated one another from the moment they met. What is *with* that?"

"Beats me, but it is kinda funny. Didn't you know he was invited to your party?"

"Mum took control of the guest list. I figured this is more her party than mine in some ways."

"Because of your dad?"

I pull my lips into a line. "She'll be feeling it tonight that he's not here."

"How about you? Are you doing okay?"

A knot forms in my belly as my chest tightens. I glance at the small collection of perfume bottles on my dressing table. Dad gave me my very first one when I was twelve years old, and I've been collecting them ever since. Most of my collection is at my Fulham flat, but I keep a few here for when I visit and want to admire their beauty.

"I wish he was here. That's all."

"I bet you do." Emma pulls me in for a quick hug. "There's something so special about a father-daughter relationship. He's the only one you've got."

I turn my gaze to hers and see understanding in her eyes. Tears spring to my own eyes, and I quickly brush them away with my fingertips. "I don't want to mess up my makeup. It took me ages to get these stupid eyelashes in place."

Emma pulls a couple of tissues from a box on my bedside table. "Here. Your lashes are still in place."

I dab my eyes. "Being a daddy's girl sucks when your dad's not around."

"It does," she replies softly, and I know she feels it, too. She lost her dad to a heart attack some years ago, and she named her activewear line after him in his honour.

"Knock knock."

I look up to see Kennedy, Lottie, and Tabitha in the doorway. They're all holding colourfully wrapped gifts in their hands, dressed in black, each of them in a different style, and all of them look absolutely radiant. "Hello, chick-adees," I say with a watery smile.

"Oh, honey. What's wrong?" Lottie rushes over to me in two seconds flat and plonks herself down on the four-poster bed beside me.

I blow my nose into one of the tissues Emma gave me. "I'm having a dad moment, that's all."

"Of course you are," she soothes. "And you're perfectly entitled to have as many moments as you want about what-ever you want. This is *your* party."

"And you'll cry if you want to," Tabitha finishes for her as she sits down on my bed, too. "That's the old song, isn't it? Not that I want you to cry of course. I want you to have an amazing night."

"She will," Emma says as she greets my friends. "Now, I'm gonna go help my hot husband out downstairs and leave you girls to talk. The party's starting soon, so I'll see y'all down there, okay?"

"I love it when you throw in a 'y'all,'" I say to her. "I sometimes forget you're from Texas."

"Born and raised," she says proudly. "And before any of you ask, no, I didn't grow up on a ranch and I don't know any cowboys."

"Pity," Kennedy says. "I could do with a cowboy right about now, Em. Do you think you could conjure one up for me?"

"My conjuring skills are pretty rusty," Emma replies with a laugh.

"Oh, get one for me, too. A tall, sexy cowboy in tight jeans and one of those big metal buckles, with a shirt that shows off his broad shoulders and magnificent pecs."

Tabitha fans herself with her hand as she leans back on my bed.

"We *all* want one of those, Tabitha," Lottie says. "Who knows? Maybe Zara will get one for her birthday?"

I glance at the three gifts my friends have placed on my bed. "You got me a cowboy?" I ask with a sardonic smile. Because of course they hadn't got me a cowboy, and if they had, it'd be a miniature one that could fit inside a small box and what would the point of that be?

Tabitha shakes her head. "No cowboy, babe. But I wish we had now. You look like you need cheering up, and that simply will not do when it's your swanky birthday party at your family's posh manor house."

"Speaking of which, I'll leave you girls to it," Emma says.

I smile at her. "Okay. And Em?"

She turns to look back at me.

"Thanks."

Her face breaks into a beautiful smile. "Anytime, sis," she replies before she leaves.

"Zara's already getting something to cheer her up. Tell them, Zee," Lottie instructs me.

"If it's not a cowboy maybe it's a fireman," Kennedy suggests. "A super-hot fireman, like in those calendars."

"Or a policeman!" Tabitha offers, her eyes shining.

I snort giggle. "If you say an American Indian next then we'll have the Village People, right here at my family's house."

Kennedy says, "Honey, you can't call this place a house. It's got a gazillion rooms and servants' quarters. It's Downton freaking Abbey."

"Tell us what you're getting," Tabitha asks. "And don't tell us it's that Asher's your back-up guy. That's old news."

"It's not about Asher, even though he has just employed ScarZar to decorate his new bachelor pad in Notting Hill. I've got my work cut out, that's for sure."

"You'll do an amazing job, babe. I know you will," Lottie says with assuredness.

She wins a beaming smile from me.

My friends are the best.

"Can we focus please, girls?" Tabitha asks. "What are you getting?"

My tummy warms at the thought of little Steve. "Well, I don't know if it's a done deal yet because they need to come over to meet Lottie and check out our place, but I did choose to go on the posse with the sheriff and apparently I'm the right coloured crayon, so that's something."

I get a confused collective look from Kennedy and Tabitha. Lottie simply beams at me because she's been in the know for days now, what with being my flatmate and having to hear all about Steve for the past few days.

I press my lips together as a grin forms on my face. "I'm getting a puppy," I announce.

"A puppy?!" Tabitha and Kennedy both squeal and then instantly pepper me with questions.

"What breed of dog?"

"How old is it?"

"Is it a girl or a boy?"

"Where are you getting it from? A breeder? A shop?"

I count my answers off on my fingers. "The dog breed is a gorgeous little Jack Russell with the most darling liquid brown eyes that gaze up at you and totally melt your heart; aged about 11 weeks or so; a little girl called Steve, which I'm changing to Stevie; and she's from Penelope's Pooches just down the road from the shop."

"See? I told you she was getting something," Lottie says. "Isn't it wonderful?"

"Oh, my gosh, yes! I'm so excited for you." Kennedy grins. "I cannot wait to meet Stevie."

"It's not as good a gift as a cowboy," Tabitha grumps. "But I suppose you could get a cowboy outfit for her. Wait, then it'd have to be a cow*girl* outfit." She shrugs. "Cute either way."

"As I said, it's not a done deal yet. Lottie and I have to put on a great show for them tomorrow afternoon."

Tabitha puts her hand on my arm. "Let's hope you're over your hangover by then, babe, because tonight, we par-*tay*."

I shake my head and laugh. Tabitha loves nothing more than to get all dressed up and hit the town, and she's always having adventures that end up with her in a variety of precarious positions—including the time she set the smoke detector off at a party because she was bored, and another time when she lost her bra and found it up at the top of a thirty-foot tree the following day. How it got there is anyone's guess, and Tabitha swears not to know.

Tabitha pulls a hipflask out of her pocket and waves it in the air. "A shot for luck," she says as she opens the lid and takes a swig. She hands it to me.

"What is it?" I ask.

"Well, it's not lemonade," she replies with a wry smile. "Grapefruit vodka. It's yummy and with the fruit, I'm sure it's good for you."

I giggle as I hand the flask to Lottie. "I'll pass, but thanks."

"But it's your birthday, Zee. You need to get cucumbered with the rest of us," Tabitha says.

"I'm not planning on getting cucumbered tonight."

"Suit yourself," she replies with a shrug.

"What the heck is 'cucumbered?'" Kennedy asks.

"Drunk," Lottie, Tabitha, and I all reply at the same time.

"And here I was thinking the only thing you Brits did with cucumbers was put them in sandwiches. Okay, I'm heading downstairs now. You girls coming with?" Kennedy asks as she turns to leave.

I leap off my bed, shocking Lottie and Tabitha who have to regain their balance with my sudden departure. "Wait! Stay here for a bit, Kennedy. I need you to—" I glance quickly around the room for an excuse to keep her from venturing back downstairs, "—help me decide which shoes to wear."

She obviously didn't run into Charlie Cavendish on her way to my room, and I want to avoid her having to do so now.

Her eyes slide to my feet. "But you've got on a gorgeous pair of shoes already. Why not wear those?"

"Because they're hurting my feet," I fib with my fingers crossed behind my back. "I need your expert eye to help me choose another pair to go with this dress. White is a very tricky colour, you know."

Lottie crinkles her forehead in confusion. "Why do you need Kennedy to help you choose shoes? She writes features for her magazine, not a fashion column."

I glare at her and mouth "Charlie Cavendish," hoping she'll get it.

She doesn't.

"What, Zee? Speak up."

"Charlie Cavendish," I say in a low voice through a clenched jaw.

"Charlie who?" she asks, and I close my eyes in resigned frustration.

Kennedy freezes. "Charlie Cavendish is here?" she questions, her voice strained.

"Mum invited him. She was in charge of the whole list, and I've been so wrapped up in this whole Karina drama that I barely gave it a second look. I'm really sorry, Kennedy. I know he's not your favourite person on the planet."

"I don't know why. I think he's fabulous," Lottie declares.

"And gorgeous," Tabitha adds. "What's the matter Kennedy, fabulous and gorgeous aren't what you're looking for in a man?"

She gives a flick of her wrist. "He's fine. Totally fine," she says, convincing a sum total of *no one*.

"Really?" Lottie asks.

Kennedy crosses her arms over her chest. "Just because he's got more money than sense and thinks he can charm a girl with tales of his yachts and houses and pet gorillas doesn't bother me in the slightest."

"Charlie Cavendish has a pet gorilla?" Tabitha asks, looking thoroughly confused. "But he lives in London. Where would he put it?"

"I wouldn't be surprised if he did have a pet gorilla. He's got virtually everything else," Kennedy huffs.

"He doesn't have a pet gorilla," I say. "Or at least I don't think he does."

"Shame," Tabitha replies with a sigh. "So far tonight we've lost a sexy cowboy for the birthday girl and a pet gorilla."

Kennedy harrumphs.

"How did we get onto this topic, exactly?" Lottie asks. "We're meant to be celebrating our brilliant friend turning the grand old age of thirty, not prevaricating over whether certain men we know have African primates as pets, which I suspect is highly illegal, anyway."

"Well said," Kennedy says.

"What time is it?" Tabitha asks. "Is the party about to start?"

I glance at my phone on top of my chest of drawers. "The party starts in three minutes." I notice a message and click on it. "Oh, look. Scarlett says she's got me the best birthday present a single girl could get. I wonder what it is?"

"I bet it's a cowboy!" Tabitha says excitedly.

"Haven't we been through this already, Tabitha? It won't be a cowboy, or anyone else from the Village People," I reply.

Lottie's eyes grow big and round. "But it might be a *man*."

We share a look and, as though we are all thinking the same thing at the exact same time, we rush over to my large bedroom window and look down onto the long, gravel driveway that leads up to the house. Tonight, it's lit by rows of burning torches, making the whole place feel like something from a Jane Austen novel—or a scene from *Jumanji*. I haven't decided which yet.

A black, shiny car crunches down the drive and comes to a stop in front of the house.

"Oooh, who's that?" Lottie asks.

We watch a blonde-haired woman climb out of the passenger seat, followed quickly by two men, both in dinner suits, and both with full heads of hair (which is pretty much all I can tell from up here on the third floor).

"That's Scarlett and the guy she's seeing right now, isn't it?" Kennedy asks.

"Harry Honeydew," Tabitha replies.

"That *cannot* be the guy's real name," Kennedy replies.

"Oh, it is. Harry is from a long, long line of Honeydews. They're really quite famous in their home shire."

Kennedy ruffles her brow. "Honeydew? Shire? You Brits are just plain weird."

"We can't all be from sunny California and look like you, Kennedy," I reply with a laugh.

As though sensing our eyes on her, Scarlett looks directly up at us, smiles and waves, pointing at one of the men at her side.

"She didn't!" I exclaim.

"Oh, I think she did," Kennedy replies.

"I wanted a cowboy for you," Tabitha grumps.

Lottie nudges me. "He looks good from up here. I wonder if he's a Honeydew as well?"

Kennedy giggles. "Honeydew."

"So, this is where the party is," a deep, American voice behind us says.

In unison, we turn around to see Asher filling the doorway with his presence. He's wearing a classic dinner suit—which he insists on calling a "tux"—and from his stubbled jaw to his floppy hair and dark eyes, he looks like Taylor Lautner and Theo James's love child. If that were a biological possibility.

My girlfriends say hello and then return their attention to Scarlett and the Honeydews.

"Love the dinner suit," I say to him.

His lips twitch. "It's a tux and thank you. What are we looking at here?" He walks across the room and peers over our heads down at the driveway.

"Scarlett just arrived with her new guy, and she brought a friend," Tabitha explains. "A *guy* friend."

"How fascinating," Asher deadpans.

"Oh, but it is," Lottie insists, "because she told Zara that she was bringing her the best birthday present a *single* girl could get and now she's turned up with her boyfriend and this other guy. You do the maths."

He counts it off on his fingers. "Let me see. Scarlett plus her boyfriend plus another guy equals an uninvited party guest."

Lottie rolls her eyes. "I can't imagine Zara is going to give two hoots about whether he was invited or not, Asher."

"Should we ask the birthday girl?" he says, and all four of my friends tilt their heads to look at me.

"I dunno," I reply in the most articulate sentence of my thirty years.

Tabitha nudges me with her elbow. "Yeah, you do."

"I'm... open to meeting him," I say.

The corners of Asher's lips curve up. "Right. So, you're telling me that the poor guy down there," he says as he gestures at the three figures moving across the driveway, "is here on a blind date with the birthday girl?"

"How does that make him a poor guy, exactly?" I ask.

"Yeah, Asher," Tabitha adds. "Any guy would be lucky to go on a blind date with Zara. Look at her, she's gorgeous, and she's also a totally brilliant person."

Asher runs his eyes over me, and it does something new and weird to my belly. I brush it off with a huff. It's only Asher. It must be the sexy dinner suit messing with my hormones.

"You do look good tonight," he says.

"Good? She looks phenomenal!" Kennedy insists.

Asher's lips lift into a smile. "Okay. She looks phenomenal."

"That's better," Kennedy sniffs. "Where's your date?"

"She's downstairs," Asher replies.

76

"Are you telling us you brought a date here and then promptly disappeared to come up to see us?" I ask him.

"She's fine. She knew one of the other guests."

"Who did Carolyn know?"

He shakes his head. "Not Carolyn."

I blink at him, incredulous. "*Another* girl? Your love life has got one fast moving revolving door, Asher McMillan. I get dizzy as a spectator."

He grins at me. "Why, thank you."

I give him my best *mother is not amused* glare. "It's *not* meant as a compliment."

"Look. More cars are arriving," Lottie says.

"Is the birthday girl ready to head down to her party?" Kennedy asks.

All eyes are on me.

I grin at my friends. "I am. Let's do this."

Chapter Six

Along with my friends—well, the girls, not Asher—I do a last-minute hair and makeup check in my floor-length mirror. I flick my hair behind one shoulder, allowing my long tresses to fall over one side.

"Perfect," Lottie coos behind me. "She's ready for her close up, Mr. DeMille. I wish I had your hair. Or your face. Or your body."

I let out a giggle. "There'd be nothing of me left. And besides, you're beautiful, Lottie."

Her cheeks colour. "Thanks."

"Enough preening, women," Asher says from his position by the window. "There are tons of people arriving now, and they'll want to see the birthday girl."

"You do realise every member of my crazy family is going to be here tonight."

"Your family is simply wonderful, especially your hot older brother. Even if he is as uptight as Mr. Darcy," Tabitha says.

I harrumph. Ever since Sebastian posed as Mr. Darcy on a reality TV show called Dating Mr. Darcy (see what they did there?), he's had women lusting over him left, right, and centre. Sadly for them, he met Emma on the show and fell head over heels in love, married her, and is now the proud father of a little girl, my darling niece.

As I'm about to follow my girlfriends from the room, Asher places his hand gently on my forearm. "I almost forgot. I got you a present."

"You did? Aw, thanks, hubby."

Lottie pauses at the door and looks back at us. "You two coming?"

"We'll be right down. I'm just giving the birthday gal a present."

"Okay, but don't be long. Your public awaits!" She flashes us her smile before she leaves the room.

"I can't top Scarlett's present, you know."

"We don't even know if she did get me a blind date. And if she did, it's a weird gift. I mean, is it even legal to gift a person to someone?"

He laughs. "I'd say that's a hard no." He reaches into the inside pocket of his jacket and pulls out a red box tied up with a hot pink ribbon. "Here, I got you this."

"Aw, you shouldn't have, but I'm glad you did." I take it from him, untie the ribbon, and pop the box open. Inside is the most gorgeous blue, pink, and purple glass perfume bottle. It's small enough to nestle in my palm, and I gaze at it as I take in its sheer beauty. "Asher. I don't know what to say."

"I was going to give you something else, but when you told me about your weird perfume bottle obsession, I figured I should get you one of those."

I look up at him and grin. "It's gorgeous. Thank you so, so much."

"Happy birthday. It's not an antique, like the one you showed me that time, but it is made of Murano glass."

"Are you serious? It's Murano?" I wrap my arms around him and give him a quick hug, breathing in his fresh scent. "You're the best."

He shrugs, his eyes bright. "Personally, I don't get the whole perfume bottle thing, but you do so..."

The word "so" lingers in the air.

"Zara! You're missing your party!" Scarlett is standing in the doorway with her hands on her hips. Wearing a silver, pleated dress that hugs her curves, her hair in soft curls around her shoulders, she looks like an up-to-date Marilyn Monroe. "Oh, hi, Asher."

"Hello, Scarlett," he replies.

I hold the perfume bottle up. "Look at what Asher gave me. Isn't it gorgeous?"

She waltzes over and takes it from me. "So pretty. Now, come with me." She hands the bottle to Asher before she hooks her arm through mine and begins to steer me from the room. "I've got someone you must meet, and he's very keen to meet you."

"You *did* bring me a blind date!" I say as she bustles me down the hallway towards the grand staircase. I can hear music and voices and laughter floating up from the ground floor.

"What can I say, darling? It's your birthday, and you've told me you're looking for Mr. Right. The least I can do is save you from having to marry Asher."

I look over my shoulder, expecting Asher to be following us, but there's no sign of him.

"Shouldn't we wait for him?"

"No time for that. You're the star of the night and your handsome prince awaits."

I giggle. I like the idea of a handsome prince, even if it is a little bit fairy-tale for my tastes. "Who is he? Tabitha hopes he's a cowboy."

"He's Harry's cousin. His name is George Honeydew, he's loaded, single, straight, and utterly hot. You're going to die."

A fluttery feeling rolls through my belly. "Oh."

By now, we're halfway down the large, sweeping staircase and the music and chatter have increased in volume.

"I showed him a few shots of you from your Instagram on the way here, and he nearly had an aneurism. He's keen."

"Right. Game on."

"Game on," she confirms.

We round the corner and are met with a sea of people, all sparkling in their evening-dress-best. Several heads turn to look up at us.

"There she is. My daughter, the birthday girl," Mum calls out, and everyone in the room bursts into spontaneous applause.

With Scarlett still clutching onto my arm, I grin out at everyone and take a little bow. Growing up in a social, aristocratic British family, it's impossible to be a wallflower. There are always garden parties in the summer and cocktail parties and luncheons and trips to the opera. The Huntington-Rosses are not hermits, that's for sure. So, I'm more than used to having to perform in public—even if I'd prefer my party to be with a few close friends at my local pub rather than this grand affair.

But it makes Mum happy, and I know she'll be feeling dad's absence today, just as much as I am.

"Speech!" someone calls out, and I'm pretty sure it comes from Tabitha.

When I look her way, she hides behind Lottie.

I burst instantly into Huntington-Ross mode, extracting myself from Scarlett's grasp and saying, "I am absolutely thrilled to have you all here to celebrate me reaching a milestone that moves me officially into 'old.'"

The older party go-ers titter while my friends nod in grim agreement.

"You know, I've been told that I'm having my mid-life crisis right now, and although I'm not exactly middle aged, I guess I am going through something. I'm growing up. So, I've made a decision and I want to share it with you."

"You're getting married?" Mum calls out, ever hopeful her only daughter will take that joyful skip down the aisle.

I let out a laugh. "No, Mum. Sorry. It's actually more exciting than that." I pause for dramatic effect and then announce, "I'm getting a puppy! Well, if Penelope says so, that is." I look out at the assembled upturned faces and await their reaction.

It's fizzled at best.

My friends applaud and whoop, my Mum's friends wait for the next, more important part of my announcement—newsflash: this is it—and my brother Sebastian shoots me an encouraging but confused look.

Undeterred, I continue. "Her name is Stevie and she's a Jack Russell, and she's just divine." I beam out at everyone. Realising this is the sum total of my announcement, Mum's and Granny's friends applaud politely while my friends call, "Woot! Zara's getting a puppy!" and, "We love you, Zee!"

"Thanks. I'm excited. I hope you have a fabulous time tonight." I offer everyone another smile before I make my way down the stairs with Scarlett in tow. Someone hands me a glass of champagne, and I take a sip. The bubbles tickle my nose and work their magic, my spirits lifting.

The party has officially begun.

Twenty minutes and three glasses of champagne later, the band is playing my favourite tunes and the party is in full swing. I've been diligently doing the rounds of all the guests, most of whom seem to be Mum's and Granny's friends who are intent on delivering one message to me and one message only.

When are you going to settle down?

Actually, not all the questions peppered at me have been the same. There have been some variants. They range from *What? You're still single? But you're 30 years old!* to *A dog is all very well, but are there any promising boyfriends on the horizon?* to *It would be such a comfort to your dear mother to see her only daughter happily married.*

The last one was from Mum.

My mother, subtle? Hmmm, not so much.

"You know you really should listen to your mother, Zara," Granny says to me when I complain to her about it. "When I was your age, I had been married for twelve years," Granny says as she leans on her old wooden walking stick. "Twelve *years.*"

"I know, Granny. You told me at Sunday lunch last week in front of half the family. Oh, and the week before that, and the week before that."

"And why do you think I told you, young lady?"

I open my mouth to respond, but it becomes clear it was a rhetorical question.

"Because you can't dilly-dally with these things anymore, wasting your time on chaps not worthy of you or, worse yet, not even stepping out with anyone."

"Stepping out? Granny, this isn't the 1950s. We don't

'step out' anymore." I feel someone's eyes on me. I glance up and notice my blind date, George, watching me with a small smile teasing at the edges of his mouth. With his sandy blonde hair, square jaw, and cheeky grin, the guy looks like Captain America, only without the suit and shield. Although by the looks of him, he'd look amazing with the suit and shield.

But I digress.

I shoot him a quick smile.

"What do you do then?" Granny asks me.

I drag my eyes from Captain America back to Granny. "I'm sorry?"

"What do you call it if it's not 'stepping out?'"

I steal another look at George. He's still got his eyes on me with that sexy grin on his face, and my belly does a little flip. "I don't know. Date? Hang out? Hook up?"

Granny makes a face. "Hooking up sounds absolutely vile. Why can't you find a nice man to settle down with? You'll be on the shelf before you know it."

"Being 'on the shelf' isn't a thing anymore, Granny. Women have choices. I've got a career and a wonderful group of friends."

"Friends," she scoffs, just as Tabitha screeches with laughter and promptly slips and lands on her butt on the ballroom floor. "Perhaps it may be time to choose a little more wisely on that front, too." She eyes Tabitha as Lottie tries to pull her to her feet, but her skinny legs splay over the floor like a newborn deer trying to stand, and both of my friends end up clutching their sides with laughter as Asher grins down at them. A moment later, he's got them both safely back on their feet, but the damage is done in Granny's eyes.

"I adore my friends, Granny, and I have no interest in replacing them, even if they can be a little...exuberant."

She purses her skinny lips. "Hmmm."

"They're like family to me."

She harrumphs. "*We're* your family."

I lean down and kiss her on her gaunt, lined cheek. "And I love you so much."

"Don't you even *want* to get married?"

I'm in a tricky spot. If I tell her the truth—that I'm more than ready to meet Mr. Right, marry him, and make babies—she'll burst into a high-spirited dance, right here in front of everyone at my party. Although that would be quite an incredible vision, I don't want to get her hopes up. I mean, I haven't even met a guy I would consider marrying, let alone following through with it.

"Someday," I reply elusively as I notice Scarlett, Henry, and Captain America George talking and laughing with Tabitha and Lottie close by. They look like they're having a great time, and I'm meant to be having fun with them and maybe even flirting with George—not getting questioned on my life choices by my family.

"Granny, let's talk about it later, okay? Right now, I'm going to go over to see my friends. I'll catch up with you soon."

"Do you want to end up a lonely old crow like your poor aunt Cecily, Zara? Because that is precisely where you're heading," she warns.

"Great chat, Granny," I reply in a bright tone. I spot a couple of her old cronies sitting down over the by the wall. "Oh, look, Granny. There's Lord Wistern. I'll invite him and his wife over, shall I?" I don't wait for a reply. Instead, I weave through the group of people, saying hello and telling them I'll chat to them later, until I reach my target.

"Hello, Lord and Lady Wistern. How lovely it is to see you both. I wondered if you'd had the chance to say hello to my granny yet? I'm sure she'd love to see you."

"Who?" Lord Wistern asks in a booming voice.

"My granny," I reply. "Geraldine."

Realisation dawns on his craggy face. "Oh, Geraldine. Doesn't she owe me money?" he asks his wife.

"No, that's Gerald, your cousin, dearest."

"Gerald owes me money? The scoundrel!"

"Yes, dearest. A rather sizeable sum."

Lord Wistern looks scandalized. "How much?"

"Dearest, we don't speak of money in society. It's unseemly."

"I don't care about all that. How much does he owe me? I've a good mind to get it back."

"Dearest—"

"How much?"

"It's about a hundred thousand pounds at last count," she says under her breath.

I pretend I don't hear. "So anyway, would you like—" I begin only to be cut off.

"How much?" he booms in outrage, his already rosy cheeks turning Rudolph the Reindeer red. "This is preposterous. Where is he? Take me to him immediately."

Lady Wistern throws me an apologetic look. "Dearest, there's no need to get agitated. He's owed you the money for thirty years."

"Thirty years?" he questions.

Okay, the Wisterns perhaps weren't the best choice.

I back away from the bickering couple only to step up against someone. I turn to apologise and come face to face with the man himself, George. "Hi," I say in a breathy voice.

"Happy birthday," he replies with a smile. His voice is

velvety soft and deep, and it sends electricity through me. "I'm sorry I didn't bring the birthday girl a gift."

"No problem. I bet you didn't even know you were coming to this tonight."

"No, but I'm glad I did. Your family home is stunning."

"Thanks." We smile shyly at one another for a moment.

"My parents are also here at this party tonight, actually. Isn't that weird?"

I blink at him, uncomprehending. "You brought your parents?"

He laughs. It's warm and sexy and it brings a smile to my face. "They know your mother, apparently. I was as surprised as you to see them here."

"Small world." Although it's not that small, especially not in the country "set" in which there's been so much inter-breeding over the years, it's amazing any of us can function as normal human beings.

Okay, that's a total exaggeration, but you get the point. We all know one another.

"So, you're Henry's cousin, right?" I ask.

"George Honeydew at your service." He inclines his head in a little bow. It's old fashioned and endearing and oh-so cute.

#Swoon

"I came down for the weekend and Scarlett suggested coming tonight. I hope it's okay that I'm here." He looks around at the party goers. "It seems like a pretty formal deal."

"That's how my family rolls. This isn't my everyday life, you know. I live in a flat in London with my friend Lottie. I'm really quite normal and boring."

"You don't strike me as 'normal' or 'boring.'"

I press my lips together to stop a ridiculously huge grin from breaking out across my face.

Thank you, Scarlett!

"Where did you come down here from?"

"I live in Edinburgh these days, although I'm originally from Surrey. I must say, it's nice to be back in the Home Counties. Although I do love living in Scotland, it's not exactly tropically warm."

"Ah, no, but then you do have Jamie Fraser."

"Jamie Who?"

"From *Outlander*? You know, the whole time travel Jamie and Claire love story?"

He shakes his head. "I've got no idea what you're talking about, sorry."

"It's a TV show. But then you're a guy so it's probably not your thing. My friends and I love it. Hashtag obsessed."

"I'll be sure to check it out, since you recommend it. Maybe I'll let you know what I think of it once I've watched an episode or two."

I smile at him. This guy is nice and sweet and funny! And hot. Definitely hot. "Okay."

"So, I might need your number to do that," he says.

"My number. Right."

He pulls out his phone from the inside pocket of his jacket and I tap in my name and number. As he takes the phone from me, his finger brushes mine and as I lift my eyes, our gazes lock.

"There you are, Zara. Your mom sent me. You're needed for the birthday cake," a voice says beside me.

With reluctance, I tear my eyes away from George to see Kennedy looking at me.

"Zara? You okay?" she questions when I don't respond.

"What? Oh, yes. Fine. The cake, you say? Sure. Let's do it."

She looks from me to George and back again. Realisation dawns on her face. "So, you met each other, huh?"

"Yup." Heat begins to burn my cheeks. I steal a glance at George. He looks awkward, too, which only makes me like him more.

"Blind dates can be super awkward," Kennedy says.

"Oh, this isn't—"

"We're not—"

We stop and regard one another before we both smile.

"I'm happy to call it a blind date if you are," George says.

"Sure. It's a blind date."

Charlie Cavendish arrives at our group and immediately kisses me on each cheek, saying, "Happy birthday, Zara. You're looking stunning tonight." His eyes drift to Kennedy. "Hello, Kennedy," he says coolly.

"Charles," she replies with a healthy dose of contempt in her voice.

It's my turn to dart looks between two people. What is *with* these two?

Charlie greets George with a handshake. "Hello, George. I didn't know you knew Zara."

"Oh, we go way back. Don't we?" he replies as he gives me a wink.

"W*aaaa*y back. It's been, what, three minutes?"

"Oh, at least four."

We share another smile, a bunch of cheerleaders doing flips in my belly.

This guy is perfect!

"They're on a blind date," Kennedy says.

"Is that so?" Charlie questions, shooting Kennedy a look that could freeze a hot coffee.

"It is, actually," she replies.

"Well, that's nice, isn't it?"

"It is. For them."

Done with glaring at Kennedy for the time being, Charlie returns his attention to me. "Tell me, Zara, how does it feel to hit the big 3-0?"

"It's totally great. It's just like in that movie *13 Going on 30*. I'm thirty, flirty, and thriving."

Both men look at me with blank expressions.

"It's a Jennifer Garner movie," Kennedy explains for me.

"Right. A chick flick," Charlie says.

Kennedy throws her hands onto her hips. "Oh, that's so typical. You would say that, wouldn't you, Charles? Guys watch rom coms too, you know."

"Oh, you're absolutely right. My cousin, Cyril has watched every rom com ever made."

"See?"

"Of course, he's a fashion designer with immaculate dress sense whose tastes run to the, uh, male end of the spectrum, but still."

Kennedy rolls her eyes. "So only women and gay men watch chick flicks? *Such* a stereotype."

"I tell you what. Since it's so important to you, I'll watch this Jennifer Lawrence movie—"

"Garner. Jennifer Garner. It's not *The Hunger Games*."

"Now that's a good movie," George interjects.

"Absolutely. Action, intrigue, a punitive totalitarian government, not to mention Katniss looking hot in black leather." Charlie taps his chin. "I wonder, can a movie about turning 30 give you all that?"

Kennedy rolls her eyes, her arms now crossed over her chest. "I'll have you know that *13 Going on 30* is a classic."

"I'm sure it is."

It's time to intervene in this little movie sparring match. I don't need bickering friends at my birthday party.

"Okay, you two. We get it. You love to fight. But you know what? This is my birthday party, so you," I point at Charlie, "go and talk to Sebastian and Emma over there. And you," I point to Kennedy, "go and dance with Lottie and Tabitha."

"Yes, miss," Charlie says with a small salute, which wins a fresh eyeroll from Kennedy. "Catch you later." He turns and leaves.

Once he's out of earshot, I ask, "What is it that bothers you about him?"

"Everything," Kennedy replies simply, and I believe her.

The lights are dimmed, and I know what's coming next. This is a birthday party, after all. Sebastian appears holding a huge cake, literally covered in burning candles. The band bursts into *Happy Birthday*, and everyone sings along as I stand there, feeling like an idiot—but a happy one at least.

By the time I've made a wish and blown out my candles, George is nowhere to be seen. I scan the room, but instead of spotting him, I'm met by a grinning Asher, who makes his way through the crowd to me, carrying a plate with a half-eaten piece of cake on it.

"This is delicious. I knew you'd choose strawberry shortcake with vanilla icing. You having some?"

"Oh, sure. I will," I reply distractedly.

"The birthday babe needs to eat cake."

"Sure. Have you seen George?"

"George, the guy who came with Scarlett and Henry?"

"Yup."

"I think he left."

I blink at him. "He left?"

"I think so. Why? Didn't the blind date go well?"

I suppress a smile. "It did, actually."

He studies my face for a beat before he says, "You know you just barely decided to find Mr. Right. You don't have to jump at the first guy you meet."

"I'm not jumping. I'm walking at a leisurely but confident pace towards him."

Asher lets out a laugh. "Is that so?"

"Oh, yes. He asked for my number."

"You know the guy's an idiot. Right?"

"He's not an idiot."

"Oh, he is."

"You're just jealous because Scarlett didn't bring you a blind date."

"I'm fairly certain I never want Scarlett to bring me a blind date."

"Well, I don't care what you think. When George calls me—and he *will* call me—I'll go out with him and have an amazing time. We had a connection."

Asher shoots me a look that tells me I'm totally delusional, but I don't care. I had a connection with George Captain America Honeydew and I cannot wait to hear from him.

Chapter Seven

Dear Dad
    Today, I think I'm getting my new puppy. I say "think" because I need to first pass the pet shop's test. Apparently, it's not enough to join the posse, not walk on hot coals, and choose to be a new coloured crayon.

I'll explain some other time.

Wish me luck!

Miss you. Love you.

Your Za-Za xoxo

I am so excited! Today is the day. Forget turning thirty and birthday parties and hot guys called George—okay, don't forget him, just put him in a box to be opened at a later date.

Today is the day that I'm getting my puppy!

Well, I hope to get her, that is. It all comes down to whether I pass Penelope's Pooches' next test.

I've got Lottie lined up and ready to go. She's under strict instructions not to say anything whatsoever. I don't want her to go telling them she wouldn't join a posse to find the bad guys, or not dive to the bottom of the ocean to find the treasure. She might not be the one getting the dog, but as my flatmate, she's going to be a part of her life. She needs to pass this.

And so do I.

I'm still plumping cushions and dumping dirty dishes I haven't had the chance to clean in an empty bottom drawer when the doorbell chimes. Although I'm expecting it, I almost jump out of my skin.

"It's them. Lottie, it's them!" I call out down the hall.

"Who?" she asks as she wanders into the living room, rubbing her eyes, still wearing her PJs. "And do you think you could speak at a little less than full-on shout volume? Some of us are a little worse for wear after a certain someone's birthday bash last night."

I run my eyes over her appearance. Her pyjamas are rumpled, her hair is flat on the side she's been lying on, and last night's eye makeup is smudged beneath her eyes. "Lottie! You need to get dressed now. Penelope's here."

"Whose Penelope?" she asks with a yawn.

"The dog people," I explain as I dash down the hall. I press the button to let them into the building, saying, "Come on up to level 2!" and pull the door ajar. I grab a brush from the bathroom. "Here," I say as I thrust it at her. "Sort that bird's nest out, get dressed, and remember not to say a word."

"Do you really think the dog is going to care if my hair isn't brushed?"

"No, but the Penelopes will."

"They sound like a cult to me."

"Or like they're in an 80s movie, like *Heathers*," a deep voice says from the doorway.

I turn and gawk. Asher's standing in the doorway

wearing a pair of jeans and a grey jacket over a white tee, holding a cardboard tray of coffees in his hands. "What are you doing here?"

"You let me in. And nice greeting, by the way. You sure know how to make your future husband feel loved, especially one who comes bearing coffee."

Lottie brushes past me. "Mmm, coffee. You're an angel sent from the heavens. Thanks, Ash," she says as she takes one.

I raise an eyebrow at her.

"All right. I'm going," she says as she remains standing in the same spot.

"Lottie, your bedroom is that way, and Asher, you're meant to be the people from Penelope's Pooches, here to assess my home," I say as he comes in and closes the door behind himself.

"Sorry to disappoint you. That's happening now?"

"Yes! And I need you to *not* be here."

He flicks his eyes to Lottie. "Is your roommate a little stressed, by any chance?"

She lets out a giggle. "Zara, stressed about getting this dog? Never!"

The buzzer sounds once more.

A flash of adrenaline bursts through me. "That's got to be them," I say. I lift the handset and say, "Hello?"

"This is Penelope from Penelope's Pooches. We've come to do an assessment," a tinny voice says through the speaker.

"Come on up to the second floor. Flat four." I press the entry button before I turn to face Asher, who should not be here, and Lottie, whose hair is still a fright. "Right, you two. Lottie, go sort your hair out and throw some clothes on, and

Asher, you're here now so you'll have to stay, but you can't say a word."

"Alright, I'm going," Lottie says as she wanders back down the hallway to her room as though she's got all the time in the world.

"Bathroom, Lottie! You need to wet your hair first."

"Sure."

I watch as she totally ignores me and wanders through the door to her bedroom instead.

"She's not wetting her hair," I say, incredulous.

Asher passes me a coffee. "Relax, wifey. It's fine. Although on second thought, maybe you shouldn't be having any caffeine right now."

I take a sip. "Has anyone in the history of time relaxed when they've been told to relax?"

"Well, if they have, I don't think you'll be joining their club anytime soon," he replies with a grin. "Seriously, though. It'll be fine. They're just gonna ask a few questions like 'did you realize dogs poop' and 'don't forget to pet them every now and then' and then be done with it. You'll have your dog and considerably less money, and we can all get on with our lives."

I let out a puff of air, my rock-hard shoulders dropping. "You're right. It'll all be fine."

"It will. I'll go sit in the living room." He strides down the hallway just as there's a knock-knock at the door.

I take a breath and then pull it open with a bright, extremely relaxed, and in-no-way-unnatural smile on my face. "Hello!" I say to not one, not two, but three people, all wearing the same light blue boilersuit and pigtails. "You must be... Penelopes."

"We are," they say in unison with identical smiles.

Wow. So unsettling.

"Do you have individual names, or should I just call you all 'Penelope?'"

"Penelope is fine," the one with blonde frizzy hair and freckles says. "Our individual identities are secondary to our purpose."

"Of course." I stand back to let them in. I avoid looking in Asher's direction, because I just know what he's thinking, and it will not be helpful right now. "Come on in. Welcome to my dog-friendly home."

The three of them walk into the entry hall and look around. I notice a cobweb up the wall at the ceiling and wish I'd looked up while I was frantically cleaning the flat moments ago.

"Where is a good place for us to sit and chat?" Frizzy Blonde Penelope asks.

"The living room's great. Follow me." I walk down the hall and into the living room, where both Asher and Lottie are sitting. Lottie has managed to get dressed in some jeans and a sweatshirt and has even brushed her hair.

Frizzy Blonde Penelope raises her eyebrows. "Hello. Do you live here, as well?"

"I do. Hi, I'm Lottie." She waves at the Penelopes. "I'm Zara's flatmate and I'm super excited about Stevie."

"And you are?" One of the other Penelopes asks Asher. She's got straight black hair and a blunt fringe.

"Oh, I'm just a freeloader. A guest. Not a roommate."

"But Asher, you *are* Zara's future husband so you're so much more than just a freeloader," Lottie insists with a smile that tells me she's having fun with this.

I shoot her a look, my lips drawn into a thin line. Why did she have to mention the back-up thing? It's not in the least relevant to me getting this dog.

"You're getting married?" Black Hair Penelope asks.

97

"Well, that changes things. We'll need to ask you a few pertinent questions before we can proceed, since your husband will also be in Stevie's pack."

"We're not getting married," Asher says. "That was just a joke. Pretend I'm not here." He rises to his feet. "In fact, I'll leave you to it."

"Sit," Frizzy Blonde Penelope says, and to my surprise, Asher sits right back down.

I stifle a giggle. I'll have to remember that next time I want him to do something.

"You both need to stay. You," she says, pointing at me, "sit with the other two."

"But—"

"Sit!"

"Okay." With my tail between my legs—figuratively because I'm not a dog, even if the Penelopes seem to think I need to be treated as one—I slink over to the sofa and plonk myself down between Asher and Lottie.

"Good doggie," Asher says under his breath, and I elbow him in the ribs.

"Ditto."

"Now, the other Penelopes are going to assess the suitability of your property while we have a little chat." Frizzy Blonde Penelope takes a seat opposite us and pulls a notebook from her bag.

"I'd be happy to show your colleagues around the place," I offer.

"Not necessary," she replies without looking at me. "They're perfectly capable to manage the process on their own." She nods at the other two Penelopes, and they immediately begin to wander around the flat.

"I have a few questions for you, Asher."

"Shoot."

"If you were a packet of biscuits, what would you be and why?"

"Excuse me?" he questions.

"If you were a packet of biscuits, what would you be and why?" she repeats.

"I can't answer that. I promised not to talk," he says.

I scrunch my eyes shut in humiliation.

"You can answer the question," Frizzy Blonde Penelope says.

"Do I have to?"

"You do."

"You know, the thing is, that's not a question I've ever actually asked myself."

I widen my eyes at him "Asher, just go with it," I say with a forced smile.

"Okay. Let me think. If I were a packet of *cookies*," he begins, emphasizing the word, "I think I'd be biscotti."

"Why biscotti?" Frizzy Blonde Penelope asks.

"Because like biscotti, I'm a quarter Italian, and I'm tough to crack but worth every bite." He grins at her, and I want to sink into a hole in the floor.

Frizzy Blonde Penelope looks up at him through her lashes. "I like that reply," she says, and promptly begins to blush.

"Thanks. I kinda like it, too." Asher shoots me a look that says *so there*.

So mature.

"Lottie, a question for you. If you could be a colour, what would you be."

"Rain," she replies promptly.

I blink at her. "She said a colour, Lottie."

"Rain is a colour. In fact, it's many colours. It's white,

it's blue, it's grey, it's taupe, it's deep, dark, foreboding black."

"Fascinating," Frizzy Blonde Penelope says as she taps at her tablet.

Is that a good sign? Please let that be a good sign.

"What if you were a fish? What would you be? This question is for both of you."

"Oh, that's easy. I'd be a tiger shark," Asher replies. "Ferocious, uncompromising, totally in charge."

Frizzy Blonde Penelope taps.

"I'd go a different direction altogether," Lottie begins. "I'd be a starfish. That way I get to observe the world around me while sitting serenely on a rock."

More tapping on the tablet.

"Tell me more about the tiger shark," Frizzy Blonde Penelope says to Asher, her blush intensifying. "I find that so interesting that you would say that."

As Asher goes on about alpha sharks and plankton, I roll my eyes so hard they're in danger of spinning out of my head. Women love Asher. Sure, he's easy on the eyes, but he's also funny and charming and has a knack for making people feel at ease. And right now, I'm thankful for him because Frizzy Blonde Penelope seems happy.

The other two Penelopes return to the room and my nerves kick up. "Is everything okay with the flat?"

"There is one concern," the Dark Haired Penelope says. "Come with me."

I spring to my feet and follow her from the room and down the hall to the kitchen. "What is it? What's the problem?"

Asher and Lottie and the other two Penelopes arrive in the room soon after.

"At Penelope's Pooches we specialise in small dogs, as

you know. My concern is that the kitchen window is too high for a dog to see out."

"Really?" I ask as my mind races. Do I need to move the window? Is that possible? Would our landlord even allow it?

"See the distance from here to here," Dark Hair Penelope says as she gestures at the floor to the window. "It's clearly too high off the ground."

"I can see that," Frizzy Blonde Penelope says. "Our dogs need to be able to see blue sky."

"Well, they probably shouldn't be living in London, then," Asher mutters under his breath but loud enough for me to hear.

"Not helping," I trill.

"It rains here a lot. Just sayin'," he replies.

"So, is there a way around this? I mean, what if I hold her up to see the sky? Or get a seat she can jump up onto."

"What kind of seat?" Dark Hair Penelope asks with a furrowed brow.

"One low enough for her to jump up on and look out."

The three Penelopes lean in towards one another and begin to speak in whispers. I hold my breath. I can't lose Stevie over a stupid window height. I've come so far with this, frankly insane, process. If my heart hadn't been set on Stevie...

"Can we have the room?" Frizzy Blonde Penelope asks.

"Sure." I bustle Asher and Lottie out of the kitchen and close the door.

"This whole thing is insane. You know that, right?" Asher says.

"I can understand it. They want to make sure their dogs go to good, loving homes," Lottie says.

"Yeah, but the window's too high for the dog to see blue sky? What's *that* about?"

"Shhh," I say to them both as I press my ear against the door, listening. All I can hear is muffled talking.

"Let's go sit and finish our cold coffees," Asher suggests.

"I'll be right there," Lottie says as she pads down the hall and into her bedroom.

Asher and I return to the living room, and I sit and wait for their verdict, my nerves clanging like pots and pans.

"This puppy had better be the freakin' queen of dogs to go through all of this for," Asher says as he stretches out on the sofa.

"She's worth it. And what was with that flirty talk back there? I wondered if Lottie and I should have left the room at one stage."

"I thought I'd try to help you out."

"By flirting?"

"By being charming. There's a difference, you know."

"I don't think Frizzy Blonde Penelope knew the difference."

He laughs. "You call her Frizzy Blonde Penelope?"

"They won't give me their names. How else do you differentiate between three women all dressed like identical toddlers who insist they're all called Penelope?"

"Good point."

Lottie arrives back in the room and flops down on a chair. "This is so weird. They're in our kitchen discussing us while we sit around and wait for them."

"It's just hoop jumping to get my puppy."

"When are you seeing George?" Asher asks me.

"I don't know. I only just met him last night. You guys have rules about how quickly you contact a girl. Don't you?"

'No," he replies.

"Oh, you so do," Lottie agrees. "I even had a guy tell me he decided to break the 'three-day rule' once. He said he didn't care if he seemed too eager and he'd be breaking the guy code, he had to do it."

"I don't have a three-day rule," Asher replies. "So, you're *not* expecting to hear from the guy for three days, is that what you're saying?"

"Exactly."

"Us girls are onto you," Lottie warns.

"Well, whether he calls in three days or three years, the guy's still an idiot."

Lottie pulls a face at me, and I giggle.

"If you say so, Asher," Lottie says.

He flicks his eyes between us. "What? I don't like the guy."

"You just don't want your future wife dating someone else. That's what's going on here," Lottie says.

"No, it's not," Asher says as I reply, "No way."

Lottie sizes us both up, her eyes dancing. "Hmmm. Very interesting. Let me know if you pull the wedding up, okay? I'll need time to get a killer outfit for it."

"You're hilarious," I deadpan. "I wish I'd never told you about us being back-ups for each other."

"She'd have found out soon enough, wifey. You know, when we're *married*," Asher says with a cheeky grin.

I shake my head at him. "You're not helping here, Ash."

The door to the kitchen swings open, making me jump. I look up to see Frizzy Blonde Penelope in the doorway.

"Come back in, Zara," she instructs, and I dart a look at my friends before I follow her back into the kitchen where I'm met with all three Penelopes.

"Have you decided if I can get Stevie?" I ask eagerly. "I mean, if I can join Stevie's pack."

Frizzy Blonde Penelope levels her gaze at me. "We have concerns."

Uh-oh.

"Does that mean...? Am I not getting...?" I swallow down a rising lump. "You're not letting me have Stevie." My shoulders slump.

"We will need to carry out a random check-in after you've formed a pack."

I ping my gaze to hers as hope bubbles up inside me. "Does that mean what I think it means?"

Frizzy Blonde Penelope gives me a curt nod. "It does. Welcome to Stevie's pack, Zara."

"Oh, thank you!" I rush across the tiled floor to her.

She immediately raises her hand and shouts, "Down, girl!"

I come to a crashing halt and raise my hands in the air. "Sorry, sorry. I don't know what came over me," I say. "I'm just so excited. When can I see her?"

Frizzy Blonde Penelope cracks a smile for the first time since Asher was flirting with her—sorry, *charming* her. Potato pot-ah-to. "Does right away work for you?"

"Are you kidding me? Of course it does."

Ten minutes and a large chunk of my savings gone to Penelope's Pooches later, I'm sitting on the floor of my flat as Asher and Lottie look on, playing with my new, adorable, gorgeous, wonderful puppy, Stevie. She's bouncing around, gnawing on anything she can, her little white tail wagging a mile a minute.

"Isn't she adorable?" I gush as I pick her squirming little body up and she frantically tries to lick my face.

"Oh, she so is. Here, give her to me." Lottie reaches out and takes her in her hands. "Who's a gorgeous girl, then? You are, yes you are."

Asher arches his brow. "Baby talk, Lottie? Seriously?"

"You cannot hold this ball of canine deliciousness and not baby-talk."

"Sounds like a challenge to me." He stretches out a hand and takes Stevie from Lottie. Holding her up, she wriggles and wags her tail, trying with every ounce of energy to lick him.

I sit back and watch as he tries not to say anything to her. It's obvious he wants to. She's simply too adorable.

"Give her a cuddle," I instruct. "You know you want to."

He cups her at chest height, and she claws her way up to nibble his ear. He lets out a laugh. "That's so ticklish."

Lottie tells him, "Okay, now hold her so you can see her face and tell her she's a good doggie."

"Do I have to?"

"Yes, you do!"

He holds her up once more and looks directly at her. "You're a good dog," he says in an extra deep and manly baritone before he immediately places her back down on the floor rug. She promptly dives on an old sock and tries to bite it. "See? There's no need to baby-talk the dog."

"And you were totally unaffected by her, weren't you?" I ask.

"Are you telling me I'm some sort of robot? Of course I think she's cute, but I still don't see the need to talk to her like she's a baby."

"Whatever," I reply with a laugh. Nothing can dent my mood now that I've got my very own puppy. I pat her little body as she gnaws on a chew toy that was part of the puppy paraphernalia pack Penelope sold me. "Good, Stevie. Good girl."

"Stevie's a better name for her than 'Steve,'" Lottie announces as she lifts her up and the puppy begins to nibble on her ear. "No, Stevie, no!"

"Oh, Stevie is way cuter. Like Stevie Nicks. I need photos. Where's my phone?" I ask.

Asher shrugs. "I dunno."

"Try the kitchen bench. You were googling how to toilet train a puppy earlier, remember?" Lottie says.

"Toilet training?" Asher says. "That'll be fun for you."

I locate my phone on the kitchen bench. When I press the home button, I notice a missed call from a number I don't recognise along with a message. I dial my voicemail.

"Hi, Zara. We met last night at your party. Sorry I had to leave. I had a thing I had to go to, so I slipped out. I wondered if you'd like to get together Tuesday? Let me know." There's a pause before he adds, "Oh, this is George Honeydew, by the way. Okay, bye." He hangs up and I stand there staring at the wall, my phone still against my ear.

He called me. George called me, and he didn't even wait a full day.

Happiness leaps inside of me.

I wander back into the living room.

"What are you grinning at?" Asher asks, peering up at me from the floor.

"I've got a date."

"With that idiot George?"

"Yes, with that idiot George, only he's not an idiot. He's wonderful."

Lottie's eyes are like saucers. "OMG, Zara! He broke the guy rules for you. He must be serious."

Asher harrumphs. I ignore him.

"He seems like a good guy." I'm totally downplaying it of course. Inside I'm happily skipping, leaping, and twerking my brains out.

Lottie tells me, "This could be the start of something big."

"Give me a chance here. I've only just met the guy," I protest, but I don't mean a word of it. We had a connection in that brief conversation, and I for one am excited to see where this thing can go.

Chapter Eight

I spend the rest of the weekend enjoying Stevie's exuberance and ability to go from running around at full throttle to totally conking out under a chair and immediately falling asleep, snoring her wee head off.

I'm utterly charmed by her and I am one hundred percent convinced that spending half my life savings on her and going through that weird Penelope's Pooches assessment process was completely worth it.

She's not perfect of course, and we have had a couple of mishaps already. More than a couple. She got a hold of one of Lottie's favourite shoes and punctured the leather around the heel to such an extent it now resembles a wonky sieve. And she has no idea that when I take her outside it's not a game to gnaw on her lead and instead, she should be focussing on doing her doggie business so we can get in out of the cool London air.

But I know it's all part and parcel of training a new puppy, and I for one am ecstatic to have the opportunity.

I arrive at work on Monday morning with her tucked under my arm. Although Scarlett knew that I might be getting Stevie, she has no clue that I've already got her. She's going to be just as excited as I am when she sees her.

"You can't mix Hollywood Glam with Country Chic and Industrial minimalism. It ends up looking like a total dog's breakfast, I don't care if you're married to the country's most exciting new football talent," she's saying into her phone as I slip past her to hang up my coat. She looks up briefly at me and waves before she adds, "Karina Designs? We're not focussing on the fact they've moved in up the road right now. We're just simply doing what we do best: catering to our clients' needs and delivering amazing designs."

I position myself in front of her with a sleeping Stevie in my arms. Thankfully, she ran herself ragged in the flat this morning, so by the time I got on the Tube, she was snoring softly and no one paid her much attention.

Scarlett eyes her in my arms. "Portia? I've got to go. Talk later. Ciao ciao ciao." She hangs up. "Is that what I think it is?"

"*She's* not a that. She's Stevie, our new shop dog. I passed the test and got her on the weekend."

She rises from her seat and comes over to get a closer look. She strokes her soft fur and Stevie stirs briefly before going back to sleep. "She's adorable. Is she really yours?"

"Signed, sealed, and delivered."

As though sensing she's being discussed, Stevie yawns, and we can see her little pink tongue and row of tiny white, sharp teeth—which I've had sunk into my hands, my earlobes, and my ankles over the last forty-eight hours—before she opens her big brown eyes. She immediately looks from me to Scarlett and begins to wag her tail and starts wriggling in my arms.

"Stevie, this is Scarlett. She's my business partner and

co-owner of ScarZar, which is where you're going to spend every single day from now on."

"She is?"

"Of course."

"But I thought you'd train her up first. Puppies are unpredictable."

"Charming, you mean. It'll be fine. She's smart, she'll cotton on fast, and people will absolutely love her. We'll be known as the interiors shop with the adorable Jack Russell, just as we said. Karina will be so dull in comparison."

"I know that's the plan. Can I hold her?"

"Sure." I hand her warm little body over and watch as Scarlett cradles her carefully in her arms as she squirms. "She's a wriggly little thing, isn't she?"

"She's a puppy. It goes with the territory."

"Oh, look. She's stopped."

Stevie goes limp in Scarlett's arms, and immediately alarm bells tone in my head.

"Quick! Put her down."

Scarlett nuzzles her. "Why? She's so sweet and snuggly like this."

"Because she's peeing, that's why!"

"What?" Scarlett pulls Stevie away from her and we both watch in horror as the last remnants of pee drip to the floor. She looks down at her silk shirt, which has a large wet patch, right in the middle, where the thin fabric is now clinging to her body. "Oh, my gosh. You have got to be joking me." She thrusts Stevie into my hands and storms out to the back of the shop where I hear her pulling paper towels from the dispenser in the toilet.

"I'm so sorry," I call out to her. "Stevie, we do that outside, okay? *Outside*."

Stevie gazes at me with her big eyes, wagging her tail

like I'm not telling her off for peeing on my business partner.

Scarlett storms back into the shop. "I'm literally covered in dog pee."

I press my lips together as I look from her thunderous face to the wet patch on her shirt. It's no good. A giggle builds up and before I know it, it squeaks out of me, making such an odd sound that Stevie instantly focuses her attention on me and begins to yap with glee. It's infectious. A moment later, Scarlett's face creases into a grin and a snort escapes from her nose. Soon enough, she's also in fits of giggles, both of us clutching our sides as Stevie's tail beats frantically against my arm.

We're so busy laughing hard that we don't notice the bell chime above the door until it's too late and a customer is standing inside the shop, giving us a stern, questioning look.

I'm the first to get my giggles under control. "I'm sorry about that," I say to an elderly woman in a completely black ensemble but for her thick, tan coloured pantyhose. I tuck Stevie under my arm. "How can I help you today?"

"Her shirt's got an unsightly stain," the woman says, gesturing at Scarlett.

"I'm just going to pop out to get that fixed," Scarlett replies. She collects her handbag and waltzes past me towards the door. "Zara will look after you. You're in good hands."

I smile at the woman. "Sorry about that. What can I do for you?"

She eyes Stevie briefly before she looks back at me. "Are you going to keep holding that puppy?"

I glance down at my dog. She's watching the woman closely, her little body trembling with excitement as though she's saying *I know this human wants to pat me. And she might have a ball! Or treats! Let me at her!* I'm already fluent in Stevie.

"I'll pop her out the back while you have a browse at all our lovely things. Back in a moment." I rush out to the tiny back room that's full of accessories, soft furnishings, and boxes, find an old fluffy cushion, and plonk Stevie down on it. Why didn't I bring in her dog bed? The fluffy cushion will have to do for now.

"Stevie. Stay. Stay." I raise my hand in the stop sign and shoot her a look that says I mean business. She gazes back up at me with her puppy dog eyes—literally—her tail wagging.

I crouch down beside her and stroke her back. "I've got to do my job, little girl. I'm sorry. I'll get it all set up for you after. Promise."

She lifts her ears and cocks her head to the side in the most heart-melting of looks and it takes all my will power not to scoop her back up in my arms. Instead, I repeat the stay command and back out of the room, closing the door firmly behind myself.

"Sorry about that," I say to the woman as I breeze back into the shop. "What can I help you with?"

Fifteen minutes and a sale of a lamp and set of coasters later, Scarlett returns to the shop in a pretty turquoise blouse.

"Did you buy a new top?" I ask her.

"I had to. The other one was peed on. Remember?"

"Sorry about that. She's only a pup. She'll learn."

"Did that lady want us to do any decorating?" she asks hopefully.

"Nope. She just bought a lamp."

"Shame. Where's Stevie?"

"She's out the back. I made a little bed for her. Which

112

reminds me. I need to pop out to get her a proper doggie bed for here as well as a pen for her to be in for the time being. Once she's older we can let her wander around the shop."

"Sure. I've got some calls to make. Hey, I forgot to tell you. George thinks you're wonderful."

"He said that?"

"We went to brunch yesterday down at that place by the river. He raved about you. Said he thought you were beautiful and smart and totally his type. Has he called you yet?"

A grin claims my face. "He did. He called the day after my party."

"The day after your party? Wow, he didn't mention that. He's keen."

"I know, right? We're going out on Tuesday evening."

"Zara, you sly dog. You didn't mention that."

"I was a little preoccupied with Stevie. But I am excited about it. He seems great."

"Oh, he is. He and Harry are really tight. They do extreme sports together. You know, things like skydiving, and scuba diving."

"All the divings, huh?" I grin. "He sounds like James Bond."

"Only better, because he's the real thing."

There's a muffled crash from out the back of the shop. We glance at one another in alarm.

"Uh-oh." I dash trough the shop and pull the door open and gawk at the room.

The scene is not pretty.

It turns out placing a puppy on a fluffy pillow and expecting her to stay was not only wishful thinking, but utterly delusional. In the last fifteen minutes, she's yanked the fluff out of the cushion and strewn it across the floor,

113

knocked over a glass vase that's in several pieces on the floor, and tugged on a bolt of material that's now resting precariously against a wall. I quickly collect it and put it up on the shelf it came from.

How can one small puppy do so much damage?

"Stevie Huntington-Ross! What have you done?" I growl.

She looks up at me, wagging her tail furiously as though she hasn't destroyed a vase, a cushion, and almost pulled a shelf down with a bolt of material.

I scoop her up in my arms. "Bad Stevie. Bad doggy."

Scarlett arrives at the door. "What the...?"

"I'll clean it up."

"But that vase cost a fortune!"

With Stevie tucked under one arm I lean down and collect the broken bits of glass. "I'm sorry. I'll come up with a better solution."

"Like leaving her at home?"

"No. We agreed she'd be a shop dog. She's going to be part of our style signature, remember?"

"*Dog* being the key word, Zara. She's still a puppy. She can't be trusted yet. You need to train her before she can come back."

"But people love puppies."

"Not ones that pee on your shirt, they don't."

It's a good point. "I'll pay for your new one."

"Maybe you should schedule your mid-life crisis for after work and on weekends only. That way we can get on with our jobs without this happening." She gestures at the mess.

"Again, it's not a mid-life crisis. It's a puppy," I say levelly.

What is it with people thinking I'm having a mid-life crisis?

"She's an out-of-control puppy, Zara."

I force out a puff of air. "I'll go out now and get a little pen for the shop. People can look at her and pat her, and she'll be under control."

"Maybe."

I sense she's softening, so I leap on it. "Come on, Scar. You know it makes sense."

"We can't afford to have any more incidents. We've already got our backs to the wall with losing half our business in the last few months."

I grin at her. "You're the best. I'll pop into Penelope's on my way back from Asher's later today. I've got to show him what I've designed for him and measure up."

"How is your future husband?"

"Not a mid-life crisis, and not my future husband."

She waggles her eyebrows at me. "Maybe that position might be taken by a certain George Honeydew?"

"It's a little too early to go planning a wedding, don't you think?" I say, feeling coy.

"Babe, George is a great guy and he's from one of Berkshire's richest families. You could do a lot worse."

"Let's see how our first date goes, shall we?"

"I've got a feeling about you two."

I grin at her, excitement building inside of me. I've got a feeling about us, too.

Chapter Nine

Asher pulls the door to his flat open and immediately his eyes lock onto Stevie, snuggled into my arms. "You brought your puppy?" He tries to look grumpy as I balance my pink tablet bag and vintage Chanel handbag along with Stevie. I know he doesn't mean it.

"She's my new sidekick, what can I say?"

Stevie bangs her tail against me and begins to wriggle to get free.

"Cute sidekick, although I'm not sure how helpful she's going to be in measuring up the flat today."

"She's going to be incredibly helpful. Aren't you, my little pooch?" I nuzzle her warm fur.

Asher arches an eyebrow. "Here, let me take those for you." He unhooks my bags from my shoulders and holds them for me.

"That's better. Thanks." I follow him into his sparse living room, still holding my now frantically squirming puppy. "Is it okay if I let Stevie run around your flat? She's been a bit of a naughty girl today, and I think she could do with letting off some steam."

"Isn't that what dog parks are for?"

"She's too little for a dog park yet and besides, she needs her final shots before she can go near one of those places."

Asher eyes Stevie. "Has she done her doggy business already?"

"Absolutely." I don't mention it was on Scarlett's shirt. There's no need to get into details.

"Okay. I've got hardwood floors, so if she has an accident, it won't be hard to clean up."

"Oh, I'll take care of it if she does."

"Yeah, I meant you," he replies with a laugh. "Let me go close some doors first." He leaves the room.

I hold Stevie up to give her some clear instructions. "Play nice. Don't eat anything. Definitely don't pee on anything." I lower her to the ground then pick her up again and add, "Or worse."

Asher returns to the room, closing the door to the hallway behind himself.

I put Stevie gently down on the floor and watch as she immediately dashes around the place sniffing, her oversized paws slipping in all directions on the shiny floor.

"That puppy of yours sure has some energy."

"She's been cooped up at the shop. We can't let her wander around the store, so she's been in the back room. I'm getting a pen for her until she's grown up a bit."

"By 'grown up' do you mean toilet trained and less likely to gnaw on people's things?"

"She doesn't gnaw on people's things."

Asher gestures at Stevie. She's tottering towards us, proudly dragging one of Asher's shoes along the hardwood

117

floor. She stops and immediately drops to the ground and begins to gnaw on the shoe.

"Stevie, no!" I say as I swipe the shoe from her and examine it for damage. There's a distinctive set of puncture marks in the shape of a small dog's mouth. I hold it up. "I am so sorry. I'll get you a new pair. I promise."

Asher takes the shoe from me. "Maybe I should give her the other one so she can even things out?"

"Very funny."

"When is she going to puppy school?"

"I grew up with dogs. I know how to train her."

He shoots me a sideways look. "Do you, Zee?"

"Yes!" I insist. "This is just teething problems, nothing more."

"Pun intended?" He gestures at the shoe.

We both watch as Stevie scrambles across the floor down the hallway. We follow her into the bedroom where she comes to a crashing halt in front of a floor length mirror. She gazes at her reflection, moves to one side, and her ears prick up. She presses her nose up against the mirror and jumps back, shocked from the cold when she was expecting a warm, wet nose. She gives an excited yap and starts bouncing around. She barks and growls and hurtles herself at her reflection.

I glance at Asher. He's got a smirk on his face, which he quickly wipes away. "Call a puppy school today, Zee. That dog is a danger to herself."

I give him a mock salute. "Yes, sir."

He pulls a face. "I'm not being bossy. Just sensible."

"You're totally being bossy, but Stevie and I love you for it. Now, let's sit down and I'll show you my ideas for this place. I'll need to measure up, too."

We return to the kitchen where we sit on his two stools

—black leather and chrome, naturally—at his kitchen bench, and I place my tablet in front of us, touch it, and the screen lights up.

"What have you got for me, wifey?"

"You know how you said you liked the grey colour palette? Well, I thought of combining these elements for your living room." I pull up one of the mood boards I made with images I cut and pasted from our suppliers, including examples of furniture, a rug, light fittings, a colour palette, and a few accessories. "This is the one I thought you'd like the best, but I did another couple for contrast."

He points at one of the accessories. "What's with the horse's head? I may be one a quarter Italian, but..."

"I thought it was stylish and bachelor pad-y."

His lips quirk. "Is that an official interior designer word? 'Bachelor pad-y?'"

"Who's the interior designer here?"

"What else you got?"

I pull up the other mood boards. "I also did this board, which is less contemporary and more traditional," I begin only to be interrupted by growling.

We both turn around to see Stevie's teeth sunk into Asher's black leather sofa. She's pulling with all her might—which isn't a whole lot considering she weighs as much as a couple of cans of baked beans. I leap off my stool and say, "Stevie! No!" as I sweep her up. She immediately lets go of the edge of the sofa and focusses instead on furiously licking my neck, making me giggle.

Asher watches us with an amused look on his face. "You two are a perfect team. She destroys the client's existing furniture so you can replace it all with new stuff."

I survey the sofa, looking for damage. There's a row of

neat tooth marks on the bottom corner, but luckily no tears. "Sorry about that. She's a liability right now."

"I'll say it again. One word: puppy school."

"That's two words."

"It was a joke."

I straighten back up. "Next time you tell a joke, why don't you warn me in advance so I can prepare to laugh at the right time."

"You're a comedian, did you know that?"

I throw him a winning smile. "One of us needs to be, babe." I return my attention to Stevie. "Maybe if I give her some food she might settle down and have a sleep."

"Yeah, because fuelling her up will definitely not give her any extra energy. I'm just glad she didn't go for one of my boards." He nods at the three surfboards he has leaning up against the wall.

"She couldn't get her jaw around one of those if she tried. Look at her," I thrust Stevie at him and to my surprise, he takes her in his arms.

"She's so soft and warm," he coos, his bossy edge from moments ago softened into a mush of puppy love.

"I'm going to get a bowl. You two get to know one another."

I begin to rifle through his half-empty kitchen cupboards, looking for a bowl. Locating one on my fourth cupboard, I pull a packet of dog biscuits from my handbag, pour some out, and place the bowl on the wooden floorboards. "Stevie, want some food?" I ask, but she's too busy playing with Asher who's now sitting on the sofa with her bouncing over him.

I stop and watch. It's cute to see them together having some fun. Asher's eyes are soft and warm as he watches Stevie bounce and fall and get back up. He lifts his gaze to mine, and grins at me. "I want to find her annoying, but she's super cool."

"I knew you'd love her."

I sit and the two of us play with Stevie until she begins to slow, flops down on her belly, her eyes growing heavy. Before long, she's fallen asleep on Asher's lap, exhausted from her frantic playing.

"She likes you," I say.

"What can I say? All the girls do."

"That's what I love so much about you, you know. Your modesty."

"Show me the other moody things."

"They're called 'mood boards' and you know it." I grab my tablet from the kitchen bench and come back and plonk myself down next to Asher. I show him the other mood boards I put together, and he points to features he likes across all three. I take a note and agree to show him the final scheme later in the week.

"Can you get me that exact sofa?" he asks, pointing at a brown leather mid-century modern style sofa.

"I can. I've seen them at a supplier. It's so comfy."

"Sold."

"But...you don't even know how much it costs, and we haven't even talked budget yet."

"What can I say? I want what I want, and right now, I want that sofa. Email me your full quote and we'll take it from there."

I narrow my eyes at him as I recall a conversation we had some time ago. "You told me when we went to Sebastian and Emma's vow renewal that you would have to save up your pennies to be able to afford my services. No offence, but it won't be cheap."

He gives a totally nonchalant shrug. "I want to get it right. Go ahead and quote me. For all of it."

"Okay," I reply uncertainly. I move on. "This is the high-level design for the wardrobe. Loads of shelving and hanging space, and a spot for a floor length mirror for you to gaze at yourself in.

"I do a lot of gazing at myself," he replies with a grin.

I laugh. "I'm sure you do."

I glance down at Stevie. She looks so comfortable as she snuggles up to Asher. "I'm going to have to measure up your place. You okay sitting here with the puppy?"

He glances at his wristwatch. "Actually, I need to get back to the office shortly. I've got a meeting soon. Hey, can you bring me my cell?"

"You could move her, you know."

"I don't want to interrupt her sleep."

I laugh. "You big softie. Where's your phone? I'll go get it for you."

"Hallway table."

I collect his phone and notice he's got a bunch of alerts. As I hand it to him, I tell him, "It must be so hard to be as popular as you are."

He flicks through his messages. "They're mainly work."

I peer over his shoulder and read one of the messages out loud in a sultry voice. "Asher, I'm thinking about you as I lie in my bubble bath.' That does *not* sound like a work message to me, unless I've got no idea what being a lawyer actually entails."

He slaps his phone against his chest and looks up at me. "Zara Huntington-Ross, you might be my future wife, but that doesn't mean you can go reading my personal messages."

I raise my hands in surrender. "All I'm saying is that is

not a work message. That's all. And who's Fenella, anyway?"

"I brought her to your birthday party, remember?"

"You're such a serial dater it's hard to keep a handle on which girl it is this week. Seriously, you've got a problem."

He chuckles, and Stevie lifts her head briefly, her eyes firmly shut, before she flops back down again and begins to snore. "I didn't ask her to think of me while lying in her tub."

I cock an eyebrow. "You sure about that?"

"Who made you my mom all of a sudden?"

"I'm not being motherly. All I'm saying is you're getting on. Isn't it about time you settled down? Found a nice girl?"

"If I do that, I won't get to marry my back-up girl, will I?"

"Don't count on it. I plan on meeting Mr. Right way before then."

"Don't tell me you're thinking that guy George with the ridiculous last name could be him."

Heat fills my cheeks. "No," I reply, convincing no one, let alone Asher.

He looks me square in the eyes. "He's an idiot."

"So you keep saying, but so far, there hasn't been any evidence of his alleged idiocy."

He crinkles his brow. "When's your date?"

A smile teases the edges of my mouth. "Tomorrow night."

He pushes out a puff of air. "Have fun," he says. And it's so disingenuous it makes me burst into laughter. "What?" he asks as he shakes his head.

I lean down and kiss him on the cheek. "I love that you've gone all big brother on me, which is weird considering you think I'm acting like your mum."

"And one day, we might be married. How's that gonna work?"

I giggle. "Who knows. Hey, I need to go and measure up your wardrobe. You message the girl in the bubble bath and whatever other girls you've got on a string."

"I don't date more than one at a time, and they know it's just for fun. Nothing serious."

"You tell them that? Like, straight up, 'this is just for fun?'"

"Yup."

"And they still go out with you?"

"Sure. It's best to be up front with them from the get go."

I size him up. With his official status as a bona fide member of the Tall, Dark, and Handsome club it's obvious to see how he attracts all these women. But I know it's more than that. He's fun and charming and easy to be with. It's a killer combination, that's for sure.

"What?" he says, his lips curved into a smile.

I shake myself back into the room. "Nothing. I need to get on with this."

I collect my handbag from the kitchen bench and make my way into Asher's bedroom. I pull the double doors to his wardrobe open and stop and examine the space. It's so crammed full of boxes and junk, it's almost impossible to measure.

"Hey, Asher. Can I move some of your boxes in here?" I call out. "I'm in your wardrobe."

I hear footsteps and then he appears beside me, a sleeping Stevie nestled up against his chest. "Let's swap. You take the sleeping dog and I'll measure."

"It needs to be accurate for the wardrobe company to fit their design."

124

"Are you questioning my ability to measure four walls? I am a guy, you know. It's part of the man card: you've got to know how to measure stuff, put stuff together, and read a map."

"I'm glad I'm not a guy, then."

He hands me Stevie. "Measuring tape, please."

"It's in my handbag."

He begins to rifle through my bag. "You've got a wallet, a set of keys, a bunch of receipts, and five lipsticks." He looks up at me. "Five?"

"What can I say? I change my lip colour with my mood."

"Clearly. No measuring tape."

"Seriously? I was sure I brought one."

He holds my bag open for me to see.

"Can I use yours then, please?"

"Sure. It's in one of those boxes."

We both look up at the stack of boxes, reaching all the way to the ceiling.

"Useful," I say.

"Sorry. I didn't know my decorator would come to measure up my closet without a measuring tape."

"I guess I'm going to have to come back."

"Which reminds me." He reaches into his back pocket and pulls out something. "This is for you."

I eye the silver key as it catches the light. "A key to your place, huh? That's going to confirm every one of Lottie's suspicions, you know."

"It's practical, that's all. I'm about to be super busy with work. You having your own key means you can come and go whenever you need."

I take it in my hand. "Sounds like a good idea."

"You can start with remembering a measuring tape next time."

"Yeah, got it."

"If you're all done, let's go. I need to get back to the office."

"Sure." I collect my things and together we leave the flat and head down the stairs to the street.

"So, I can use my key whenever I need?" I ask as we walk down the street towards the Tube stop.

"Well, within reason."

"Maybe you need to leave a tie around the doorknob so I don't intrude on you when you're 'entertaining' Fenella." I use air quotes to make my point.

His eyes are dancing when he tells me, "Just text before you come over. That way I've got time to hide all my women."

"You pretend it's a joke, but I know you, Asher McMillan."

"Do you?" he asks, and the look on his face morphs from light-hearted banter to something else.

Intrigued at what he means, I open my mouth to reply when Stevie wakes up and immediately begins to squirm to get down. I hook on her lead and put her on the ground, where she sniffs around excitedly.

Asher's phone rings and he glances at the screen. "I've gotta go, wifey. Go get me that sofa, 'kay? Oh, and a tape measure."

"I'm on it," I say and I wave goodbye as I make my way down the street, Stevie pulling me along.

Chapter Ten

Dear Dad
  I'm going on a date with someone I really like! I know, it's been a while, especially if we don't count Zack (and I definitely don't count Zack).

George is deadly handsome, from a family even Granny would approve of (a miracle, right?), and he's messaged me a bunch of times already. I'm not going to get ahead of myself and say something outlandish like 'he's the one,' but Dad, he might be the one!

We'll see. Wish me luck!

Miss you. Love you.

Your Za-Za xoxo

I'm pulling on my outfit for my date with George when my phone buzzes for about the fifteenth time in the last ten minutes. It's another message from the man himself, Gorgeous George as I'm now calling him.

I'm into power, and that's what the men have got.

We've been discussing the finer points of tennis, specifically why women's tennis is so much more interesting to watch than men's (me), and why the current World Number 1 man is technically incredibly accurate but actually kind of boring (him).

I tap out my reply.

Hello? Have you seen Serena Williams play?

Good point. There is one thing to say that women's tennis has over men's. Two words: short skirts.

I giggle as I reply.

I can't believe your flirting technique is to talk about other girls' clothing.

I watch as dots appear on the screen, telling me he's messaging me back.

I'd be more than happy to flirt with you over any topic.

I grin as I read my screen. I haven't even laid eyes on him and already this evening's date is going brilliantly.

Another message pops up.

See you in fifteen. Just getting in my Uber now.

I glance at the time on my phone. Eek! I'm running late. I zip my dress up and slip my feet into my heels. Collecting my phone from my bed, I order an Uber, apply another layer of lipstick, and head out into the living room. I find Lottie, Kennedy, and Tabitha lounging on the sofa watching *The Real Housewives of Beverly Hills*, our usual Tuesday evening ritual which I've had to forgo for tonight's date.

It's not been a tough decision.

"Can you believe that woman?" Lottie is saying. "She's so rude."

"That's the show, babe," Tabitha explains, stroking Stevie's fur as she sleeps on her lap. "They say things the rest of us might be thinking but would never actually come out with."

Kennedy adds, "And they look so good while they're

doing it, too."

"Some of them are a little 'caught in a wind tunnel' for my liking," Tabitha says as she pulls her face taut with her palms.

"They've got to have something to do with all those stacks of cash," Lottie tells them.

I stride over to the TV and turn to look at my friends. "How do I look?"

"Beautiful," Lottie declares as Tabitha says, "Perfection," and Kennedy says, "So pretty."

Tabitha pauses the TV show and I beam at them.

"I'm so nervous about this date. I want it to go so well."

Tabitha replies, "You fancy the pants off one another. It'll go well. Believe me."

"No, we don't," I protest, but I know it's true. Every time I think of Gorgeous George, I get a wonderful fluttery feeling in my belly and I find myself smiling. If that's not a good sign, I don't know what is.

"Go, have a great time, and report in," Lottie instructs.

"But only if you can tear your eyes from his for more than two minutes," Tabitha adds.

"Or her lips," Kennedy teases as she nudges Tabitha.

The thought of kissing Gorgeous George has a smile almost cracking my face in two. "Well then. If you don't hear from me, you'll know I'm having a good time."

My phone alerts me to the fact my ride is one minute away. "Gotta go, girls. Be good, Stevie," I say as I dash from the room and collect my handbag on the way to the front door.

"Don't do anything I wouldn't do," Tabitha calls out.

"Babe, that rules out *nothing*," Lottie retorts.

"Hey!" is the last thing I hear from Tabitha before the front door slams shut behind me.

Twelve minutes later, I arrive at the restaurant, thankful the traffic was light enough to get me here on time. I step out of the car and look around. I've not spent much time in this part of London, but I take a mental note to come back. The street is lined with boutiques and cafés, and the restaurant itself is one of those friendly neighbourhood places that's welcoming and unpretentious, but you just know the food is going to be fantastic.

The white and blue colour scheme tells me it's a Greek restaurant, and the music coming from inside fits.

Being a warmer than usual evening, there are a bunch of people at tables on the footpath, sitting under a wisteria-covered trellis with gorgeous purple hanging flowers. I glance at either side of me, looking for George as I head for the entrance.

Something catches my attention out of the corner of my eye.

"Zara!"

I turn to see George walking towards me, a grin on his handsome face, and I catch my breath at the sight of him. He's wearing a pair of jeans that fit him just right, a lilac and white striped shirt that's open at the neck, and he's wearing his sandy blonde hair a little scruffy and a lot sexy.

He plants a kiss on my cheek, and I breathe in his woodsy and masculine scent. "You look so beautiful tonight."

I grin at him as my tummy does all kinds of flips and flops. "Thanks. You look pretty good yourself."

"I've got us a table over here." He gestures at a table covered in a classic blue and white check tablecloth with white chairs over at the far side. "That is if it's okay to sit outside?"

"It's perfect."

He slips his hand into mine and leads me through the crowded outdoor tables. I notice a well turned-out middle-aged couple at the adjoining table smiling at me, and I return their smile as George pulls my chair out for me and I take my seat.

"I'm so glad we're doing this," he says once he's sitting opposite me.

"I am, too. Is this your local? I've not been to this place before, but I love that wisteria." I tilt my head up and look at the beautiful flowers, hanging from the trellis.

"Is that what's it called? It's just flowers to me."

I giggle. "You're such a guy."

"You say that like it's a bad thing."

"It's not at all."

"Good."

Our gazes lock and things zing around me at a hundred miles an hour. Oh, my, is this man hot! I feel giddy just looking at him.

"So, you're a tennis player, I take it?" he asks as he waves his phone in front of me.

"Oh, not really. I like to play sometimes in summer, and I've been to Wimbledon a couple of times, but that's mainly for the strawberries and cream really," I reply, referring to the famous Wimbledon dessert.

"There are a lot of cheaper and easier ways to get strawberries, you know, Zara."

"But it's not as fun to go to the supermarket and just simply buy a punnet. Where's your imagination?"

He laughs and it reaches inside and tickles my belly. I pick up my menu. "So, what's good here to eat? I'm starving."

"I always have the moussaka. It's so good. Creamy and delicious."

My mouth waters. "Sounds good to me."

His eyebrows ping up. "What? No salad? No 'I'm on a diet so I can't afford all that cheese?'"

"Who says that?"

"Women, that's who. Not you, and I like it."

"You like the fact I want to eat moussaka? Wow, you're easy to please."

His eyes dance. "What can I say? I like a girl who eats."

"Well, I'm definitely a girl who likes to eat, so I guess we're a match made in heaven."

His gaze intensifies. "I feel like we might be."

I ogle him in disbelief. This guy is one in a million! No game playing, no beating about the bush. He wants me to know he likes me and he's serious about me.

I feel like pinching myself.

Thank you, Scarlett.

"Don't you?" he asks.

"Yeah. Maybe." We grin at one another.

A man with a thick black moustache approaches our table with a notepad and pen in hand. "You ready to order?"

George looks up at him. "How are you doing, Nick?"

The waiter's eyes dart uncertainly from George to me and back again. "Good. Good. You?"

"I'm great, Nick. Just great. This is Zara, my date."

Nick turns his attention to me and says, "Hello." It's obvious to me that he's got no clue who George is, but I'm not going to say anything to embarrass him.

"Hi, Nick. Nice place you've got here."

"Yes, is very good. You order now?"

George collects my menu from me and hands them to Nick. "I'll have my usual, thanks, and Zara here will, too."

"Your usual?" Nick questions, his features tense.

George laughs. "Nick, you're killing me. The *moussaka*,

my man. You know I always have that here."

Nick's face morphs into a smile. "Moussaka! Good choice. Two moussaka coming up. You want bread, olives, dolmades?"

"A bowl of olives?" he asks me, and I nod. "One bowl for the lady."

"Okay. Olives, moussaka."

"Thank you, my good man."

Nick throws us a final uncertain look before he turns to leave.

"Well, that was embarrassing," George says once he's out of earshot.

"I know. I felt so bad for you. But I wouldn't let it bother you. He must see hundreds of customers a day. You can't blame him for not recognising you."

George's jaw locks. "I meant that he couldn't remember my usual order."

Right.

I need to back pedal. "Oh, that? Yes, that was embarrassing for him, not for you. Obviously."

He regards me with suspicion. "That's right," he says slowly.

I need to salvage the situation, and fast. "Anyway, let's get back to what we were talking about before the waiter arrived. Strawberries. That was it." Where can I take the conversation from strawberries? What are your top three berries? Are you a banana man? Actually, that last one has probably too much potential innuendo for a first date with a guy I might want to get serious with some day.

In the end, George swoops in and saves the day. "I know what. Tell me about what you do. You work with Scarlett, right?"

My job. Yes. That'll work.

"We own an interior design business together called ScarZar. We've got a shop in Kensington and we both consult. It's so fun working with a friend."

"Could you do my place?"

A smile spreads across my face. "Of course. What do you need doing?"

"I don't know. All of it? It's old and needs updating, but I think it has what they call 'good bones.' You know, high ceilings, crown mouldings, big windows. That sort of thing."

"It sounds amazing."

"I'll have to show it to you. You know, so I can get your professional opinion of course."

"Of course."

We grin at one another, and I take a sip of my water.

"And maybe so we can sit on my sofa and snog," he adds, and I splutter my glass of water over him in surprise.

"Sorry," I say as I grab my napkin and dab at his shirt.

He takes my hand and holds it still. "Don't worry about it. I caught you off guard, didn't I?"

"A little."

"The thing is, I'm very attracted to you, Zara, and I hope you feel the same way about me."

My belly does so many flips it's a miracle I'm not thrown from my seat. "I am," I reply coyly.

His smile spreads across his face. He removes the napkin from my hand, turns it over, and places a soft kiss right in the centre of my palm.

I swear, every nerve in my body instantly redirects to that spot.

Nick arrives at our table to deliver our wine and olives, and I reluctantly pull my hand away.

Conversation flows between us over a bottle of wine and the moussaka, and before long we're talking and laughing, our fingers laced together on top of the table. I feel close to him already, and we've got so much in common. We both went to uptight boarding schools, we both escaped our well-meaning but sometimes overbearing families to live a life of freedom in London, and we're both old enough to have got the London party scene out of our systems and want something more from life.

"You know, Zara, my parents will absolutely adore you."

Warmth spreads through my limbs. "You think?"

"Oh, I know," he says assuredly.

Him telling me his parents will adore me is a massive seal of approval. "That's a nice thing to say."

"Would you like to meet them?"

"I would."

"How about now?"

Wait, what?

He wants me to meet his parents *now*? On our first date?

"Why don't we order dessert and plan it for another time?" I say with a laugh, because he can't be serious. Surely not.

"I always say there's no time like the present." He reaches over to the middle-aged couple at the adjacent table and places his hand on the man's arm.

"What are you doing?" I ask, my brows knitted together. Has he lost his mind?

The man looks directly at me and his face breaks into a smile. His face that looks a lot like.... *No!* It can't be!

"Hello, Zara. It really is lovely to meet you, and we feel like we've learnt so much about you tonight."

"Maybe too much, at some points," the woman at the table with him says. "Although I do respect your providence as a sexual being."

My what as a *what*?

"George, what's going on?" I ask, hoping the conclusion I've jumped to is way off base.

"Oh, how rude of us, Mary," the man says. "Anthony and Mary," the man says as both he and the woman rise to their feet.

"Anthony and Mary?" I question.

"That's right, dear," the woman says. "We're George's parents."

My jaw almost hits the table in utter horror. "You're...what?"

"Oh, look at her, George. She can't quite believe it," the woman, Mary, George's mother says with a laugh to her son.

Her *son*.

George's grin is gigantic. "No, she can't. Can you, Zara? Isn't this wonderful?"

Uh, no?

"Come and give me a hug, dear," Mary says as she opens her arms and beams at me. "You passed the test with flying colours."

I blink at them with incomprehension before I slide my eyes back to George. He too is beaming at me as though he's won the lottery. "These are your parents?" I ask him, my eyes wide. "And there was a test?" Humiliation trickles down my limbs.

This can't be happening.

"Go on, give Mum a hug," George instructs as he looks proudly on.

Like a zombie, I rise to my feet and get enveloped in Mary's arms. She smells of garlic and lily of the valley, and she hugs me tight while my head spins.

"I have to say, Zara, I liked you from the moment I saw you at your birthday party. I know your mother through bridge, of course, but never met you or Sebastian. You gave a lovely speech. Didn't she, Anthony?"

"She did. You certainly like dogs, don't you, Zara? You'll do well in the Honeydew family. We like dogs, and we like a woman to speak her mind. Don't we, eh, George?"

"We do indeed, Dad," George replies.

"Th-thank you," I mutter. Because I'm too dumb-founded by this whole thing to know what else to say right now.

George is still grinning like a cat with an endless supply of cream.

Me? I'm like the cat that's been turfed out of the house into the pouring rain for no good reason.

Have I really just had a first date with a guy's parents sitting at a nearby table, listening to every last word we've said, right from the very moment I arrived?

I search my memory banks. We talked tennis. Fine. Then there was that whole berries conversation. Also fine. Then he kissed my palm and told me he wanted to snog me on his sofa.

Not so fine.

Hang on. He said those things to me knowing his parents could hear everything we said?

Not so fine at *all*.

"Let's pull the tables together, shall we?" Mary suggests.

"Great idea, darling. That way we can have a jolly good chat." Anthony begins to move the chairs back. Together, he and George lift the table and plonk it down next to ours as I blink at them in disbelief.

And here I was thinking this evening couldn't get any more bizarre.

I was wrong. So very wrong.

"There we are," Anthony says, admiring his handiwork.

I dart my gaze between the three of them. They're acting like this is a completely normal thing to do. And what's more, George seems to think so, too.

He's gone from Captain America to Homer Simpson in two seconds flat—and there's no way on this sweet Earth I want to snog Homer Simpson.

It's all too much.

"Can you excuse me for just a moment?" I ask, reaching for my handbag that's looped over the back of my chair.

"Of course," George says.

"Hurry back, though. I want to hear more about your interior design business," Mary says.

I hook my handbag over my shoulder, shoot the three of them a quick, mortified smile, and then make my way past the tables, through the door, and straight to the ladies' out the back. I slam one of the cubicle doors closed and stand and stare at the blank wall.

What just happened?

One minute we were on a date, the next minute it took a turn for the mortifying.

My urge to run kicks in with a steel-toed boot.

Am I overreacting? Should I instead be happy I've found a cute guy who wants to introduce me to his family?

I pull out my phone and stare at the screen. I need to tell someone what's happened and check that running away is the right thing to do. My instinct is to text Asher, but the last thing I want to do right now is have him say *I told you so*. Which he would undoubtedly do. He thought George was an idiot from the get go.

So, instead, I do a group message to my girl besties: Lottie, Kennedy, and Tabitha.

On my date with George. All good except he just announced his parents have been at the next table all night and then he introduced me to them, and now they want to sit with us. This is weird, right? I'm not being overdramatic?

The responses are swift and emphatic.

Lottie: So weird!

Tabitha: Total mummy's boy in a sick, sick way.

Kennedy: OMG, girl. Run!

Well, that's clear. None of them think it's a terribly good sign, to say the least. Then, another message pops up.

Lottie: But you know what they say about guys and their mums.

Tabitha: What? That if they invite their mums on a first date, they're totally sick?

Kennedy: Tabitha's right, Lottie. Don't put a positive spin in this, and don't you listen to her either, Zee. Run. Now.

Tabitha: Agreed.

Lottie: But this is Gorgeous George we're talking about here!

Tabitha: Stop it, Lottie! It's beyond sick.

Kennedy: Run! And don't look back!

I slot my phone back in my handbag, my mind made up —and I can tell you now, it's not to continue my date with Homer Simpson and his family.

I pay for my meal and half the bottle of wine, and then I stop by the table where George is sitting with his parents. "I'm so sorry, George. Thank you for the date, but I don't think this is going to work out. It was absolutely—" weird? horrific? beyond humiliating? "—lovely meeting you both, Anthony and Mary. Enjoy the rest of the evening. Bye!"

And before they say another word, I turn on my heel, stride out of the restaurant, and bolt down the street as fast as my heels will take me.

Chapter Eleven

Dear Dad
    So, I'm definitely not going to become Mrs. Zara Honeydew any time soon. Or ever.

On the plus side, my darling puppy is such a blessing! Stevie is bouncy and fun and totally full of the joy of living. She makes me smile every time I look at her. Okay, not every time exactly. Sometimes she chews my shoes. Sometimes she poops on the hand knotted woollen rug I 'acquired' (okay stole) from Martinston's study to remind me of you. But the rest of the time? She is absolutely divine.

I so wish you could meet her.

Miss you. Love you.

Your Za-Za xoxo

I arrive at the shop with Stevie the following morning, bracing myself for the inevitable onslaught of questions from Scarlett. George must have said something to her boyfriend, Harry, last night because she peppered me with messages about my date after I got home.

The shop is empty when I arrive. I glance at the time on my phone: 9:45am. For once, I've beaten Scarlett in. I unlock the door and put Stevie down on the floor. She immediately scampers around, sniffing everything as though this is the last moment of her sense of smell before it's gone forever and she needs to smell *every*thing.

I eye the dog pen I bought from Penelope's Pooches after my visit to Asher's place. "You'll need to go in your pen when Scarlett gets here, little girl. So go crazy."

She doesn't need telling. She *is* a puppy, after all.

I wander to the back of the shop, flick on the lights, and power up the computer. I scan the day's appointments, and my heart sinks at how few there are. I chew on my lip, deep in thought. How can the little guy beat the big guy? I mean, you hear these stories about how it can happen, how the little guy—or girls in our case—fight back. But how are we going to do it? Karina has scale. They've got a bunch of designers, relationships with all the suppliers, and a killer store that screams *you're in safe hands with us!* We've got a tiny, but charming shop off the beaten track with only two designers—and a dog who is admittedly extraordinarily cute, but who pees on people and destroys the stock.

It's not exactly a fair fight.

I'm just about to Google *how David managed to beat Goliath* when the bell above the door chimes. I look up, expecting to see Scarlett, and am surprised to see a couple of girls about my age. They're both wearing long skirts, ankle boots, and cute tops, with long mousy brown hair hanging down their backs. I blink a couple of times, thinking I'm seeing double for a moment before I realise they're identical twins.

"Hi, girls," I say with a warm smile as I slot my phone

into the back pocket of my wide-legged pants. "Welcome to ScarZar. Can I help you with something?"

As the words leave my mouth, Stevie comes bounding over to them and hurls herself at one of the girl's legs, yapping excitedly.

"Oh, what a cute puppy!" she says as she leans down and pats her. Stevie bounces around and the girl only manages to get a hand on her for a split second.

"She is cute, but she also needs to go in her pen," I say.

"Oh, leave her," Twin #1 says. "She's too cute. Look at her, Prue. We should get one."

"Oh, yes. We so should," Twin #2 replies.

The two girls coo over Stevie as she vaults between them doing what she does best: being an adorable and excitable puppy. One of them picks her up and Stevie starts climbing up her top to get to her ear where she promptly begins to lick and nibble on her lobe. As she giggles, I ask the other twin what I can help them with.

"We're trying to decide what to get our mum for her birthday. She's turning fifty and utterly depressed about it," one of them says.

"So, we thought we'd buy her something gorgeous to make her feel better about getting so old," the other one finishes.

"Can you imagine being fifty?" Twin #1 asks before she bursts into a fresh wave of giggles with Stevie's licks. "Puppy, stop!"

"Being fifty would be so awful," Twin #2 says with a shake of her head.

I smile at them. "It'll happen to us one day too, you know. What sort of thing are you looking for?"

"We were thinking a few things to brighten up the living room."

"Scatter cushions? Lamps? Ornaments?"

"All of those," Twin #2 says.

"Tell me what the living room looks like now and what your mum's taste is."

"Oh, her taste is awful," Twin #2 says.

Twin #1 nods her agreement. "Truly awful. She needs a total style makeover."

"We like the sofa in the window," Twin #1 says, referring to the gorgeous green velvet sofa.

"It's divine, isn't it? Why don't I get some of the cushions and put a few things together while you have a wander around? There are some beautiful things on the shelves in the back." I suggest and the girls agree.

As I pull a few items together from around the shop, the two girls give a cursory look at the shelves before they sit down on the floor and spend the rest of the time playing with Stevie. I smile to myself. This is exactly what I wanted to happen with having a shop dog. Stevie adds fun and personality, and she'll help differentiate us from the big Karina's of the world.

I stand back from my display and call the girls over. "What do you think?" I ask as Twin #2 hands me Stevie.

"I like it, but I don't love it. You know?" Twin #1 says. "Remember we saw that design on line?" She says to her sister. "Pull that up."

Twin #2 takes her phone from her bag and stares at her screen. After a beat, she turns the phone around and I inspect the image.

"That's much more of a Boho look," I say as I examine the image. I notice it's a design by Karina. "I can totally do that for you. We've got some things out back. Give me two minutes."

"Leave the puppy, please. It's my turn for a cuddle," Twin #2 says as she reaches out toward me.

"Sure." I rush out back and rummage through a pile of cushions, looking for the ones I know will fit the scheme.

When I return, the two girls are talking quietly between themselves. "Here we are. What do you think of these paired with the throw and that large vase?" I remove the original cushions and replace them with the new ones. I stand back and look at the display. "Gorgeous, don't you think?"

"Oh, totally," Twin #2 says as her eyes dart to Twin #1.

"Thanks for all your help, but we've, ah, got to go," Twin #1 says.

Twin #2 crinkles her nose. "Yeah, sorry. Thanks, though. You've been super helpful."

"Super helpful," #1 echoes as the two of them edge towards the door.

"Are you sure? I've got a bunch more ideas."

"We're good. Thanks though. Your puppy is gorgeous."

"So gorgeous."

One of them pulls the door open, and then they both turn and scramble out of the shop as though it's on fire, and I'm left holding the proverbial baby—okay, cushions—wondering what the heck just happened.

I spy Stevie, curled up in a ball on a leather armchair, and on instinct, I follow them and hang back enough so that they can't see me—but I can see them. They walk out of the mews, turn right, and walk until they reach a shop about three doors down, turn, and walk inside.

Karina.

I chew on my lip. That image was from Karina. While I was out the back searching for cushions, they probably realised that and decided to simply head there.

144

With a deflated feeling in my chest, I trudge back to the shop. I push through the door and glance at the display I'd put together for them. Another customer lost to the big, flashy shop down the road. Sure, all the twins were after was a few accessories to brighten a room, but it hurts all the same.

The bell tinkling pulls me out of my reverie. I look up to see Scarlett.

"We just lost another customer to Karina," I say without preamble. "They literally got up and left in the middle of a design conversation. Can you believe it?"

She cocks an eyebrow. "A little like you got up and left in the middle of a date with George Honeydew?"

"Don't start. He brought his parents to our first date. Enough said."

"Only because they're a really close-knit family."

I shoot her a *you cannot be serious* look. "Riiiight. There's close and then there's weird."

"I told you George is a catch, Zee," she replies, ignoring my response. "You should call him and apologise."

"Apologise?" I say with a surprised chortle. "No, thanks. George and his eavesdropping parents might just be the universe's way of telling me to forget about finding Mr. Right and instead be happy being a spinster with Stevie."

"You don't mean that."

I push out a breath of air. Another failed romance. Only it wasn't even a romance. Just a first date gone wrong. "I know I don't, even if it is tempting."

"You'll never find the perfect guy, you know. He doesn't exist. So what if George invited his parents on your date. Do you think he would have done that if he wasn't serious about you?"

"Scarlett, he kissed my hand and told me he wanted to

snog me on his sofa, all the while knowing his parents were listening to every word he said." I shudder at the memory. "I'm not going back there."

"Your loss, babe," Scarlett says as she waltzes past me.

Maybe it is, but also maybe it's not. Scratch that. It's definitely not.

The bell chimes and I turn to see who it is. It's the Kensington Uniform mother and goth daughter combo from a week or two ago. "Hello. Victoria and Chloe. How lovely to see you both again."

"We were in the neighbourhood, and we thought we'd pop in to see if the sofa we ordered had come in yet," Victoria says.

"It's due in about a week," Scarlett answers.

"Good. Now, in the meantime, I'd like to have a chat about window treatments."

"Of course. I've got some ideas about those. Do come and have a look."

As Scarlett and Victoria gather around the laptop on the counter, I smile at Chloe. "How's the new flat?"

"S'all right," she replies in her characteristically articulate way.

"No swords on the walls, though, right?" I ask with a wry smile.

"Nope." She pulls her lips into a line and begins looking around the shop.

Giving up on trying to make conversation, I refocus my attention on rearranging some of the items on the shelves.

After a couple of minutes of listening to Victoria and Scarlett discussing the scheme, Chloe declares, "Look at this cushion. It's shaped as a dog. I want one, Mum."

A dog cushion? I don't remember having one of those in the shop.

"Where, darling?" Victoria asks as she walks across the shop to where her daughter is standing by a leather armchair. "Oh, it's so realistic." She reaches out to pick it up.

It's then that I realise they're not talking about a cushion. They're talking about Stevie. She's curled up in a ball on the armchair, sleeping soundly. "Oh, that's not a cushion," I begin, but it's too late. Victoria has pinched what she thinks is a cushion to pick it up, and immediately Stevie's eyes ping open. Her surprised gaze darts from Victoria to Chloe. Dressed all in black with her pale white face and black-rimmed eyes, Stevie gets the fright of her life and leaps to her feet, yapping and yapping and yapping as she backs away from the two, her teeth bared.

Chloe recoils, stepping back and landing on her mother, who immediately calls out in pain and hops on one foot, losing her balance and falling backwards into a shelving unit. Down come the scented candles, down come the Buddha heads and book ends and vases and all kinds of ornaments. Down they fall until they land on the floor, and I watch in horror as Victoria clutches wildly for the shelves and them promptly crashes to the ground herself.

"Mum!" Chloe yells as Scarlett races over and crouches down beside her.

"Victoria! OMG, are you okay?" Scarlett asks.

"I'm sorry," I shout over the noise. "It's my dog, Stevie. She's not a cushion. I should have said something." I reach out and pick Stevie up. She yaps and yaps, and even me holding her tight and cooing soothing things in her ear isn't enough to calm her down.

"I can see that. Make it stop, will you?" Victoria demands as she peers up at me from the floor. "And you.

147

Help me up." She reaches out for Scarlett, who hoists her back onto her feet.

"I'll take her out the back," I say, and Scarlett shoots me a look as I turn and dash to the back of the shop and into the storeroom, where I shut the door firmly behind me.

By now, Stevie has calmed down, so I pop her on the floor and watch in horror as she decides now would be a good time to relieve herself. All over a stack of placemats.

"Nice, Stevie. You've totally outdone yourself," I mutter as I grab some paper towels from the adjacent toilet and begin to soak her mess up.

Scarlett pulls the door open, her face like thunder. "She has got to go!" she declares.

"I'll just keep her in the pen. I shouldn't have let her sleep on the chair. It was dumb. I'm sorry, Scarlett."

She glares at me, her hands on her hips. "If she's going to stay in the shop, you need to get her trained."

"I can manage her," I insist at the precise moment Stevie clamps her sharp little teeth into the edge of my skirt and begins to yank on it as she growls menacingly. Well, as menacing as a small dog can be. "Stevie, no," I grind out through clenched teeth. She doesn't listen, so I pick her up and lift both her and my skirt. "Let go," I tell her as I tug on my skirt. I get it free after a minor tussle, only to look back at an empty doorway. "Scarlett?" I call out.

"Puppy school!" she yells back from the shop, adding a threatening, "Or else."

I look down at Stevie. She gazes up at me, her liquid brown eyes as innocent as the day she was born. "Do you want to go to puppy school?" I ask her.

Her response is to wag her tail and nuzzle me before she scrambles up my chest and bites down on my earlobe.

* * *

That evening on my way home, Asher calls and I share the story of how Stevie brought down a Kensington Uniform mum.

"Zara, that's unbelievable!"

"It wasn't her finest hour, but to be fair to Stevie, the daughter's a goth. She looks quite scary."

"Let me get this straight. You got the dog to add to your business and bring new customers in, right?"

"I know what you're going to say. So far, she's destroyed stock and sent clients running."

"You said it, Zee. You know you need to take her to puppy training school, right?"

"I suppose so."

"No 'I suppose so.' More 'I will, Asher. Whatever you say, Asher.' That's what I'm looking for here."

"But I know how to train a dog."

"Do you really?" he asks, and I can imagine the look on his face right now. He'd have his eyebrows raised, a subtle smile on his lips, looking at me intently. "Come on, Zee. I'll go with you to the classes. Will that help?"

"You'd do that for me?"

"Nothing would make me happier than to be in a room filled with untrained, out of control puppies," he deadpans.

I giggle. "You'd love it."

"It's set then. You book it, I'll be there, and we'll train that dog of yours to be Kensington's best behaved canine."

I reach my block of flats, balance my phone between my ear and shoulder, and slot my key into the lock. "How about we aim a little lower, like say, she won't pee on the merchandise or frighten the clients?"

He lets out a laugh. "Good goal. So, how was your date with George the idiot?"

"He's not an idiot. He's actually a really nice guy."

"Who also happens to be a complete idiot."

I open my mouth to reply and then close it again, doing my best fish impression.

I hate it when he's right.

"You see? You don't want to say it, but you agree with me."

I pinch my lips and harrumph, which only serves to make him ask, "What happened?"

I push out a breath as I climb the stairs to my flat. I'd may as well come clean with him since my other friends already know, thanks to our online group chat as I cowered in the Greek restaurant's toilets. "He invited his parents to our date," I say and I scrunch my eyes shut as I wait for Asher's inevitable reaction.

"Wait, what?"

"They sat at the table next to us all evening and I had no idea they were listening to every word we said until he asked me if I wanted to meet them and turned to them to introduce me."

"You have got to be kidding me."

"You were right. He was an idiot." I look down at Stevie and cringe as I think of Victoria crashing to the ground. "A bit like me, really."

"You mean the shop incident."

"Yup."

"You just had a momentary lapse of dog responsibility. George is a terminal idiot. You know what you need?"

"A nun's habit and veil?" I ask as I unlock the door to my flat and push it open. I'm immediately met with the aroma of chocolate cake. "Uh-oh."

"What?" he asks.

"Lottie's baked a chocolate cake."

"And that's bad how, exactly?"

"It means she's been to see her mother and needs carbs." I slip off my heels, let Stevie go, and pad down the hallway where I find Lottie sitting at the kitchen bench, shovelling chocolate cake into her mouth like she hasn't eaten in a month.

She looks up and gives me a half smile, her teeth covered in chocolate icing.

"I don't get it," Asher says in that bloke-y way of his. Because of course he doesn't get it. He's not a girl.

With my eyes on Lottie, I say, "I'd better go, Ash. I'll explain the whole mother-daughter dynamic another time."

"That sounds like a laugh a minute."

"Oh, it will be."

"Promise me you'll book the puppy school."

"I will."

"Say it. Say, 'I will book the puppy school.'"

"I will book the puppy school. Happy?"

"Delirious. Give Lottie a brotherly pat on the back for me. Catch ya later."

I hang up and plonk myself down beside Lottie. "You saw your mum, huh?"

"Yup."

"What did she say this time?"

"She only told me that I'm wasting my life and that I should be more like my sister and why was I still living with you and not married with three kids by now and didn't I know that she gave up so much for me so I could have this life I'm now wasting."

"So, the usual."

"Yup." She scoops some more cake on her fork and piles it high with chocolate icing.

"I'm sorry, Lottie. Will it help if I tell you Stevie wrecked a bunch of stock and scared away a client and Scarlett is annoyed with me and I told Asher I'd take Stevie to puppy school?"

Without a word, Lottie offers me a fork, and I plunge it into the cake and take a large bite, savouring its chocolatey yumminess. "Mmm, dabth gooo," I say with a full mouth.

"Whoever said you couldn't solve your problems with chocolate cake has got to have been a guy."

I clink my fork against hers. "Preach it.

"Stevie scared off a client?"

"Oh, yeah."

"And you're going to puppy school with Asher?"

"Yup."

She pushes the cake towards me. "Eat up."

And we do eat up. The whole dang cake.

Dear Dad

You know how I said Stevie is a total blessing? Well, it turns out she's equal parts blessing and liability. Don't get me wrong, she's totally adorable and I know how much you'd love her, but I've come to the conclusion that we need some help.

And Asher and Scarlett telling me to take her to puppy school had nothing to do with it.

Miss you. Love you.

Your Za-Za xoxo

Chapter Twelve

I arrive at the shop with a reconciliatory cup of coffee for Scarlett the following day. She's staring at the computer screen in the empty shop and looks up at me as the bell above the door tinkles. Her eyes glide down to Stevie at my side. "I see you brought the terrible terrier."

I place Stevie in the pen and turn to face her. "I'm so sorry about yesterday. Stevie will be in her pen at all times in the shop until she's fully trained and grown up. And I booked puppy school for her, too. We start next week." I thrust one of the cups in my hands at her. "Here, I got you a coffee to say sorry. A cappuccino with extra chocolate."

She takes it from me. "Thanks. I think we might have lost Victoria and Chloe."

"Seriously? Let me call them. I'll offer them something for free."

"Don't offer them Stevie," she says with a smile teasing the edges of her mouth, which tells me she's begun to soften.

"Ah, no," I reply with a giggle. "They've got that sofa ordered, so we haven't lost them entirely."

"True." She takes a sip of her coffee. "Your mum was here."

"Mum? Oh, no. I totally forgot I was meant to meet her for coffee this morning."

"You can still go. It's not like we're run off our feet here."

I glance around the empty shop. The stark comparison with the buzzing Karina shop down the road is undeniable. "Are you sure?"

"I'm sure. Take your liability though." She nods at Stevie who's chewing on a toy in her pen.

"Okay." I message Mum and arrange to meet her at the Starbucks near the Tube stop. Half an hour, and much cooing over Stevie later, Mum and I are sitting together with the dappled light from a nearby maple tree playing across our table.

"Really, she is such a little darling. Is she a huge hit with the customers?" she asks as she stirs her cup of tea.

"What little we have these days. But yeah, some of them love her." I neglect to tell her about what happened yesterday. Along with the rest of my family, Mum already thinks I'm a touch on the immature and irresponsible side of the equation.

She crinkles her brow. "Why don't you have many customers?"

"That big chain store, Karina Design opened up the road."

"Oh, I love their things," she declares before the look on my face tells her that's not exactly what I want to hear right now. "Sorry, sweetie. How are you and Scarlett going to deal with them?"

I shrug. "I don't know. We're just busy trying to keep our heads above water right now, Mum. Stevie is meant to help add personality, so we get known as the fabulous interiors store with the cute dog. So far all she's done is cost us."

"Why is that?"

"She broke some stuff," I reply elusively.

"With all due respect, sweetie, you can't rely on a dog to keep your business running."

"That's not all we're doing, of course," I reply with a scoff. "There are other things in the pipeline, too." I cross my fingers under the table because other than hoping, we're not managing to do anything to attract new customers. We've been too busy reeling from our sharp decline in business. We need to get off our bums and do something about it.

"Oh, yes?" Mum questions.

"Things I can't talk to you about right now, I'm afraid." I lean in conspiratorially. "Walls have ears, you know." I shoot her a meaningful look.

"Oh. I see, darling," she replies with a knowing look. "Well good luck."

We're going to need a lot more than luck.

"Thanks, Mum."

She plays with her coffee cup. "Now, tell me all about your love life. Anyone special on the scene I should know about?"

Oh, great. The question every single thirty-year-old wants from her mother. Although Mum is hardly as pushy as Lottie's mum, the message is the same: find yourself a suitable man and get yourself married. Stat!

"It's been so long since we met any of your beaus," she adds, using a term from the Dark Ages. "The only young man we ever see you with is that friend of yours, Asher."

"He's not a 'beau,' as you put it. Just a friend."

And a back-up guy. Another thing I'm not going to

mention to her. We don't want her getting her hopes up for something I plan on never happening.

"Pity. He is very handsome and such a lovely chap."

"Sure, Mum." Asher has clearly charmed my mother, too.

"So? Any news?" She looks at me with such hope in her eyes, it feels like clubbing a bunny to tell her the actual truth.

"No one special."

"I had a call from Mary Honeydew," she leads.

Oh, no.

"Did you?"

"She mentioned that you and George had been seeing one another and took exception when he introduced you to her. Really, sweetie, it's a compliment when a young man wants to introduce you to his mother. You should see it as a good sign that he's serious about you. I can't imagine George Honeydew would introduce his floozies to his mother. Can you?"

"'Floozies,' Mum? Really?"

"You know what I mean. He obviously likes you."

"Did Mary tell you *how* he introduced me to her?" I ask and she shakes her head. "She and her husband were sitting at the table next to us, listening in on our entire conversation and I was kept in the dark until George announced their presence, which was *after* we'd spent a couple of hours talking. And on our first, and only, date."

She sits back in her seat. "Oh. Mary didn't mention that."

"I'm sure she didn't."

"Could you have misconstrued the situation? I mean, perhaps there's a rational explanation?"

"Mum."

"All right. I thought I'd ask. I do so want to see you happily married, Zara. You are thirty, after all."

"Are you going to tell me that you were married with kids by the time you were my age like Granny did?"

"Well, it's true, but I do know times are different now. But really, isn't leaving it all until you're in your 30s taking it a bit far, sweetie? It might be time to grow up, you know."

"I'm grown up," I grump with my bottom lip protruding as though I'm a sulky toddler. It's not doing my case any good. I pull it in quickly.

"Of course you're grown up, darling. How about I ask around, see if I can find you a suitable young man? Jennifer Harcourt has a son about your age. Simeon is his name. Do you remember him? I think he bit you on your arm when you were three. Left quite a mark."

"Mum, I don't want to get set up with the son of one of your friends, particularly one who bites arms. I'm perfectly capable of finding my own husband, thank you very much."

"Simeon is awfully good looking," she leads. "Well, if you look past the patchy premature hair loss and that odd snaggle tooth he should have had fixed a long time ago. Modern dentistry can do wonders, and I'm certain he could find someone to make him a toupee or two. You're okay with a man being a foot or so shorter than you, aren't you?"

I shake my head. "No, Mum. I'm not going to get set up with Simeon or anyone else for that matter."

She pushes out a puff of air. "Pity."

"I do want to find The One, but—"

Her face lights up and her hand flies to her chest. "You do? Oh, how marvellous."

"—*but* I'm going to do it in my own way and in my own timeframe."

157

She lifts her cup to her lips and takes a sip. "Well, don't leave it too long."

"I know, I've got my biological-clock tick-tocking."

"I was going to say if you leave it too long, all the good ones would have been snapped up."

I dwell on that fact for a moment. "I hadn't thought of that."

"Hmmm." Mum shoots me a meaningful look.

Stevie yaps at a passing dog and I look down to see her lead completely twisted up like macramé around the leg of my chair. I lean down to untie her, scoop her up and plop her on my lap.

"You know what would be a whole lot more useful to me? Talking to your wealthy friends about ScarZar and seeing who we might be able to do some decorating for."

"Of course. I'll have a think."

"Thanks, Mum. I've got to go now. I'm decorating Asher's place and I need to measure his walk-in wardrobe before I order the new units for him."

"Well, send him my love." She gives me a quick hug.

"Oh, he's not going to be there. I've got a key."

Her eyebrows lift towards her hairline. "Do you now?"

"Don't go reading anything into it, Mum. We're friends, that's all."

"He is rather dishy."

I laugh as a shake my head. "He's Asher, Mum."

"Should I call Simeon's mother for you?" she asks hopefully as we stand to leave.

"That's a hard no, Mum." I kiss her on the cheek. "See you soon. Love to Granny."

After taking Stevie to a patch of grass where she does her deed, I take the Tube to Notting Hill Gate and walk the short distance to Asher's block of flats. Once inside, I let

Stevie off the lead, and she scampers towards the living room as I head to the wardrobe.

I pull the double doors open and survey the space. It's just as jam-packed as it was when I was first in here, with boxes and plastic tubs stacked on top of one another to the ceiling.

"Asher, you hoarder," I mutter as I pull my metal measuring tape out of its case and stretch it out to reach the ceiling. I note the height in my notebook. Now for the depth. With all these boxes, I know that's going to be trickier to get. I look at it from a bunch of different angles, but I'm not going to be able to get an accurate measurement unless I move some of those boxes.

I return to the kitchen where I collect one of the bar stools and plant it firmly in the wardrobe. I kick off my heels and climb onto the stool in bare feet. Standing to my full height, the stool wobbles beneath me, and I steady myself by clamping onto one of the boxes. A couple of seconds later, I'm feeling more stable and a whole lot more confident.

I reach up to move the top box. I give it a tentative pull. It's lighter than I anticipated, and I let out a relieved puff of air. This isn't going to be as hard as I thought it would be. I pull the box from the shelf, and holding it carefully in my hands, I steady myself against the other boxes as I kneel down on the bar stool. It's a tricky manoeuvre and not one I'd recommend, but I manage it. Almost. With one knee on the stool, I remove my other foot only to lose my balance. I drop the box and scramble to grab on to something—anything—and somehow manage to get the edge of a box before the stool gives way and I fall with a heavy thud onto the carpeted floor.

"Ow!" I declare as I rub the thigh that made contact with the uncompromising ground.

A little head appears around the door, and the next thing I know Stevie is all over me, as if me being on the floor is for her enjoyment. She climbs on me and licks whatever skin she can find.

"Stevie, stop," I say with a laugh as I protect my face from her incessant licks. She's relentless, leaping up to get at her favourite part of my anatomy to attack: my earlobes.

Cradling her, I push myself up into a seated position and place her on the floor to survey the damage. The cardboard box that I dropped has split, and its contents have spread out on the floor. With a sigh, I collect up the documents and books and random papers and slot them back in the box. I spot a silver-coloured album on the floor and reach over to pick it up. As I do so, I flip it over.

I stop and stare at the photo in the picture window on the cover.

What the...?

An image of a smiling Asher gazes back at me. Looking handsome in a suit and tie, he's grinning out at the camera as a woman in a bridal dress presses her cheek against his, beaming out at me.

The cogs in my brain begin to whir.

Asher's married? He's *married*?

But...

How...?

When...?

Who...?

What?!

I lean back on my haunches, gripping the album in my hand. This makes no sense. Asher's Asher. He's not married to some woman who looks like...like his *bride*.

Asher's single. He's a flirtatious serial dater who never gets serious about anyone.

Except he has.

And the evidence is right here in this album I'm clutching in my hands, staring back at me in a big white dress.

My fingers itch to open the album, but I know that would be a terrible breach of his trust.

So, before I have the chance to change my mind, I push the urge away and stuff the album back in the box and fold the corners in, pushing it away with my bare feet.

I remain on the floor, chewing on my lip as I assimilate this new, shocking information.

How could I not have known this about him? How could he not have told me? We've been close for years, ever since we met two years ago, in fact. *Two years*. We've spent so many hours together talking at the pub, having coffee, watching movies, ambling through parks. Heck, he even had a mani-pedi with me and Lottie at Harrods that time when we were celebrating getting a lease on our new flat.

But never, ever has he mentioned a wife.

I think I would have remembered that.

Numb, confused, and in shock, I sit and stare at the box until I've had enough. I need to get this place measured up —and I really, really need to leave.

I hop back up on the stool and remove another box and another, this time with much more care, until I've got a clean line of which to measure. I take the measurement twice to make sure I've got it. Then I slot each box back where I found them, the last of which is the broken wedding box.

I stand on the stool and look down at the innocuous box in my hands.

Who knew such a secret lies within it?

Deep in thought, I close the doors to the wardrobe, tell Stevie we're leaving, and close and lock the door behind me.

Asher is not the guy I thought I knew. He's got a secret. A big one. And now that I know, I can't un-know it.

As I rush down the street, one thought overrides all the others: I wish I'd never touched that box.

Chapter Thirteen

Asher and I enter the room at the back of a vet clinic that's hosting puppy training school with Stevie straining on the lead to get inside. Somehow, despite our massive weight differential, this little canine powerhouse is managing to pull me along, virtually yanking my arm out of its socket.

"She's excited," Asher observes.

"You could say that," I reply with a laugh as Asher pulls the door open for me and we charge inside. "Stevie!" I say as I tug on her lead.

I glance at him out of the corner of my eye. He flashes me his Asher grin, and I rearrange my mouth into what I'm hoping is a breezy smile.

He crinkles his forehead. "You okay, Zee?" he questions.

Well, that's clearly a smile fail.

"I'm fine. Just nervous about puppy school, I suppose."

"It's Stevie who should be nervous," he replies, and we both look down at my dog. She's pulling on her lead so hard that she's choking herself, her front paws completely elevated off the floor as she strains to get to the other dogs in the room.

"True," I reply with a forced laugh.

I'm trying my best to be as normal as possible around Asher tonight. It's the first time I've seen him in the flesh since I unearthed that whole marriage bombshell a few days ago, and I'm finding it virtually impossible not to hear wedding bells and picture the happy bride from that photo careening down the aisle towards him every time I look his way.

I need to get a grip.

The room is lined with a bunch of humans with their puppies, ranging in size from a teeny tiny chihuahua in a pink tutu—an interesting choice of outfit for puppy school, but who am I to judge?—to a St. Bernard puppy whose paws are almost bigger than its head. Each of the dogs is on a lead, and all but a couple are yapping and bouncing and straining at their leads to get to one another.

"At least Stevie's not the only excited one," Asher says under his breath.

"All right?" says a woman with a square face and a body to match, wearing a pair of taupe dungarees and a hot pink utility belt around her waist. She smiles down at Stevie. "Who've we got 'ere then, eh?"

"This is Stevie Huntington-Ross," I say as Stevie notices her for the first time and takes a flying leap at her leg.

The woman raises her knee a few inches off the floor and Stevie slaps into her shin, falling onto her back before she immediately repeats the manoeuvre. "She's a feisty one. Isn't she?" she says, looking up at me for the first time.

"She sure is. I'm Zara, Stevie's mum. And this is Asher."

Asher raises his hand in greeting and the woman says hello.

"I'm Dog Diva Denise and I'll be training you this evening. Find a spo' over by the wall, and strictly no socialising."

"We can't talk to the other owners?" I question.

She looks at me as though I've asked a totally dumb question. "I meant for the dog?"

"Oh, right. Got it. No dog socialising."

She raises her brows at me. "Go on. Off you go," she instructs, and she says it in such a way that we immediately do as she says.

"Dog Diva Denise?" Asher questions under his breath with a wry smile, as we find a spot between a darling King Charles and a cute little caramel coloured Spoodle.

"Shhh. She might hear you," I reply through gritted teeth. "I don't want to get in any trouble."

"What can she do? Tell you you're a bad doggie and not give you any treats?"

I snort laugh. "Something like that."

Stevie strains on her lead to get at the King Charles, and I smile at the owner as if to say *puppies these days*.

"Hey, did you get what you needed for the new closet the other day?" Asher asks me as we stand waiting for Dog Diva Denise to begin the session. "You hadn't mentioned anything."

"Yeah, I did, thanks. All measured up." I concentrate on staring at a dog scratching its ear on the other side of the room. *I got the measurements* and *a bombshell of information about your past, buddy.* Of course I don't mention it. I mean, I'm not exactly going to blurt out that I know he's married. Or was married. Or has a wife hidden in an attic somewhere, Rochester-style. *Argh!* Whatever. It's all so disconcerting, and I'm still struggling to process it.

He regards me out of the corner of his eye once more. "You seem weird tonight."

I glance up at him. He's got a quizzical expression on his face. "I'm fine," I reply with a shrug.

"Look. I know you don't want to be here, and I know you think you know everything about dogs, but you're doing the right thing."

My face breaks into a relieved smile. He thinks I'm being weird over the puppy training. I play into it. It's a whole lot easier than dealing what I'm really feeling weird about. "I know about dogs. Stevie's just young, that's all."

"All I'm saying is I think it's great you're doing this."

I lift my eyes to his once more. We lock gazes, and my chest tightens. "Okay. Sure. Great."

He opens his mouth to say something, when Dog Diva Denise—I still can't believe she actually calls herself that—thankfully interrupts.

"Let's get star'ed then, shall we? I'm Dog Diva Denise and I freely admit I'm a dog lover."

"That should be illegal," Asher whispers in my ear and I nudge him with my elbow.

"I suspect most of you lot in this room are dog lovers too, which is why you're 'ere with your little fluff balls of love tonight. Am I right?"

There's a wave of agreement within the room.

Dog Diva Denise raises her hand to silence us, and we all do exactly that.

This woman is gooooood.

"You," she says, looking directly at me.

"Yes?"

"What's wrong with what I just said?"

I look uncertainly around the room. Everyone is watching, even some of the puppies—although I could be being paranoid about them. "I'm...ah, not sure."

"Anyone else?" she questions, scanning the room.

No one ventures a reply.

"Allow me to educate you all. The only problem with what I said is these puppies you've brought 'ere tonight are not little fluff balls of love." She pauses for dramatic effect before she adds in a deeper, more serious voice, "They're dogs."

"This woman is insightful," Asher mutters under his breath and I stifle a giggle.

Dog Diva Denise begins to pace the room, fixing each person with her beady-eyed stare. "And dogs need to be trained. Don't they?"

"Err, yes, they do," a guy with a beagle replies when she comes to a stop in front of him.

"Trained good and proper. Am I right?" she asks a young woman, who looks thoroughly terrified.

"Yes," she squeaks.

"Little fluff balls of love don't need training. Oh, no. Little fluff balls of love can sit there and look all fluffy and whatnot until their wee hearts' content." She comes to a stop, her hands on her hips as she glares at us all. "Tonight, we begin. Tonight, we take these puppies and we mould them into the dogs of tomorrow. Tonight, we make history."

Wow. Just wow.

"Dog Diva Denise is a big old drama queen," I say to Asher.

"I'm scared of her," he jokes.

"You!" She zeroes in on Asher and me. "Did you have something you wan'ed to share with the rest of the class?"

It's like being back in high school.

"No. I'm good, thanks," Asher replies nonchalantly. "Great speech, though. Super moving."

Dog Diva Denise's hardened features dissolve into a smile. "Thank you," she replies, all breathy and fluttery. "That's nice of you to say."

I roll my eyes. Freakin' Asher and his power over women. The moment he chooses to turn it on, they seem to fall at his feet in a frenzy of hormones. It must be something to do with the fact he's American. All smooth and confident and...foreign. Or something.

I flick my gaze to him. He's got a sexy smile on his face, and I'll admit, the way he's dressed tonight in a pair of jeans and a plain white T-shirt that hints at his athletic torso and broad shoulders beneath isn't hurting him, either.

Yeah, okay, he's handsome. Far too handsome for his own good, if you ask me.

But he's still secretly married. Or divorced. Or *something*.

I blow out a frustrated puff of air. I need to push that new gem of knowledge firmly from my mind. It's weighing on me and it could come between us.

And that's the last thing I want.

Dog Diva Denise manages to pull her gaze from Asher long enough to start the class in earnest, and before long we're all walking our dogs across the room—with varying degrees of success.

"The goal, people, is to walk your dog with a loose lead. A *loose* lead."

I tug on Stevie's extremely taut lead as she strains to get to the St. Bernard I've learned is called Derek. "Stevie, heel," I say in an assertive voice.

She ignores me completely.

"He's too big for you," I tell her as I give her lead

another gentle yank. "You'd need a crane to get close to that one."

"I see you're talking to your dog as though she were a human," Dog Diva Denise says as she sidles up next to me. "Another mistake, everyone," she announces to the room. "Dogs are dogs. Treat them as dogs."

I offer her a weak smile. "Got it," I say.

We move onto sitting and staying and some of the puppies seem to catch on pretty fast. Not Stevie. She's too busy straining at the lead to get anywhere but by me, and I spend my entire time saying, "Stevie, no. No, Stevie."

"Have you tried using a deeper voice?" Asher offers "Who knows? It might help."

"Sit, Stevie," I say in as low a voice as I can manage, but all she does is peer up at me as though I've been possessed and then continues to scramble around, pulling on the lead.

"You know what you sound like, Zee?" he asks me. "You sound like Anna Farris in that movie *The House Bunny*."

I shoot him a sharp look. "You've watched *The House Bunny*?"

He shrugs. "Yeah. Years ago, with a girlfriend, I think."

Or a wife.

With my attention momentarily on something other than my insane dog, Stevie seizes the opportunity to yank hard on the lead and it pops right out of my hand. She screams across the room, her little legs splaying in all directions. She reaches one dog and pushes her face right in theirs, then takes off and trips up, doing some sort of canine interpretation of a ninja roll across the hard, shiny floor, until she reaches another dog. She begins to leap excitedly in its face. The dog responds by bouncing around just as eagerly, and much like my little escape artist, manages to worm its way free from its lead and the two of them career around the room, eliciting excited yaps and barks from all the assembled puppies.

"It's a puppy mutiny," Asher declares as I dash past him, chasing Stevie and her accomplice as they wreak havoc.

"I'm so sorry," I say to the room as I lean down to swoop Stevie up in my arms. But it's like she's shape shifted into a slippery eel, slithering expertly through my fingers and taking off in the other direction.

"Never chase a dog!" Dog Diva Denise barks, which is ironic, because we're in a roomful of barking dogs.

By now, all the puppies in the room are going insane with excitement, wrapping their leads around their owner's legs, trying desperately to break free to join in the fun with Stevie and her new friend.

"What am I meant to do?" I ask Dog Diva Denise in exasperation as Stevie and the King Charles—whose name is clearly Pepper, thanks to the number of times her owner has yelled the name in the last minute—roll around the floor together, nipping and growling and yapping and generally acting like the out of control puppies they are.

In one fell swoop, Dog Diva Denise separates the dogs, picks them up, slots one under each arm and yells, "Stop!" in such a way that everyone in the room, be them human or canine, stops and stares at her as silence falls.

"If your dog is on a lead, tighten it now." She points at me and says, "You. Hand me the lead."

I don't quibble. I hand it over pronto.

"Go and stand over there with your boyfriend."

"Oh, he's not—" I begin, but think better of it when Dog Diva Denise's face turns from thunderous to outright cyclone. "I'll move." I slink over to Asher with my head bowed.

"That was *spectacular*," he says to me as I lean up against the wall next to him.

I glare at him in response. "Don't say another word."

"I'm not sure what else there *is* to say, Zee." His lips twitch in that teasing way I know all too well.

"We don't want a repeat of that little fiasco, now do we?" Dog Diva Denise says as she holds onto Stevie's lead, which is now clipped onto her collar.

I watch in dismay as Stevie sniffs around her feet and promptly drops down and does a pee, right in front of everyone.

"Nice work Stevie," Asher says quietly to me. "You must be super proud."

I snort with laughter, and immediately cover it up with a cough when Dog Diva Denise shoots me an accusatory stare.

Without even mentioning Stevie's little deposit, she moves away from the patch of yellow on the floor and begins to give her instructions. I watch in astonishment as Stevie does everything she tells her, her gaze firmly set on Dog Diva Denise, her little tail swooshing from side to side.

"That little blighter," I mutter through a tight jaw.

At the end of the class, Dog Diva Denise hands Stevie's lead back to me, and Stevie sits down at my feet and gazes up at me as though waiting for further instruction.

"How did you do that?" I ask her in astonishment. One minute she's roaring around here like her pants are on fire— you know, if dogs wore pants—and the next she's the world's most obedient and well-behaved puppy.

"It's all a matter showing her who's boss," she replies. "Which is clearly something you've been struggling with." She shoots me a meaningful look.

"I thought it was an incredibly impressive display on

your behalf, Dog Diva Denise," Asher says as he wraps his arm around my shoulders. "My girlfriend and I have clearly got a lot to learn."

I slide my questioning eyes up to Asher's.

He flicks me a quick smile before he says, "I guess we'll be back next week."

"With the right leadership, your puppy will grow up to be a fine dog," Dog Diva Denise replies, trying to sound assertive while her cheeks turn pink under Asher's gaze.

"Oh, I'm sure she will. Thank you, Dog Diva Denise," Asher says.

"Oh, call me Denise," she replies, her blush turning Santa-suit-red.

"See you next week. And...sorry for you know," I say.

"Do better next time," she sniffs at me before she flashes a smile at Asher.

With Stevie prancing like a prize pup in a dog show, we leave the room and make our way out onto the street.

"What the heck was that about, Stevie? Why did you do everything she told you to do and absolutely nothing I told you to do?"

Stevie sits and looks up at me, concentrating hard on what I'm saying.

"Stevie, up," Asher instructs and she immediately rises to her feet. "Sit." She sits.

"It's a doggie miracle," I say as I watch in wonderment. "Come on, Stevie, heel," I say as I begin to walk down the street and she trots beside me as if she's been following my lead all her life. Which we all know she hasn't.

"Is this the point where I say, 'I told you so?' Or should we wait until we're having a drink at the pub down the road first?" Asher asks.

The thought of sitting with Asher in a pub without the

distraction of the puppy class makes me feel uneasy. It's just him and me, nothing to pull our attention.

That photo of him and his bride weighs heavily in my mind.

"I'd better get home. I'm sure Stevie's pretty knackered, and I've got an early start in the morning."

"Zara, you open your shop at 10am. That's only early to rock stars."

"I've got some other work I need to do for a client, actually." I neglect to tell him *he's* the client. Details.

"Okay, well let's call it a night. Great work, Stevie. You may have embarrassed your mom, but you got it together in the end. Good work." He gives Stevie a couple of firm pats then leans in and plants a kiss on my cheek. "See ya, girlfriend." He pauses and adds, "That's a demotion from 'wifey,' you know."

I let out a nervous laugh, and it sounds more than a little hyena-like. He shoots me a quizzical look, but before he gets the chance to comment, I turn on my heel and call out,

"See you later," as I dash down the street.

What am I going to do about this? We've got this bride-shaped wedge between us now, and things feel weird. Wrong.

And I'm not sure how to get past it.

Chapter Fourteen

ear Dad
   *You know when you think you know someone
and then you find something out about them and
it changes* everything? *Well, that's happened with Asher.
One minute he's my fun-loving single friend, next he's this
guy with a past. A past he's kept secret.*

   *The problem is, every time I see him now I can see that
photo of him on his wedding day, happy and in love.*

   *How do I get past this? How do I get us back to the way
we were?*

   I wish you were here. I could do with some Dad advice.
   Miss you. Love you.
   Your Za-Za xoxo

A few days, and a whole lot of obsessing over what to do
about the whole Asher's marriage-gate later, it's Saturday
afternoon and Tabitha, Lottie, Kennedy, and I are in a room
at the top of an old church in south-east London. We are

standing at the top of rows of tiered seating, looking down at an old, beaten-up wooden table.

"I don't care whether this is historically significant or important or whatever, Lottie. This place is super creepy," Kennedy declares with a shiver.

"I totally agree," Tabitha says.

I nod my head. "Yup. Totally creepy."

Lottie turns to us, her face bright. "But isn't it so *interesting*? I mean, this place is at the top of an old church and people used to sit on these levels and watch actual surgeries. That blows my mind."

"Surgeries with no anaesthetic, babe," Tabitha replies. "It's barbaric."

"Which is why it's so creepy," Kennedy adds. "Think about it. People were operated on without any anaesthetic, and they did it in front of an audience. It's a nightmare."

The four of us are on one of Lottie's *get to know London and improve your mind* tours she insists on us doing. Lottie grew up in Oxfordshire and moved to London for a job three years ago now, becoming my roommate when we were introduced through a mutual friend. With the way she gets all excited about London, you'd think she was a tourist, here for a week. We Londoners might visit the odd tourist spot, but it's usually when we've got someone visiting from out of town—or by total accident.

Today's expedition involves visiting the Old Operating Theatre, Museum and Herb Garret, which is not proving to be nearly as popular as last month's outing.

And yes, it's just as creepy as you think.

"I want to go back to Madame Tussauds," Tabitha complains. "At least there aren't any skeletons there, and we can perve at whatever celebrity we want up close."

"And there's no operating table that looks like it's used for torture, either," I add.

Lottie launches into the speech she's given many times. "Come on, girls. London is rich with history, and this place is a part of it. Imagine being in here, watching a surgery in utter wonder back in the day."

Kennedy raises her hand. "No thanks. I do not want to imagine that. In fact, I would quite like to think about pretty much anything else right now."

"I've got something for you to think about," I blurt out before I can stop myself.

This whole "Asher was married" thing has built up and up in my mind and I've increasingly needed to talk to someone about it. These three girls are my best friends, and they all know and love Asher as much as I do.

"What is it, Zee?" Lottie asks, her brows pulled together in concern.

"You look like you've seen a ghost," Kennedy comments.

Tabitha shudder. "Which is pretty likely in this place."

"I-I found something out a few days ago and I'm in a weird place about it."

"I'm worried about you now, Zee. What is it?" Lottie asks.

"Is it more George weirdness? I still can't get over what he did." Tabitha shakes her head.

I chew on my lip before I reply, "It's not George. It's...Asher."

"What did he do?" Tabitha asks, her eyes wide.

"Oh, my gosh. You kissed!" Lottie exclaims. "I knew it. From the moment you became one another's back-up person, I knew it."

Kennedy gazes at me. "You kissed Asher?"

"Oh, I bet she did," Tabitha says. "He's her back-up guy so she probably wanted to give him a test run."

"A test run?" I guffaw. "Are you serious? Who does that?"

"How was it? Is he a good kisser? Tell us everything. And I mean *every*thing. Lip texture, plumpness, tongue." Lottie clasps my arm. "Oh, Zee. Tell us there was tongue!"

A mother with two young children standing by the operating table looks up at us with a scowl on her face and then hurries her children out of the room.

Tabitha places her hands on her hips as she watches them leave. "I bet those kids will be more traumatized by this place than some conversation about snogging a hot guy. Priorities, woman."

"Can you please focus, Tabitha?" Kennedy asks. "This is juicy stuff. Come on, Zee. Tell us about you and Asher."

"There's no 'me and Asher.' And there's definitely been no kissing."

"Shame," Lottie says as Tabitha asks, "Are you sure?"

I give a firm head nod. "I'm sure there's been no kissing. I would have noticed that."

"You could have sleep kissed," Lottie offers. "You know, the snogging version of sleep walking."

All three of us shoot her a look.

"What?" she protests. "It could be a thing."

"So, what's been going on with Asher?" Kennedy asks.

My stomach churns with anxiety. "I feel weird talking about it, but it's got in my head, and I need to get it out."

"Tell us!" Tabitha, Lottie, and Kennedy insist at once.

I take a deep breath and begin. "I was at his place taking some measurements for the new custom wardrobe I've got going in and, well, I found something. Something...unexpected."

Lottie sucks in air. "You went through his things? That's not cool."

Kennedy shakes her head. "That doesn't sound like something Zee would do."

"No, no. Definitely not," I insist. "I had to move some boxes so I could measure up and one of them dropped on the floor and broke open. Something fell out."

Tabitha's eyes are wide. "It's a blow-up doll, isn't it? Asher's got a blow-up doll."

She wins a bat on the arm from Kennedy. "It won't be a blow-up doll." She pauses and then asks, "Right?"

I give a grim nod. "Right."

"A blow-up doll would be so weird, and Asher's not weird. He's a player, with far too much female attention, but he's not weird," Lottie surmises.

"You see here's the thing. He might be a player now, but he was—" I pause, wrestling with this new information I've learned about our friend. The Asher I thought I knew is no more, replaced with this married guy who hasn't been straight about his past with any of us.

"What?"

"Tell us!"

"You can't just stop mid-sentence like that!"

I take a deep breath and blurt out, "I found out Asher's married. Or was married. I'm not sure. All I know is there was a wedding."

Lottie and Tabitha recoil from me in shock, their eyes the size of Christmas baubles, their mouths forming perfect 'o's.

"Are you serious?" Lottie asks.

"He's married? As in, like, to a woman?" Tabitha asks.

"He's not gay, babe," Lottie says.

"Yes, and yes," I reply with a grim nod. "Not to the gay

part. We all know he's totally straight. And I don't know what to make of it. I mean, this is *Asher*. We all know him to be this fun, easy-going, single—emphasis on the single—guy, right? He's not married. At least, I didn't think he was until I found the album."

Lottie shakes her head, her lips pulled into a thin line. "Wow. Just wow."

"You think you know a person," Tabitha says.

I hang my head. "I feel bad telling you girls, but it's been eating me up."

"Don't feel bad," Lottie says. "I would have done the same. This is big news. None of us knew about some wife, and he might be closest with you, Zee, but we're all friends with him. None of us knew about this."

Tabitha nods. "That's true."

"I knew," Kennedy says quietly, and we all turn to gawp at her in astonishment.

I pull my brows together. "You did? Why didn't you say anything?"

"I figured it was his story to tell, not mine."

I push my hair behind my ears. "Well, that makes me feel terrible for telling you."

"How did you know?" Tabitha asks.

She shrugs. "He's from San Diego and so am I. It's not a huge place. You hear things."

"How long have you known?" Lottie asks.

"I heard about it when I was home and caught up with some friends over the holidays. One of them knows his wife."

"His *wife*," Lottie echoes, and we all stand still and dwell on that fact for a while.

"My friend told me that Asher had left San Diego to come here for a fresh start after his marriage fell apart."

"So, he's divorced?" I ask.

Kennedy lifts her shoulder. "I think so, but I don't know for sure."

I blink a few times as I process this new information. "Oh, my gosh. He was married and it fell apart."

"It's been two years. I bet he's divorced. It would make sense if he was," Tabitha states with confidence.

"Tabitha's right. It does make sense he'd be divorced, particularly if she broke his heart and he moved on," Kennedy says.

She broke his heart. The idea makes me feel odd. Unsettled.

Protective.

Lottie voices what we're all thinking when she says, "Things must have been pretty bad for him to leave the country."

"Or it could have been a coincidence," Tabitha offers. "He might have been offered a job just as things got bad with his wife, so he decided to take it. It might not be as dramatic as we think."

Tabitha is counting off on her fingers and comes to a sudden stop. She looks up at Kennedy. "Hold on a second. Let's back up the bus here for a minute, Kennedy. You're telling us that you've known about this for over *six months?*" she guffaws. "Why didn't you tell us?" She turns to Lottie and me. "That's the sort of thing friends tell friends, right?"

"It's because I figured he would tell us if he wanted us to know. But now that you've discovered his secret, Zee, we all know."

I give a grim nod. "And we can't *un*-know it."

"Exactly."

I think of the smiling, happy faces in the picture

window of that wedding album, and my heart squeezes for my friend. "Poor Asher."

"Yeah, poor Asher," Tabitha echoes as the others nod their agreement.

We stand together, lost in thought, when Lottie punctures the silence. "That explains so much."

I crinkle my brow. "What do you mean?"

She holds up a finger. "Number one, he's a super fun guy. Number two," she says as she raises another finger, "he's never serious about girls. And number three, he's run away from a woman who hurt him. It all fits."

"Where are you going with this exactly?" I ask.

"Can't you see? He's avoiding getting close to anyone because he's been hurt by this wife of his."

"Makes sense," Kennedy says.

We look up as a group of men walk into the room, talking and laughing loudly about cutting open patients on the operating table.

"Let's go to the pub and finish this conversation there. After this whole weird operating theatre thing, I need a glass of wine," Kennedy suggests.

"Not to mention the whole Asher-is-married thing," Tabitha adds as she and Kennedy walk down the stairs towards the exit.

I place my hand on Lottie's arm. "Sorry, babe. I don't think this place quite hit the mark today."

"That's okay. I'll find something lighter for next month. How about the London Dungeon?"

"Where they used to torture people? Lottie, I think you need to reassess what you think of as 'light.'"

"Yeah, okay."

Together, we walk down the steps, past the old operating table and skeleton, and out of the room. Downstairs, the four of us head out onto the street in search of a pub. As luck would have it, we find one only a street away, and we each get a cold drink before sitting outside under an umbrella.

"I feel weird about it," Lottie says. "Like, we know Asher because he's Asher."

"Exactly," I say.

"But now he's not the Asher we thought he was. Is he?" Tabitha says.

"He's the same, but different." I scrunch up my nose. "Does that make sense?"

"Oh, totally." Lottie nods in agreement. "Do you know what happened between Asher and his wife, Kennedy?"

"What my friend Kyla said is that his wife did the dirty on him."

Collectively, we suck in air at the shock.

"That's horrible," Lottie says.

"Poor Asher," Tabitha says.

"No wonder he ran away," I add.

We sit in silence for some time as we each digest the information.

"That does it," Lottie says as she bangs her hand on the table, startling us all. "We need to help him."

"How?"

"We need to find him a new wife."

I chortle. "Where? Online?"

Lottie rolls her eyes. "Not that kind of wife. We need to find him a woman he can fall in love with, a woman worthy of our amazing friend. Someone who's not going to hurt him like that dreadful wife of his."

"She'd have to be someone super special," Kennedy warns.

"I think it's a great idea in principle," I begin, "but I

don't think he wants to find someone. I mean look at his dating record. He's hardly a stable relationship kind of guy, is he? How many girls has he dated since we've known him?"

"It's only because he's been hurt," Lottie says.

Kennedy nods her head. "Lottie's probably right. The guy's had a rough time."

"Which is why we should stay out of it altogether. He clearly doesn't want another wife," Tabitha says with authority. "Otherwise, why would he have agreed to be Zara's back-up guy?"

My friends turn to look at me.

"What?" I say.

Lottie narrows her eyes at me. "Interesting."

"It is, isn't it?" Kennedy replies.

I flick my gaze between them. "What's interesting?"

"Are you sure there's been no kissy kissy between you guys?" Lottie asks.

This again? *Awesome.*

I lay my hands palm-down on the table. "Asher's been hurt and now he's sowing his wild oats. He might have agreed to be my safety net in the distant future, but there's no way that I'm one of those oats for him."

Tabitha giggles. "Now I've got an image of two oats kissing each other. It's weirdly hot."

"Oh, I don't think you're one of his oats," Lottie says.

Whatever. I know we're just friends. And I know he's withholding a big secret from me.

"I think we need to pretend we don't know about this and act normal around him," I begin. "He ran away because something horrible happened with his wife, and we need to give him the space to deal with that. After all, he hasn't told any of us about it."

"Zara's right," Tabitha agrees.

"I still want to find him a new wife," Lottie says as she shoots me a meaningful look.

"Stop!" I say with a laugh.

We spend the rest of the afternoon sitting in the sun, putting the world's wrongs to rights. By the time we head home my mind is made up. I'm not going to talk with Asher about what I know. Instead, I'm going to ignore it and get back to our old, fun-loving, easy friendship.

Even if my heartstrings have been well and truly yanked on by what I now know. He's still just Asher, and we're still just fun-time friends. And that's the way it's going to stay.

Chapter Fifteen

I say goodbye to a customer as Scarlett comes through the door, looking especially bright and breezy in a bright orange shift dress and matching heels.

"You look nice. Special occasion?" I ask as I slide the purchase receipt into the folder on the desk.

"I just felt like wearing it today, that's all. Did that customer want any design work?"

I shake my head. "She bought a throw and a couple of pill boxes. Apparently, she collects them, and she was over the moon that we had some in stock. She said she'd tell all her pill box collector friends about us."

"Oh, goody. That means we'll make about four pounds fifty this week." She slumps her shoulders and pushes out a breath.

"I know, it's depressing. If only there was a way we could destroy Karina's new shop in some freak accident or something. Then we could get back to actually turning a profit, like we used to."

"What are you suggesting? We hire a car and drive it through the window? Because no one would ever know it was us with all the CCTV cameras filming your every move in this city."

"There is *that*." I wipe some dust from a shelf and then turn back to her. "You know, I could ask Kennedy if she could feature our designs in her magazine. She's a features writer at *Claudette*. Maybe she could write an article on what it's like to be a start-up interior designer in London?" I feel a twinge of excitement at the prospect.

"Sure. I guess." She sits down at the computer.

"You guess? It could be a really great idea." My twinge builds into a fully-fledged feeling as I begin to pace the shop. "*Claudette* is a national magazine. *National*. It could do amazing things for us. Get our shop featured, and we'll be made. I don't know why I didn't think of this before." I glance at Stevie. She's safely tucked up in her pen, sleeping off a frenzied energy burst from earlier in the day.

"I know *Claudette*. I wasn't born yesterday, you know. But you might be getting ahead of yourself there, babe." She peers at the screen. "You haven't even asked her."

"Semantics," I reply with a grin. "I've got a feeling about this. Leave it with me. Okay?"

She lifts her eyes to mine briefly. "Let me know how it goes," she replies with a lot less enthusiasm than I'm feeling.

"I bet it'll work."

"Yup." She doesn't lift her eyes from the screen.

"I'm going to call her now." I breeze past Scarlett to collect my phone from my handbag. "This game is all about networks. We need to use them to our advantage."

"I suppose it's worth a shot."

"It is," I insist.

I'll show Scarlett. She might be on the brink of giving up, but I'm not. This business means the world to me.

I pull up Kennedy's details and press *call*. A couple of rings later, she answers.

"Hey, Zee."

"Can I ask you a big favour?"

"Shoot."

"Is there any way you could get ScarZar in *Claudette*? It wouldn't have to be a big feature or anything, just something to help get our name out there. That big, new design store on the high street is killing our business. "

"I don't know, Zee. It's not my usual area."

"Could you at least float the idea past your boss? We've done a bunch of gorgeous redesigns that you could photograph, plus Stevie would look so cute in those photos."

"Let me see what I can do for you."

Hope pings about in my like a pinball. "Thank you so, so much. I owe you one." I say goodbye and hang up. I turn to Scarlett. "The wheels are in motion."

"Zara, don't you think every small interiors shop in the greater London area has thought of doing that already? You're dreaming."

"I'm not dreaming. Not everyone has Kennedy as a close and personal friend, you know, and not everyone has a cute-as-a-button shop dog, either."

"Well, I'm going out." She sails past me towards the door.

"But you just got here."

"I've got an appointment with that couple who want some design work done on their place up in Hampstead. Remember?"

I wrack my brain for who she's talking about and come up with no one. "But I've got to go to Asher's place to meet the delivery guys. He's getting his new living room furniture today."

"Who's going to be here at the shop?"

We both turn and look at Stevie in her pen. The idea of Stevie running the shop while we're both out at appointments brings a smile to my face.

"Shame Stevie can't do it. I mean, how cute would that be?"

Scarlett, on the other hand, doesn't quite share my amusement. "Come on, Zara. You need to get serious. We can't run a business if you don't look in the shared calendar to see what's happening each day."

"But—"

"No buts," she replies, sounding exactly like my mother. "I'll see you this afternoon." She breezes out the door and disappears from view.

I pull out my phone and check our shared calendar. I was certain she didn't have any meetings in there when I checked it this morning, let alone one that's going to take several hours. But still, there is it in bold blue: *Scarlett in Hampstead.*

How could I have missed that?

An hour and only two dismal customers later, neither of whom wanted anything but small items from the shop, I hang a hand-written sign on the door that tells people I'll be back by two thirty and climb into an Uber. I place a vase and plant carefully in the seat well on one side of the car and hop in the other and place Stevie on my lap. I notice the driver peering suspiciously in the rear-view mirror at me.

"She'll stay on my lap and she's totally toilet trained." I cross my fingers under my skirt. I don't usually get Ubers because of the cost, favouring instead the cheap and usually efficient Tube. But today I've got a few things to deliver to Asher's place, so I'm putting the cost of the ride on the shop's credit card.

As we move slowly along London's busy streets, I scroll through my messages. Spotting one that reads *Call me!* from Kennedy. I dial her number and hold my breath in anticipation.

"Zara," she says.

"Have you got us a slot in your magazine?" I ask without preamble.

"You know I'd love to say yes to that, but I asked my boss and she said no. Sorry."

My heart sinks. Being featured in *Claudette* would be a game changer for ScarZar. "I understand. Thanks for asking."

"I do have some other news, though. I spoke to Kyla. My friend in San Diego who knows Asher's wife? She told me the whole story."

"You asked her?"

"I thought we should get the full picture rather than filling in the blanks. I figured that would be fair to Asher."

"I suppose it is."

"I don't have to tell you if you don't want to know."

My chest tightens. "I wish I'd never found that photo."

"But you did, babe."

I let out a heavy breath. "Okay, tell me about it."

"She cheated on him with his best friend."

I suck in air. "No! Oh, that's terrible!" I picture the photo of the happy couple. "The poor guy."

"I know, right? Kyla said he was blindsided by it. Never suspected a thing. Apparently, they'd been together for a few years, and he was totally in love with her. When it happened, he fell to pieces and the next thing everyone knew, he'd moved to London."

I stare out the window, my heart breaking in two for Asher. He was in love with a woman and she tore his heart out of his chest and stomped on it. Tears prick my eyes as an uncomfortable feeling claims my belly.

"Zara? Are you there?"

I sniff and Stevie looks up at me in alarm. I give her a reassuring pat on the head. "I'm on my way to his flat now. I've got a delivery happening. I've got to go."

"Sorry to tell you this. I figured we might be able to help him or something? I don't know."

"You and me both."

"Talk soon?"

"Talk soon." I hang up the phone and stare straight ahead of me, lost in thought, feelings churning like butter inside.

Asher had his heart broken by his cheating wife.

He was so hurt, he ran away.

I blow out a breath.

I shouldn't know any of this.

All too soon, the Uber comes to a stop outside Asher's building. I thank the driver and climb out with my plant and vase with Stevie's lead hooked over my wrist. Using my key to unlock the front door, I climb the stairs. At Asher's door, I place the plant and vase down on the floor and let myself into the flat. The place is deadly quiet and just as empty as usual. I'll give Asher one thing though: he might live in a totally bland bachelor pad cliché, but he's tidy. Nothing is out of place.

I take Stevie to Asher's bedroom, and I avoid looking at the walk-in wardrobe. I don't need to be tempted to look at the album. I tell Stevie to stay and then close the door.

Asher told me he'd move the current furniture out of the living room and true to his word, the place is now empty but for the oversized bloke-y TV on the wall and the surf-boards in the corner.

I inspect the new grey, panelled wall I had installed yesterday. It looks sleek and modern, and I know Asher will love it.

The front door buzzer sounds, and I press the intercom button. "Hello?"

"We've got a delivery down 'ere for Asher McMillan. Where do ya want it?"

"Fantastic. Third floor, please. Flat number seven."

I hear the guy grumble about having to lug the furniture up three flights of stairs before I hang up. I wander over to the large living room window and look out across the rooftops and trees as I wait. Being here in Asher's flat feels strange. The last time I was here was the day I discovered that my friend has a difficult past. I push out a breath as I watch a small flock of birds fly by in a v-formation.

I hear someone out in the corridor, so I walk over to the front door and pull it open. Asher is standing in the door-way, a key in his hand. Wearing a navy suit and a white, open neck shirt that shows off his creamy olive skin, he looks professional and confident—and handsome, too, I'll admit. You know, for a guy who's had his heart broken in two by some wife he's hidden from us for years, that is.

The shock of seeing him hits me in the chest and my churning emotions from earlier swoop back in. "Wh-what are you doing here?" I ask breathlessly, clutching onto the door.

He glances from my face to my white knuckles and back again. "You need to work on your greetings, Zee. Try this on for size: 'Hey, Asher. You've come home to help out today. You are a truly amazing human being, and I am so grateful for all that you do.'" His lips lift in amusement, and I loosen up a notch or ten.

This is Asher. He's my friend. He's fun and easy going

and I love hanging out with him. So what if he's not been one hundred percent honest with me and my friends? He's been hurt. The least I can do is be his friend.

"A truly amazing human being, huh? Someone thinks pretty highly of themselves."

He glances back at my hand, still holding onto the door. "Are you gonna let me into my own flat, or do I need to wait for the formal written invitation?"

I pull my hand from the door and step back for him to walk inside. "Your royal highness," I say with a mock bow.

He grins at me. "That's better. Keep it up."

"Did you see the guys are about to deliver your new living room furniture? I thought you were going to be them just now."

"I was hoping I'd get back here before they arrived. Perfect timing." He pulls off his jacket and places his keys on the kitchen bench. "I'm gonna go hang this up so I can help them. BRB."

He disappears from the room. I can hear the delivery guys down the stairs giving one another instructions as they make their way up. "You guys okay?" I call out.

"We'd be be'er if you lived on the ground floor, love," one of them calls back.

"Sorry about that. See you up here in a second."

"Yeah. A second. That's all this'll take," is his sarcastic reply.

"I see I've got a bedroom visitor," Asher says as he walks back into the room. He's got the sleeves of his white shirt rolled up, exposing his strong, muscular forearms, ready for some physical labour.

"I hope it's okay that Stevie's in there?" I ask.

"It's fine. She seemed pretty chill, sniffing her way around the room."

"Dogs do that."

"You don't say?" I lean over the top of the staircase and see the delivery men on the floor immediately below. "They're almost here."

Some huffing and groaning, and an unpleasant waft of a combination of sweat and cigarette smoke later, the delivery men place a plastic-wrapped three-seater sofa on the bare living room floor and return to their truck to bring up the matching chairs.

"Let's unwrap this baby," Asher says. "It feels like Christmas and my birthday all rolled into one."

We set about peeling the plastic off the sofa, and by the time we're finished the delivery men have brought up a chair each and we've got more to unwrap.

Within about ten minutes flat, the entire living room is transformed with the sofa and chairs, a large floor rug we've rolled out and put into position, a coffee table, and the vase and plant I brought up with me.

Asher tips the delivery guys and then we both stand and stare at the transformed room before us.

"It needs scatter cushions and maybe some shelving over there," I say, pointing at a blank, white wall, "but other than that, it's amazing."

"No mafia horse's head."

"Do you really want one of those?"

He shrugs. "I liked it."

"I'll get you one, then."

"You know, it looks so different from my other stuff." He runs his hand across the top of the sofa. "I mean, I know this is still leather, but it's got a totally different vibe."

I jump on his words. I know I shouldn't. I know I should let it be and allow him to tell me about his wife in his own time. But he hasn't told me anything about her. Not even that she exists, let alone how she broke his heart. And dang it, I'm curious. So sue me.

"Does it feel like a fresh start to you?" I lead.

He looks around the room. "It does."

"Do you think you needed that for any reason in particular? You know, like the old furniture had bad memories or something?"

He regards me through the corner of his eye. "I did spill some chips and dip on the sofa last week, if that's what you mean?"

"I was meaning more...*emotional* memories than, you know, *food* memories." I watch him closely, but the guy's not giving anything away.

"Emotional memories?" he questions with a smile lifting the edges of his mouth. "I'm not sure I could have many emotional memories about furniture I inherited from the guy I rented my last flat from."

"So, you didn't bring any of it over from the US?"

"Nope. I'm just happy to have the change. You did a great job on this room, Zee. Thanks."

He's not biting, so at the risk of blurting something out I oughtn't, I drop the subject.

"It's not done yet," I say.

"Ah, the cushions and shelving."

"And one other thing I think you'll like."

"What?"

"It's a surprise."

"Is this surprise going to cost me a lot of money?"

I give a wave of my hand. "Hardly anything at all."

"Intriguing."

"All will be revealed in due course. By which I mean within the next couple of weeks."

I hear a series of yaps coming from Asher's bedroom. "I'll get Stevie."

"You do that. I'm gonna take a load off. We've been standing here looking at the new furniture, but we haven't tried it out."

I gesture at the sofa. "Be my guest."

He flops down in the middle of the sofa and lets out a contented, "Ahhh."

"Good?" I call out as I walk down the hall and pull the bedroom door open.

Stevie immediately zips past me and takes a flying leap at Asher, almost making it onto the sofa, instead falling backwards onto the ground.

"Are you okay, little pup?" I ask.

But she's like a rubber band, simply jumping back onto her feet and bouncing on the spot. I pick her up and she squirms in my arms, eager to get on the sofa.

"I don't think Uncle Asher wants you anywhere near his new furniture," I say to her.

"It's fine. As long as she doesn't try to eat this one."

"Are you sure? I mean, Dog Diva Denise's training has worked amazingly, but she's still a puppy."

He pats the spot at his side. "Sit. Both of you."

I plonk myself down next to him and Stevie wriggles to escape my grasp. I let her go and she bounces onto the cushion between us and leaps up onto Asher. "She didn't want to be on the sofa. She wanted to be on *you*," I say with a giggle.

Asher nuzzles her and it makes my heart melt. Just a little.

Okay, a lot.

There's something about seeing a hot guy holding a cute puppy he clearly adores.

Wait. *Hot guy?*

I shake my head. Asher might be hot, but to me he's just Asher. My *friend* Asher.

But the problem is, now that I know what I know about him, I'm beginning to see him in a different light. He's no longer just my good-time guy friend who's got a way with women. He's been in love, and he's been hurt—deeply enough to feel the need to run away to another country. It's shifted something inside of me.

And if I'm honest, it's awakened something, too.

Something I don't want to think about.

Something I *can't* think about.

"Ah, this is the life." Utterly oblivious to my internal emotional turbulence, Asher stretches out his arm behind me, resting it on the top of the sofa as he lifts his feet onto the coffee table. "I could lounge here all day."

His hand brushes my shoulder and I freeze, every muscle in my body suddenly taut with tension.

How can I stop this feeling so weird? Two friends together, enjoying sitting on a new sofa is perfectly natural. But here I am, filled to the brim with a plethora of emotions about the guy at my side. I'm sitting with a ramrod straight back, wishing I could just chill the heck out.

But I can't.

I can no longer deny that things have changed between us—and I've got absolutely no clue what to do about it.

Chapter Sixteen

I rub my eyes as I lean back against the rocking chair, Lottie regarding me with a concerned look from her yoga mat on the living room floor. "But that's the thing, Lottie. It feels like everything's changed and I don't even know how to *be* around him anymore."

She shifts her weight and moves into warrior pose, looking strong and Amazonian in her shorts and form-fitting top—if Amazonians wore Lycra and were only 5 foot 3 inches tall, that is.

"I want things to go back to the way they were before—when we were just us, Asher and Zara, hanging out, having fun together."

"It's only natural that you feel different about him. We all do and it's because we know what he's been through."

"So, you're saying I feel bad for him?"

"Of course you do, babe." She glides into another pose I don't know the name for.

"Hmm." I turn the idea over in my head. Knowing that Asher has been hurt so deeply by a woman has made me feel sorry for him. That fits.

"Next time you see him, make sure to have some fun, and keep it light. You know?"

"Keep it light. Oh, you're so clever, Lottie. I've been twisting myself up over this for no good reason at all. I just feel bad for him. That's all."

"Exactly." Lottie readjusts her position, moving into downward dog. I get an eyeful of bum. Good bum, but bum all the same.

Stevie wakes up from her curled-up position on her bed in the corner, spots Lottie with her face close to the ground, stampedes over to her on her oversized puppy paws, and promptly plants a big lick on her nose.

Lottie bats her gently away with one hand. "Ugh, Stevie!"

"Stevie, come here, girl," I say, and my newly obedient—mostly—dog bounds over to me, her tail swooshing. I pick her up and plant a kiss on the top of her warm, soft head.

Really, Dog Diva Denise might have one too many screws loose for my liking, but she's doing wonders for Stevie's behaviour.

"Of course, there is another possibility." Lottie pushes herself back up to a standing position, her face doing an imitation of a strawberry from the yoga effort, and then immediately flops down onto the sofa in a heap of limbs. "Thank goodness that's done."

"I'm impressed you're actually doing it."

"I'm trying to be healthy and Zen." She pulls a face. "It's a work in progress."

"What's the other possibility?"

"Have you ever thought that maybe you could be in love with the guy?"

I choke out a surprised laugh. "In *love* with him? With Asher? Where the heck did that come from?"

"Why not? You get on really well and you spend loads of time together. You're practically an old married couple at times. We've all noticed it."

"You mean the type of married couples who don't have sex?" I reply with a wry smile.

"You know what I mean. You fit. You work. Plus, there's the small matter of the fact you chose *him* to be your back-up guy, and he said yes. I mean, how convenient would it be for you to fall in love with the guy who's agreed to marry you in less than five years' time? Very, is the answer, Zee. *Very* convenient."

I shake my head at her vehemently, instantly rejecting the notion as utterly preposterous. "You've lost your mind. There's no way I'm in love with Asher. No way! For starters, he's *married*," I shoot her a meaningful look.

"Separated and probably divorced," she corrects.

"We don't know that. And if that's not enough of a reason, then there's the fact that he ran away after she cheated on him. Who knows? Maybe he's still in love with her. Plus, he's...well, he's Asher. You know?"

She shoots me a meaningful look. "Oh, I know."

"What does *that* mean?"

She ignores my question. "Do you realise that the two main reasons why you say you're not in love with the guy are to do with how you think *he* feels?"

"That's one hundred percent not true," I huff.

She counts them off on her fingers. "He's married, and he's probably still in love with his wife."

She's got a point.

"How do *you* feel about him? That's what you need to ask yourself. Forget all the stuff about his wife."

I arch my eyebrows. "Did you just hear yourself?"

She waves her hand. "Oh, you know what I mean. They're not together."

"Unless he's got her stashed away in the attic."

She shoots me a sardonic smile. "Does his flat even have an attic?"

"Well, no. It's more of a metaphor than anything."

"A metaphorical attic?"

"The point is, I'm not in love with him. I'd know if I was," I reply with assuredness. Because the idea is beyond ridiculous.

Isn't it?

I can't fall for my back-up guy. No one does that. They're a back-up for a reason. They're not the first choice. In fact, they're the very last palatable choice after you've exhausted other, more attractive avenues.

Only somehow, knowing what I now know about him, Asher's morphed into my only avenue.

And it's scaring the living daylights out of me.

* * *

The following night at puppy training, I'm wound up so tightly I could ignite into an impressive fireworks display at any moment.

Asher is his usual self, of course. He's relaxed and easy going, happy to flirt with Dog Diva Denise and chat with the other dog owners. Me? I'm more of a mannequin than anything else tonight, with a frozen smile plastered across my face, my actions rigid. I'm concentrating so hard on *not* thinking about what Lottie said about me being in love with him that the real estate of my brain is almost entirely closed off. I'm left with a brain that has the capacity of a small, understairs cupboard.

He's wearing a pair of form-fitting jeans and a T-shirt that shows off his impressively wide shoulders, long legs, and hints at the firm torso beneath.

It does nothing to me. Really. *Nothing.*

"Good girl, Stevie!" Dog Diva Denise says as Stevie sits on command, having completed an obstacle course in front of the whole class. "That's how you do it. See the loose lead?" She brandishes Stevie's pink lead at the class. "This dog has come a long way," she adds, smiling at Asher and me. Well, at Asher. To her I'm just some irritating impediment. An irritating impediment that can't even be trusted to walk their own dog in the puppy class.

"We're so very proud of our girl," Asher replies as he casually slinks his arm around my waist.

I freeze, his touch causing an unexpected jolt of electricity to charge through me at full speed.

He smiles down at me. "Aren't we, honey?"

"Oh, uh, yes. We are so proud of...of Stevie," I confirm with a rapidly moving head.

Asher shoots me a quizzical look and I force a smile.

"All right, you two," Dog Diva Denise says. "Take the reins and show me how to do it. Completing this task will mean Stevie will graduate." She proffers Stevie's lead, and I take it in my hand. "Make her sit, make her stay while you move to the other side of the room, then call her and make her sit once more before you reward her with a treat."

I eye Stevie. That's a lot for me to remember, let alone a puppy who's only a matter of months old.

"You got this," Asher says to me.

I lift my gaze to his and the warmth and kindness in his eyes has my heart leaping into my mouth.

That's when it hits me. Hard.

I've got it bad for my best friend.

I suck in air. How the heck could I have let this happen?

"Chop chop!" Dog Diva Denise instructs, and I drag my eyes from Asher's and spring into action.

I tug on Stevie's lead and do the hand gesture Dog Diva Denise taught us to instruct her to sit, which she does instantly, her eyes trained on me. I resist the urge to lean down and pat her for being such a good doggie, and instead tell her to stay, say a little prayer as I drop the lead, and walk over to the other side of the room. I stop and turn and call her over to me, and she comes bounding towards me with such joy, a massive smile bursts out across my face. Immediately, I instruct her to sit, and after a moment in which I fear she'll fail at the last hurdle, she promptly plops her doggie bum down on the floor and gazes up at me.

"She did it!" I declare in excitement. I pull out a treat from my pocket and feed it to her as I give her a congratulatory pat. "Who's a good girl?" I coo.

Later, I'm clutching onto Stevie's graduation certificate as Asher and I walk down the street.

"Stevie, you hit it out of the park!" Asher says.

"She was amazing. Personally, I think she was so scared of Dog Diva Denise back there that she did whatever I told her, just so she wouldn't take over her control again."

"She's a smart dog."

I smile down at Stevie as she happily trots along the footpath beside me. "You're telling me."

"Hey, are you okay?" he asks me, and I'm instantly back on guard, Stevie's glory no longer providing me with the protective shield of mere seconds ago.

"Yeah, I'm just a little tense. That's all." Tense because I'm pretty sure I've got feelings for you that go way beyond friendship and you're married to a woman who cheated on you with your best friend and you left the US to come here and now I don't feel like I know you at all even though you seem like my good friend, Asher and you look so hot...

There's a chance I may be a little wound up.

"Is it work stuff?" he asks, giving me an easy out.

I leap on it. "Oh, yeah. Work is pretty stressful right now."

"It's that demanding client in Notting Hill, isn't it? The devastatingly handsome and charismatic one."

"You think rather a lot of yourself, don't you?"

"I'm just saying what you're thinking," he replies with a grin.

I slow my pace outside his building, and he pauses and looks back at me after bounding up the steps to the front door. "I thought you were coming up to watch the game with me."

"Oh, I should probably get going."

"Come on, Zee. You promised to watch baseball with me and so far, all you've managed is one measly game weeks ago. Plus, I've got a great looking flat now by this cool new London designer."

"Don't you have any guy friends you can watch it with? I mean, not only am I British and know next to nothing about baseball, but I'm a girl, in case you hadn't noticed."

"I noticed," he replies with a laugh. "Look, I'll furnish you with good snacks and beer." He shoots me his smile, and I let out a breath.

"Sure. Why not."

How awkward can it be sitting alone in close proximity to a guy I've just recently realised I've got some major feelings for?

Very, is the answer. *Very awkward indeed.*

With a bunch of guys in baseball clothes on the TV—which is fitting, considering we're watching a baseball game and all—and Stevie sound asleep at my feet, I try my best to relax against the back of the sofa with Asher next to me. He got us a couple of beers when we arrived, and I'm clutching onto mine and taking frequent sips to try to quell my nerves.

Asher regards me through questioning eyes. "Are you practicing the Alexander technique or something tonight?"

"The what now?"

"You know, the standing tall thing Lottie was into a while back? You're all tense." He slaps the back cushion next to him. "Lean back. Take a load off. Your dog graduated at the top of her class and I'm sure she'll be invited back to give a valedictorian speech sometime soon. So chill, 'kay?"

I let out a giggle, loosening up a notch. "I can totally see Stevie in a cap and gown."

"Don't go getting any ideas. I've seen the costumes in that Penelope's Pooches store. Stevie will have to give back her cool dog card if you put her in one of those."

"Aw, you think Stevie is cool."

"I'll admit it. The little tyke's grown on me."

I lean slowly back against the cushion and shoot him a smile.

I can do this. This is Asher. That's all. I'm making a much bigger deal of this whole thing than I should be.

I flick my eyes from the TV to his face and get a start when I see him watching me with a weird look on his face I can't quite decipher. "What?" I ask, as though I haven't been wrestling with my feelings for him.

"Nothing. Can we watch the game now, please?"

"You're the one interrupting it. I'm beyond excited to see whether the white stripe-y team is going to beat the blue team. That's a nice blue, by the way."

"How dare you," he mocks. "We're Padres supporters here."

"Padres?"

"The San Diego team. They're the white team. I told you this last time, remember?"

"Yeah, sure, but Padres? Isn't that Spanish for priests?"

"Check you out, knowing stuff. You're totally right. Padre does mean priest. San Diego was where the first Mission was located in California. Hence the name."

"I'm getting a history lesson, too?"

He grins at me. "It's all part of the baseball experience." Looking back at the screen he says, "What a hit!"

The ball sails right through the air into the stadium seats, where people in the crowd scramble to retrieve it.

"Is that a six?" I ask him.

"Zara, we've been over this. A six is when a player hits a ball over the boundary in *cricket*. It's not called a six in baseball."

"Because it's *so* different."

"It is," he insists, and it makes me laugh. "What?"

"You're funny."

"I'm trying to watch the game here."

"Okay. Tell me what's happening as it happens, and I will try my best to follow."

As he launches into explaining how many swings a batter gets and how the bases work, I relax into my seat. It feels like the two of us hanging out, just as it always has, and my weird, perplexing feelings about him begin to fade.

Before long, I'm whooping with him when the Padres score, commiserating when their batters are out, and genuinely involved in the game.

Things get tense when it's down to the wire. One bad pitch and the Padres could lose. We're both on the edge of our seats, watching the final play closely, when the Cubs' batter swings and misses and the Padres instantly jump up and down and race around the field.

Asher and I both leap up in excitement from our spots on the sofa, Asher punching the air and me bouncing up and down on the spot, cheering.

"Yes!" he says as he turns his bright face towards me. "We did it!"

"Go Padres!" I reply, and he scoops me up in his arms and bounces me around in a circle until I'm dizzy.

"Do you have any idea what this means?"

I throw my head back and laugh. "No, I don't."

"It means everything," he replies as he sets me back on the ground and beams at me.

And then, without a breath of warning, the atmosphere around us changes.

It could be the softness in his eyes as he looks at me, or the excitement in the air, or the simple fact that we're standing facing one another, his arms still around me, the heat from his body pressed against mine, heightening my senses.

Whatever it is, whatever has brought about this change, when I look up at him, I know that it's not pity I feel for him. It's something else. Something big.

And I need to know if he feels it, too.

With my heart hammering in my chest, my throat dries up, and I try to swallow. We hold our gaze for a beat, two, and then, without warning, he breaks it, pulling back from me.

And just as soon as it began, the moment has gone.

"Great game, huh?" he says as he runs his fingers through his hair.

I clear my throat, my heart rate still thinking I've sprinted to the top of Primrose Hill. "Yeah. Great game."

He collects the empty beer bottles from the coffee table and moves across the room towards the kitchen. "Supporting the Padres can be challenging, but times like this sure make it worthwhile."

I draw my lower lip between my teeth, emotions and thoughts forming a confused rabble in my mind.

Was that a moment?

Does he feel it too?

Did we almost...*kiss?*

I remain rooted to the spot as he returns to the living room and picks up the empty bowl of chips. He stops and looks at me, and as though in a daze, I lift my gaze to his.

"Are you heading home now? I've got an early morning breakfast meeting tomorrow that I need to be sharp for."

I spring into action. "Breakfast meeting. Right. I'll, err, I'll go then." With heat rising in my cheeks like the mercury on a hot Southern California day, I slip on my shoes, fling the strap of my handbag over my shoulder, and scoop a sleeping Stevie up from the floor.

Asher follows me to the door and pulls it open for me.

I glance at him to try to work out what the heck just happened, but his face is impassive.

He reaches out and pats Stevie's head and says, "Well done again, champ. See you both soon."

I avert my eyes and mumble my goodbye before I bolt out of his flat, a cocktail of confusion, humiliation, and regret churning inside of me.

He doesn't feel anything for me. It's all in my head.

And the sooner I get over him, the better off we'll all be.

207

Chapter Seventeen

I've been at the shop for a couple of hours, dealing with a bunch of customers and putting together a quote for a client who wants their conservatory redecorated, when I begin to wonder where Scarlett is. She hadn't mentioned going to any meetings today, and after the Hampstead debacle, I've checked and double checked the shared calendar. There are no entries.

After handing a customer a gift-wrapped metal Buddha head, I pick my phone up from behind the counter and call her. It rings and rings and goes to voicemail.

"Hey, Scarlett. Just checking in to see when you'll be in. I've got the wardrobe delivery at Asher's today and need to get there to let them in. Call me!"

I hang up and drum my fingers against the counter. This isn't like Scarlett. Usually she's the efficient, on top of it one, the one chasing business and working her heart out to make this venture a success. If I'm honest with myself, lately she's been a little distant, like she doesn't care as much as she once did. And I totally get that. It's not easy to have to deal with a failing business. It's hard graft, it's anxiety provoking, and it's not for the faint-hearted—as I've been discovering.

Stevie's yap captures my attention. She's looking at me through the bars of her pen, her little body waving from side to side as her tail swings.

"Do you want to go out, little pup?" I ask as I collect the shop keys and her lead from a hook behind the counter.

I connect the lead to her collar, lift her out of the pen, and lock the door behind myself after sticking the *back in five minutes* sign on the door. We make our way down the mews, stopping every few feet for Stevie to sniff and do her doggy business. I note with satisfaction, as she trots around the corner and onto the main street, that the lead is loose and she keeps checking in with me to see if I've got any further instructions for her to follow. Dog Diva Denise might have singled us out for humiliation, but puppy school has worked wonders on my little dog.

As we walk, the tempting aroma of coffee ekes its way into my consciousness, and spotting Starbucks a couple of shops away, I make the decision to treat myself to a cinnamon latte with extra cream.

We pass Karina, and I gaze begrudgingly in the window at the plethora of customers and staff in the plush surrounds, oozing an air of success and expense. I'm about to continue my trek to Starbucks next door when a flash of bright orange and a mop of blonde hair captures my attention.

Is that...?

No!

It can't be.

What's Scarlett doing in Karina?

Like I'm a spy in a movie—if spies have Jack Russell puppies on pink leads—I move to the edge of the large picture window so I can see her, but she can't see me. I watch as she tosses her tresses, beaming her pretty smile at an elegantly dressed woman in black. They talk for a while, and then shake hands before Scarlett turns to leave. I step quickly back against the wall, hoping she hasn't seen me spying on her.

"Come on, Stevie," I say in a low voice, and we rush next door to Starbucks and push through the door.

From the safety of the café, I watch in wonderment as Scarlett struts past, her head held high.

I pull out my phone and call her as I poke my head out the door. She opens her handbag, takes out her phone, and a second later I hear her voicemail telling me she can't take my call right now.

What the...? She busied me?

I hang up, deep in thought.

What would Scarlett be doing at Karina? Maybe she's come to a deal with them? Maybe she's agreed to something with them that's going to save ScarZar? A *you take these customers and we'll take those so we can co-exist* kind of thing.

But why wouldn't she tell me about it?

My coffee fix forgotten, curiosity gets the better of me. Stevie and I step out onto the footpath and follow Scarlett down the busy street. In a hundred or so yards, she stops to look through the window of a makeup shop, and I dash into Mark's and Spencer's, nearly knocking down a hunched-over elderly woman moving at a pace that would make a snail complain she's moving too slow.

"Watch where you're going, love," she scolds.

"Sorry. Are you okay?" I say as I take a hold of her shoulders to steady her.

"Other than you nearly causing my ticker to have a fit,

yes, I am okay." She narrows her gaze at me. "What are you doing lurking here, anyway?"

"I, err, I'm checking in on someone," I reply, as I peer around the corner and watch Scarlett turn from the window and walk into the makeup shop.

"Oooh, is it your fella? Are you checking up on him to make sure he's not carrying on with another girl?"

"No. It's my business partner. I need to know what she's up to."

Her eyes widen. "Well, that sounds exciting. Do you think she's up to no good, love?" She glances down at Stevie. "What a sweet dog."

"I honestly don't know what she's up to." I shoot her a smile. "I need to keep an eye on her. Sorry to nearly bowl you over." I begin to move away when I feel a dry hand on my forearm.

"Do you need a sidekick?" she asks. "I could be Robin to your Batman or...what other sidekicks are there, love? Oh. I can't think of any."

I regard her with surprise. "You want to be my sidekick?"

She nods, the loose skin around her jawline swinging from side to side with each movement. "Why not? All I've got planned for my day is taking home dinner for one and watching *Coronation Street* on the telly, which is all very well, but I do that every day."

Seriously?

"I wouldn't want to take you away from that." I tilt my head around the entrance and watch for Scarlett to reappear. There's no sign.

"Bucky!" the woman says with a look of satisfaction on her face.

I blink at her with incomprehension. "Excuse me?"

"Bucky is another sidekick. He's Captain America's sidekick."

We're back to sidekicks? Ones that remind me of George Honeydew, at that. "True."

She knits her thin grey brows together. "But then things didn't work out so well for Bucky, did they? What with the turning evil and the dying and the whatnot. So maybe not Bucky."

I offer her a weak smile, wondering why this woman is still talking to me, nice as she seems to be. "Look, with all due respect—"

"I used to be a detective in the Metropolitan Police, you know," she says with obvious pride. "Cracked many a case in my day, I did. I got awards and whatnot for my efforts."

I skim my eyes over her. She's wearing a beige floral dress with a brown cardigan, thick skin-tone pantyhose, and flat, sensible, old lady lace-up shoes. Which makes sense, considering she's got to be at least my granny's age. I'm having a hard time marrying the woman before me with a police detective who's "cracked many a case." "Wow. That's impressive. Well done," I reply, because what else is there to say?

"So, can I help you, love?"

I glance down the footpath. There's no sign of Scarlett. Is she still inside the shop? Where is she going? What is she up to?

I turn to the woman. "Look, I need to go and find her."

Her wrinkled face lifts in a beaming smile. "All right then. Let's go. I'm Mavis, by the way. Mavis Cooper."

I extend my hand and we shake. "Nice to meet you, Ms. Cooper."

"Oh, call me Mavis, love."

"Okay. I'm Zara. Shall we go? I'd hate to lose her."

She waves her hand as though shooing me away. "Off you go, then."

Together, we walk out of the entrance to the shop and onto the footpath, heading towards the makeup shop. Well, when I say "together" what I mean is we both do it, just one of us does it considerably faster than the other.

No points for guessing who.

Halfway to the makeup shop, I look back over my shoulder at Mavis. She's wobbling along the footpath with a determined look on her face, her nostrils flaring with the effort.

How exactly did I get myself into this situation?

"I'll nip ahead and check," I say to her as I quicken my pace.

"Don't get spotted, love," she calls out.

I reach the entry to the makeup shop and sneak a look inside the glossy white store with its rows and rows of makeup. I scan the surrounds but she's nowhere to be seen.

A panting Mavis arrives at my side. "Any sign?" she asks between breaths.

"I can't see her, but there are so many aisles in the shop that she could be behind any of them."

"What's her description?"

"Why?"

"Because I can go in and have a look-see, can't I? She doesn't know what I look like."

My lips curve into a smile. "Good thinking, Mavis. She's about my build and an inch or two shorter with blonde hair to here, and she's wearing a bright orange sleeveless dress that comes to the knee."

"She's a Barbie doll."

"Well, I suppose, but she does have a normal length neck."

"Sounds like a Barbie doll to me, love. You stay here with your little doggie. I'll be back in a mo'."

Slowly, as though she's one of the slower students at sloth school, Mavis moves past me and into the shop. After a few excruciatingly slow paces, she pauses and turns back to face me. "Am I apprehending her?"

I'm not sure Mavis could apprehend a turtle—or a fellow sloth school student, for that matter. "Let's just watch her for now."

"You sure, love? I apprehended a few big blokes in my time, you know. They called me Muscles Mavis back at the station."

I press my lips together to stifle a giggle. "Quite sure."

"Right you are."

Muscles Mavis makes her creaky, wobbly way into the brightly lit shop, and I lean back against the wall and glance down at Stevie, who's busy sniffing the ground.

"What is Scarlett up to, Stevie?" I say, and she tilts her head in question. "You wish you knew, too. Don't you?"

I take another furtive glance inside the shop. There's no sign of either Scarlett, or Mavis, for that matter. I return my attention to the street and wait, tapping my hand against my thigh.

That's when I hear it—a loud, piercing, demanding voice, drowning out the shop's soundtrack. "What are you doing? Let go of me now!"

Scarlett.

I turn to see her bustling towards me with her hands held behind her back by none other than Muscles Mavis. My jaw drops open. What the...?

"Settle petal," Mavis says in her gruff voice. "I've got someone who needs to have a word with you."

Scarlett's eyes land on me and realisation dawns on her

face. "You set this *person* on me, Zara?" she demands as they come to a stop in front of me. "What the heck is going on?"

I hardly know myself right now.

"Will you let go of me?" she says to Mavis. "You really are surprisingly strong for an old woman."

"I'm not letting go until Zara has asked you a few questions, missy," Mavis says, speaking deliberately slowly in a vaguely threatening tone.

"What? Why?" Scarlett questions.

"Mavis, it's okay. You can let go of her," I tell her.

"It's my experience that you often get a better response from these types if they're under some pressure, if you know what I mean," Mavis replies.

"These types? I take offence at that. I'm not some common criminal," Scarlett sniffs.

"It's fine, Mavis. Please, let her go."

Mavis does as I ask, and Scarlett sucks in air as she rubs her wrists. "What the heck is going on? Why did you set this insane old lady on me?"

"I'm not insane, thank you very much," Mavis replies haughtily. "I'm a pensioner."

"Scarlett, stay put," I tell her. "Mavis, thank you so much for all your help. I think Scarlett and I need to have a little chat now. But I do really appreciate all your help."

"You've given this old chook something to live for today. Thank you, love," she says as she grips my hands in hers.

I beam at her. Muscles Mavis is a real sweetheart. "Come by my design store whenever you like. It's ScarZar down the street in the mews."

"Oh, I know that place. Lovely green sofa in the window."

"That's right."

215

"All right, love. You take care now." She eyes Scarlett and then adds, "And make sure you get your answers from her."

"I will."

She throws Scarlett a final scowl before she says, "Ta ta, love," to me and toddles off slowly down the street.

"Zara, I cannot believe you just did that to me," Scarlett huffs. "I was humiliated."

"I'm really sorry. I think we should talk. Don't you?"

She looks up at me through her lashes, shamefaced. "Okay."

Five minutes later, we're sitting at a small table at Starbucks, a couple of cups of steaming coffee before us, and Stevie sitting on my lap looking around the café.

"Okay, spill. Why were you in Karina today shaking hands with one of their designers?" I question.

"I was checking out the competition, of course."

I shoot her a look that tells her very clearly that I don't believe her.

She lifts her hands in the air. "Okay. I'll come clean. Look, we both know ScarZar is over. We can't fight the big guns and win, Zara. You know that as much as I do."

"So, you're just giving up?" I ask, aghast.

"No. I'm not giving up."

Relief washes through me. "Oh, thank goodness. I thought you were giving up on us. You don't know how good it is to hear that."

She twists her mouth, rendering her face hard. "What I mean is, I'm not giving up on my interiors career, but I am taking my skills elsewhere."

I pull my brows together. "What do you mean?"

"Zara, get with the programme, girl. ScarZar is dead in the water. No one wants to work with us, we're haemorrhaging money, and pretty soon we'll both be in such serious debt, not even your wealthy family will be able to bail us out."

My hands fly to my hips. "For the millionth time, they're not wealthy."

"Pull the other one, will you? Your brother posed as Mr. Darcy on that reality TV show and he's a blooming *lord*."

"That doesn't mean my family's got any money, especially not money they're going to throw our way."

"Which is why I've got no choice but to leave."

"You're leaving ScarZar?" My voice is almost a whisper.

"I start at Karina on Monday. They love me. They will give me the clients I deserve."

"You're going to work for the enemy?"

It all falls into place. Her absence from the shop lately, her chic new clothes, spotting her shaking hands with the Karina designer. Especially the last one.

"Oh, don't act so surprised. One of us was bound to do it at some stage. I just beat you to it, that's all."

"I would never go to the competition!"

"Really?" she questions with a supercilious look on her face. "Look, let's agree to close the shop and dissolve Scar-Zar. We can work the details out later." She loops the strap of her handbag over her shoulder and collects her cup of coffee from the table in front of her.

"But what about our existing clients?"

"Darling, we've only got a handful of those, and they're all chomping at the bit to come to Karina with me."

I suck in air. "You're taking our clients?"

"Of course. They're mainly mine, anyway. You've been too busy working on your boyfriend, Asher's place to put any work into finding *real* clients." She leans in closer to me and adds, "You do realise you're just a charity case for him, don't you? He's only being nice to you because he feels sorry for you. You can decorate his place for as long as you like and make him your silly back-up guy, but he'll never fall in love with you. Men like him go for women like me."

My jaw drops open in total shock. There are so many things to unpack in her little speech, all I can manage is to gawk at her, my mind aswirl with thoughts.

I think of the way I've been feeling about Asher lately, about my discovery about his past, about how we had that moment after the baseball game the other night when I thought he was going to kiss me.

She rises to her feet. "You can have the business if you want it. What's left of it, anyway, which isn't a lot." She scoffs, her face twisted into a nasty smile. "Good luck."

And then she turns on her heel, and I'm left gaping as she waltzes out of the café door.

Chapter Eighteen

D*ear Dad*
    I hardly know how to write this. Scarlett is gone. As in gone and never coming back. She's gone to the competition that's been strangling our business now for months, and she's taking her clients with her. I feel like a failure.

What am I going to do?
Miss you. Love you.
Your Za-Za xoxo

I spend the rest of the day in utter shock. Sure, I deal with customers, I order stock, I even arrange to meet a potential new client next week. But the whole time I grapple with questions.

How could Scarlett do this?

How could she just up and leave?

Didn't she owe me at least a scrap of loyalty?

And, most importantly of all, what the heck am I going to do now?

At closing time, with a heart as heavy as a dumbbell, I lock up the empty shop early and Stevie and I begin our daily trudge back to my flat. But, as though on an autopilot that has other ideas, I find myself not in Fulham, but in Covent Garden on the street where Asher's legal offices are.

Okay, there might have been a little forethought that went into my decision to come here rather than go home, but I'm not going to unpick that.

I'm here, and Asher's the only person I want to see right now.

I stand on the footpath and stare up at his building's tall, classical architecture with its plaster columns, and large windows. I scoop Stevie up and put her in my oversized handbag. "Be a good girl and stay nice and quiet so we can get into Uncle Asher's office without anyone seeing you, okay? I'm not sure they're as dog-friendly as they ought to be here,"

She gazes up at me as though I've just told her something in Swahili, but she stays quiet enough as I check in at security and take the old, caged lift to the fifth floor.

I scan a new glass sign at the door as I walk through into the reception area. *Grover, Thompson, and McMillan.* Asher was promoted to partner not that long ago and I bet he loves seeing his name on that sign each day.

I approach the reception desk where a girl of about twenty, with her hair tied up in a top knot so tight, it looks like it's holding her whole face in place, looks up at me and says, "How may I help you this afternoon?" in a syrupy voice.

"I'd like to see Asher McMillan. I'm Zara Huntington-Ross." Stevie squirms in my handbag, and I press my arm against it. I shoot the receptionist a smile as though I'm not currently smuggling a puppy into the office.

She flicks her eyes to my handbag. "Is Mr. McMillan expecting you?" she asks, but my attention is diverted by Asher striding into the room.

The sight of him has my belly doing a flip.

"I'll take it from here. Thanks, Lola," he says.

"Hi," I murmur, the pent-up emotion I've been keeping at bay threatening to breech its walls and come pouring out.

His face creases in concern. "Come with me," he says, and he whisks me from reception, through some opaque-glass double doors, and down the hall to his office. Closing the door behind us, he turns and says, "What's wrong?"

I'd like to say I put on a brave face. That I hold it together to tell him what Scarlett has done and ask him for his sage advice.

I don't. Far from it, in fact. In two seconds flat, I burst into loud, ugly, heaving sobs, my whole body wracked with misery.

In two short steps, Asher is across the room and collecting me in his arms. He pulls me close and I bury my face in his warm, firm chest, breathing in his reassuring Asher scent, comforted by his strong arms wrapped around me. I feel comforted, protected, safe.

"Zee, what's going on?" he asks softly into my hair.

Once I can trust myself to speak, I pull back and lift my eyes to his, my arms still held around his waist. "Sorry," I murmur.

"Do you want a Kleenex? Because...*ew*." He pulls a face.

I let out a choking laugh. "Yes, please."

He moves over to his windowsill and takes a couple of tissues from a box. Stevie makes her presence known by squirming around in my handbag, so I pop her on the floor and she immediately begins to run around the room to investigate this new, exciting place.

"Hey, there," Asher says to her as he manages to pat her little body before she darts away. "Best we don't tell anyone you're here, Stevie." Returning to my side, he hands the tissues to me and I wipe my eyes and blow my nose noisily.

"Sorry to bring her here."

"It's fine."

My eyes drop to his light blue shirt where a wet patch with mascara stains has spread. "I wrecked your shirt. I'm so sorry."

"Don't worry about it. I've got a back-up." He nods at an open wardrobe against the wall that's lined with about ten shirts.

"A back-up girl and a bunch of back-up shirts." I attempt a smile.

"What's going on, Zee?" he asks me with a tender voice that has fresh tears threatening my eyes once more.

"Scarlett."

His features harden. "What has she done?"

"She's left. She's gone to the competition, and she's taking her clients with her."

His jaw locks. "She's done what?" he grinds out.

"I caught her at Karina today and we followed her, and Muscles Mavis apprehended her without me asking her to do that, but it was good that she did because I ended up confronting her, and in the end, she came clean about it all."

He cocks a brow. "Muscles Mavis?"

"It's a long story."

"I'm so sorry, Zee. Truly, I am. You deserve so much more than this."

I sniff. "Thanks."

"I wish I could say I'm surprised, but I'm not."

"Why?" I ask.

"Scarlett has always been interested in number one. It was obvious to me from the get go. I've never really liked her."

"I didn't know that."

"I wasn't going to say anything about it. She was your business partner so I figured it was your choice, not mine. I'm just sorry she's done this to you."

I push out a breath and slump my shoulders. "I'm so stupid, Ash. Really, really stupid."

"No, you're not at all. Sure, you trusted someone who didn't deserve your trust, but you're far from stupid."

I shake my head, my lips taut as my self-pity swells to the size of an elephant. "Nope, I am stupid. I'm stupid with a capital 'S.' You know what I am? I'm a girl whose business is failing and who can't even hold on to her business partner. What's more, I'm a girl who's so desperate to find love, she's got a back-up guy. A girl who writes emails every day to her dead dad." I sink down the wall until my butt hits the cold, hard ground. "I'm a mess, Asher. Not even a hot mess. Just a plain, old, everyday stupid mess."

"*I* think you're a hot mess."

I look up at him and scoff-laugh. "That's not the compliment you think it is, you know."

He leans against the wall and slides down it until we're sitting together, side by side on the carpeted floor. "You write to your dad?"

I nod, no longer trusting myself to speak. It's hard to think of Dad and not feel a great gaping hole in my heart. Writing to him has been a way to fill that hole. Now that I've told someone for the first time, I feel ridiculous, like a pre-pubescent girl who can't accept that her much-loved dad is gone and never coming back home.

Asher places his hand gently on my arm. "I think it's a really beautiful thing that you write your dad, Zee."

Tears prick my eyes once more. "He doesn't reply a whole lot. Or at all, actually." I try out a smile. "He's not the best communicator."

"You can't blame the guy, wifey." He nudges me with his elbow, and my smile begins to slowly claim the real estate of my face. "But you know what? I bet you a million bucks he's looking down on his girl, totally proud of who you are and what you've achieved."

My throat heats up. "I don't know. What have I got to show for it all? I mean, I used to think it wasn't such a big deal that I hadn't found Mr. Right because I had my career. Now that's falling around my ears, too. I've got nothing, Asher. A great big fat old nothing."

"You want to know what I think?

"What?"

"I think you're way better off without Scarlett."

"You do?"

"Absolutely. And you'll pick yourself up and start over. I have faith in you, just like you know your dad would have faith in you, too."

The heat in my throat begins to burn. "I miss him."

"I know you do, and I'm so sorry. It's got to be so hard to lose your father."

"It's no West End musical, that's for certain."

"I wish I'd known him."

"I wish you had, too. He was a great dad. I mean, he lost all my family's money gambling of course, but I know he was only trying to help us. Running a house like Martinston costs a massive amount each year. He was only trying to protect us all, I'm certain of it. I only wish he'd lived long enough to know that Sebastian saved our home for generations to come."

"I'm sure he knows."

I lift my watery eyes to his and see the kindness behind his eyes. "I hope so." I lean my head against the wall, comforted by Asher's presence despite the sense of loss squeezing my heart.

"You know, I've got some money put aside. I'd be happy to help you out with your shop. Maybe I could invest or something?"

I sniff in an unladylike manner Granny would be appalled at. "I can't expect you to do that. It's going to take a lot of money and you've just bought your flat. You're probably as skint as I am."

"Skint is such a good word," he replies with a laugh. "But I do all right. If you want my help, I'm here for you, Zee." He pauses before he adds, "Always."

I flick my gaze up to meet his. His eyes are burning into me with such intensity, it causes my breath to catch in my throat.

And then, just like that, without a hint of warning, the atmosphere between us shifts.

It could be the heat in his eyes. It could be the fact that he's offering to invest in my business. Or it could be the simple fact that I'm an emotional mess, sitting side-by-side with the guy I think I might be falling in love with.

Love?

I let out a ragged breath, our gaze still locked. It's love that I feel for this man beside me. I know it is. And as I gaze into his eyes, I know in that instant that he feels something for me, too. Something beyond friendship.

I need to know if he loves me.

With my heart hammering in my chest, my throat dries up, and I try to swallow. "Asher, I—" I what? I found your wedding photo album and now I think I'm falling in love with you? I thought I was feeling pity for you to start with, but then I realised I saw a new depth to you that I didn't know existed and it's got into my head and sparked love inside of me?

I can't say any of that. It sounds insane.

"What?" he asks, his voice low and breathy, his eyes still trained on me with that intensity that makes my belly flip over again and again.

"I...Is it just me?" I bite down hard on my lip and wait for his reply, sitting on the metaphorical edge of my seat, wishing, hoping he'll tell me he feels it, too.

He brushes a loose strand of hair away from my face with his fingertips, and the lightness of his touch against my bare skin sends a shiver through me. "Zara," he says, and there's such emotion in his voice, such need, that I know. I just know.

And then in an instant, we're tangled up in one another and his lips come crashing against mine, sucking the air from my lungs with such passion, I feel as though I could explode. He runs his hands up my back and tangles his fingers in my hair as my hands grab at his strong, warm, muscular back and taste his lips for the very first time.

We're kissing like we could devour one another, right here on Asher's office floor.

And you know what? It feels freaking amazing.

After he's sent me to the stars, he drags me back to Earth as he pulls away from me and presses his forehead against mine. "Oh," he breathes against my mouth, his fingers toying with my hair, my heart beating out of my chest. He brushes his lips softly, tantalizingly against mine once more, sending a wave of electricity through me.

This man sure knows his way around a woman's lips.

"Do you know how long I've wanted to kiss you for?" he asks.

It's at this moment Stevie decides to crash the party, leaping up onto my lap and trying to climb up to lick our faces.

I laugh as I stroke her back. "Was it since the Padre with the impressive 'stache hit the ball into the crowd the other night?" I chance with a smile.

"Yeah, you're right. I wanted to then, but I didn't think you did."

"Oh, I did."

His face creases into a smile. "A missed opportunity?"

"Definitely."

"But you know, I've wanted to kiss you for a little longer than that."

"You have? But...you never said anything."

"What was I gonna say? Hey, babe, I know we're friends and all and we're busy dating other people, but how about it?"

"You could have."

"I never got the vibe from you. Not until the other night, and I wasn't even sure then. I didn't want to go risking our friendship. It means too much to me."

"Which is why you pulled away from me after the Padres game."

"You're an incredible woman. A guy's got to protect his heart, you know."

The photograph of him with his ex-wife flashes before my eyes.

I look down and study Stevie as she rubs her face on my thigh. "My feelings for you have been sneaking up on me lately."

He places his finger lightly under my chin, tilts my head up, and brushes another incredible kiss against my lips, making my head spin. "Well, I'm glad you got here."

"Me too." I smile shyly at him, and he grins back, both of us wrapped up in this new, exciting thing between us.

"I am so in love with you," he murmurs in my ear, making my heart squeeze tightly.

I slide my fingers up his neck and into his hair. As I look deep into his eyes, I reply, "I love you, too."

We grin at one another like a couple of love-sick teens, only we're love-sick thirty-somethings instead, and we've got to where we are through a strong and enduring friendship.

"So? How long have you loved me?" I ask with an embarrassed grin, because this is Asher I'm talking to here. Asher loving me. Asher, the man I've been kissing on the floor of his office.

"Let me see. It might have been for about two years and a couple of months, give or take."

"But we've only known one another for two years and a couple of months."

"Exactly."

The reality of what he's just said sinks in. "Oh."

"The thing is, I wasn't in a good place when I met you. I was going through some stuff, and I needed to get my head clear before I started anything new. And I knew you were different. You weren't some girl to just date with no strings. You were special, and I wanted strings with you. A whole ball of them. But I held back and we fell into just being buddies. I guess you totally friend-zoned me."

"I honestly didn't know at all. I thought we were just good friends."

"And I decided a long time ago to be happy with that. But now?" he takes my hand in his and laces his fingers through mine. "Now things are exactly where I want them to be."

I giggle. "By 'things' do you mean me?"

"I would never objectify you in that way," he sniffs in mock seriousness and another giggle escapes my lips.

"Kiss me again," I say, and as I slink my hands around his neck and pull him in to me, he does just that.

Chapter Nineteen

Dear Dad
        Where do I start? You know how I told you about Scarlett? Well, the most terrible day turned into the best day ever. Asher has told me that he's had a thing for me for a long time. As in a love *thing. Love! Ever since we met, in fact. Yes, I know it's complicated right now because he was married and got really hurt and he doesn't know that I know that about him, but it's all semantics for us. He's amazing, Dad, and I am so in love with him. And you know what? I'm not even scared, because this guy is my best friend.*
        You'll think he's Christmas, just like I do. I know it.
        Miss you. Love you.
        Your Za-Za xoxo

I am dancing on air. Dancing! Sure, it may be a scientific impossibility unless you're in zero gravity and there's not a lot of that in south-west London, but that's what I'm doing. Dancing, spinning, laughing, singing. All of it on air.

Asher loves me, and I love him. And we kissed. Oh, my

did we kiss! We kissed on the floor some more after we confessed our feelings for one another. We kissed as we rode down the escalator to the Tube stop with Stevie in my handbag, we kissed on the footpath when he dropped me back at my flat and said goodnight to me, Stevie wrapping her lead around our legs.

And now it's a couple of days after and nothing can dent my utter euphoria. Not even Scarlett deserting me for the competition.

"Tell us *everything*," Kennedy says as she lays her hands on the table. The four of us are sitting at a café near Lottie's and my Fulham flat, and I've just shared the news of Asher and me with Tabitha and Kennedy. Being my flatmate, Lottie knew something was up with me the moment I walked through the door after saying goodbye to Asher that day—least of all because my lipstick was smudged across my face. Always a tell-tale sign of some serious snogging action.

"Oh, it was incredible," I reply with a sigh.

"How did it happen? Did he kiss you or did you kiss him?" Kennedy asks.

"And where?" Tabitha adds.

"On the lips, dummy," Lottie replies with a grin.

Tabitha rolls her eyes. "Of course I didn't mean where on Zara, I meant where did the kissing take place?"

"Whose question should I answer first?" I reply, feeling completely giddy, which is how I've felt constantly for the last sixty-three hours, ever since Asher and I said good night. We've been messaging one another ever since. Cute things, sexy things, fun things, deep things. Love things.

As I said, I'm dancing on air.

"Okay. I'll start at the top and work my way through. This is how it happened. I was really upset about Scarlett and I—"

Tabitha raises her hand in the stop sign. "Don't mention that name."

"I still can't believe she did what she did." Kennedy shakes her head. "What a total rat."

"I would use considerably stronger language to describe that person if it were me," Tabitha sniffs and Lottie nods her agreement as she takes a sip of her coffee.

"Anyway," I say to bring my friends back on track to Asher and me. Wow, *Asher and me*. I'm still not used to that. "As I was saying, I was upset about you-know-who, and Asher was comforting me and telling me wonderful things and, well, it just happened. I don't know who kissed who. I guess we both kissed each other. Oh, and it happened on the floor at his office. That was the last question."

"On the floor?" Tabitha questions.

"Yup."

"And?" Lottie leads. "Tell them the rest, Zee."

Happiness bubbles up inside as all three of my friends turn their attention on me, waiting for my reply. "Well," I begin as a smile stretches across my face, "he told me he loves me."

"He what?" Tabitha screeches as Kennedy claps her hands together and beams at me.

"Oh, Zee. That's amazing. Do you love him back?" Kennedy asks.

Before I have the chance to reply, Lottie jumps in with, "She does. She told him. They're in love!"

"Seriously?" Kennedy asks, her eyes wide.

"Seriously," I confirm as my belly flip-flops at the thought of loving Asher.

Lottie places her hand over her chest. "Asher has your heart, Zee. Oh, it's so romantic. A true friendship that blossomed into a love story. Perfection."

A huge grin claims my face, and I feel my cheeks warm because it's true. Asher has my heart. I play with the handle on my coffee cup, hoping my friends won't notice my blush.

They do.

"Look, our girl's blushing," Kennedy teases, which only serves to intensify the heat in my cheeks. "Oh, I'm so happy for you. And jealous. Definitely jealous."

"Yup. Jealous all right," Lottie agrees with a grim nod.

"You know what this means, girls? Zara's coming to my thirtieth birthday party next month with a *date,* and the three of us will be the sad, dateless ones," Kennedy says. "Again."

"Yeah, thanks a lot," Tabitha grumps.

"It won't be like that," I insist. "He's still just Asher and I'm still just me."

Tabitha fixes me with her gaze. "Babe, he won't be snogging any of us in the corner when he thinks no one is looking."

I giggle and it ends in a snort. "That would kind of be a deal breaker for me."

"Okay, girls. Let's make a rule," Lottie begins. "You can date him, Zee but you can't flaunt it in front of the single friends."

The other two agree.

"Fair call."

"Yup. Agreed."

My three friends turn to me.

"I promise I won't," I say with a grin, "but I cannot tell you how happy I am that I get to be the one who has to promise that."

"You know, I'm not at all surprised by this," Tabitha announces. "I've seen the way he's looked at you over the years."

"You have?" I ask.

"Oh, yeah. I have, too. You've always been the Ross and Rachel of our friend group," Kennedy says. "Will they? Won't they? Were they on a break? Okay, the last one's not relevant right now."

"I think I like being the Ross and Rachel. They end up together."

"They have a *baby* together," Lottie says, shooting me a meaningful look.

I lift a finger in warning. "Let's not get ahead of ourselves here. One step at a time, and I'm starting with dating the guy."

Lottie waggles her eyebrows at me. "One sexy, kissy step at a time, you mean."

My tummy does a flip. One sexy, kissy step at a time indeed.

"What about Asher's ex-wife?" Tabitha asks, and just like that, a sharp pin gets sunk into my happiness balloon. "Did you talk about her with him?"

"Oh, it didn't come up," I say as casually as I can.

Lottie tsks.

"You need to talk to him about it, Zee," Kennedy warns.

Tabitha just looks at me with her lips pressed together as she stirs her coffee with a spoon.

"What? I'll tell him I know about her, and we can have a frank and open conversation about it. It won't be a big deal."

My friends share a look before Lottie leans back in her seat and says, "Okay, if you're sure."

"I am," I reply with a whole lot more confidence than I feel.

Truth be told, I don't know how to bring it up. How do you say to your best friend, who has only just admitted he loves you, that you know about the past he's kept hidden for over two years?

Not easily, that's for sure.

"What if he's freaked out that you already know? It could be damaging," Tabitha warns, going all doom and gloom on me.

"I know, okay?" I snap, anxiety sparking in all directions in my head. "I'll deal with it. Can we please move on to something else?"

"*I* want to know what we're going to do about Scarlett. We need to all rally around Zara and help her out now that the turncoat has deserted our friend," Lottie says, and I shoot her a grateful look.

"I can push harder for something at the magazine," Kennedy offers.

Tabitha jumps in with, "And I can tell my relations who've got more money than sense that they need to redecorate their castles."

"Your relatives have castles?" Kennedy guffaws.

"Only some of them," Tabitha replies.

Kennedy blinks in disbelief. "Zara's family are aristocrats and your family have castles. Am I the only normal person here?"

Lottie raises her hand. "Me. I'm totally normal. Well, other than having a crazy family and a demanding, perpetually disappointed mother, that is."

"No aristocratic titles? No castles?" Kennedy asks and Lottie shakes her head.

"Nope. Norma Normal right here." Lottie points her thumbs at her chest.

"You girls are all so sweet," I coo. "What with your offers and Asher's, I am really feeling the love."

Tabitha asks, "What did Asher offer you?"

"He offered to invest in my shop, can you believe it?" I say.

"Oh, it really is love," Lottie pronounces, and the other two nod their agreement.

I beam at them, my heart completely full. It is love, and right now, I'm the luckiest girl in south-west London.

Chapter Twenty

That evening, I'm zipping up my heeled ankle boots when my phone on my bed pings. I read the screen and my heart contracts as I see it's another message from Asher.

Come meet me downstairs when you're ready xoxo

My insides turn all bouncy. I tap out a quick reply.

On my way xoxo

We've been signing our messages with kisses and hugs ever since the day at his office earlier in the week, and I'm still getting used to it. Which is not to say I don't like it because oh, my, I *love* it. With Asher being out of town for work over the last few days we haven't been able to see one another since then, so tonight is our first official date, and I am beyond excited.

I slide my arms into my cropped black leather jacket and do one last check of my appearance in the mirror. My pretty floral dress falls a couple of inches above the knee and I've styled my long dark hair so it falls in soft curls over my shoulders.

I'm ready for my first date with Asher.

I pat a slumbering Stevie in her basket and tell her to be a good girl for Aunt Lottie while I'm out. I top up her water and food bowls, then I collect my clutch from the kitchen bench and breeze down the hall to Lottie's room.

"I'm heading out on my date. Asher's waiting downstairs," I tell her.

She looks up at me from her book. "How romantic."

"Romance with Asher is such a weird concept." My belly does a flip.

"Weird but nice?"

I grin at her. "Definitely weird but nice."

"You'd better get down there. You don't want to leave Prince Charming waiting."

"Wish me luck."

"You don't need luck."

I skip down the stairs to the street, feeling as light as a feather. Once outside, I come to a sudden stop. I don't know quite what I expected to see—Asher is just as much a devoted user of the Tube as me—but it's certainly not this.

He's is waiting on the footpath, and when he spots me, a grin spreads across his face. "Good evening, Ms. Huntington-Ross," he says to me with an incline of his head. He's wearing a black jacket and a pair of form-fitting jeans and boots, which makes him look so staggeringly hot I'm amazed I don't pass out, right here on the footpath outside my flat.

"Good evening, Mr. McMillan," I reply with a giggle, playing along. I try my hardest to keep my voice steady while my heart bangs against my ribs like a caged tiger, fighting to get out.

He sweeps me up in his arms and I breathe in his delicious Asher scent as he brushes a brief but electric kiss across my lips. "Zee, you look...wow."

I beam at him, my heart doing all kinds of crazy things. "You look pretty wow, yourself."

"I thought we could go on our first date together in style." He gestures at a double decker bus, parked on the street.

"In a bus?"

"It's a totally London thing to do. How many couples go out on a date in a double decker?"

"Teenage ones who can't afford an Uber?"

"Well, there is *that*." He smiles as he reaches for my hand. "Come on. I want to sit up top."

"You are such a tourist," I reply as we step onto the bus and I nod and smile at the driver. We climb the narrow spiral staircase up to the top level, where we take a seat at the very front of the bus. "How did you get an empty bus to stop outside my flat?"

"I know people," he replies mysteriously, and I laugh.

"You know people at Transport for London? Does your influence know no bounds?" I tease.

The bus begins to rumble and pulls away from the curb.

He drapes his arm casually across the back of the seat, and I feel the warmth of his body against mine. It's weird and exciting and wonderful, all at the same time. "You have so much to learn about me, Zee. So much."

"Oh, yeah? Like what?"

"Like the fact that I know people. That's what."

He leans in and his breath tickles my neck, making my little hairs stand on end in the most delicious way. "Can I let you in on a secret, wifey?" he asks, and I nod, not trusting myself to speak at a normal, human volume as electricity tingles down my back. "I have often wondered what it would be like to take you on a real date. What we'd do, where we'd go. I've had a lot of time to plan."

"So, I should have pretty lofty expectations about tonight?"

"Is that a pun?"

I glance down at the cars and rows of buildings and trees. "Not an intentional one, but I'll take it. Where are we going on this private bus?"

"We've got the whole night, so I figured we'd go do some fun stuff. Stuff I've always thought I'd like to do in London with someone special."

I nudge him in the arm with my elbow. "You sweet talker, you."

"I try."

"Are you telling me you've never done whatever these things are with any of the multiple women you've dated here?"

"It's hardly multiple."

"Oh, it's multiple. As your BFF, I've been a silent witness to your active dating life for w*aaaaa*y too long, remember?"

He takes my hand in his and we lace our fingers together. "There's no hiding anything from you."

Other than the fact you were married.

I push the thought from my mind. We can deal with that another time. Tonight is for Asher and me. Tonight is for romance on our very first date.

We sit together and watch the cityscape change as we move through the busy streets. I lean my head against his shoulder and snuggle into him as we chat. We talk about anything and everything. From Stevie to his work to what we think of the London mayor. We cover it all, and it feels so right. Like it's us, but a new, different us—if that even makes sense.

The bus lurches to a stop and we instinctively press our feet against the front to stop from lurching forward, too.

Asher looks out the window and says, "This is our stop."

"Considering we're the only people on the bus, that would make perfect sense."

He stands and offers me his hand. "Let's go, wifey."

We thank the driver and step off the bus onto the street. I look around but don't recognise the area.

"Where are we?"

"London," is the facetious reply he gives with a grin. "Less questions, more walking, please."

We make our way down the street until we come to a stop in front of a door. I read the name on the large picture window. Stan's Bowl Land.

"You're taking me bowling?" I ask.

"I figured we'd mix it up tonight," he replies as he pushes the door open for me to step through. "The double decker bus was a touch of England, and this is a touch of America."

Once inside, I eyeball the place. It isn't anything like the bowling alley I used to visit as a kid. It's got black walls with fancy chandeliers hanging from the ceiling, purple seating, and each alley is lit up with soft blue strip lights. "This place is cool."

"I know, right?" His gaze lowers to my high heeled boots. "Let's go get you some more sensible footwear."

"You didn't tell me to bring thick socks. I'm not going to put on some yucky pair of shoes worn by stacks of other people. Because *ew*."

He reaches into the inside pocket of his jacket and pulls out a pair of plain white socks. "I've got you covered. British size five, right?"

I blink at the socks in his hand. "You really have thought of everything."

He gives a self-deprecating shrug. "I told you: I try. And I wanted to make sure I thought of everything."

"So far, you're hitting it out of the park."

His eyes dance. "A baseball expression? I'm so proud of my young Padawan."

"Aren't you mixing baseball and *Star Wars* there?"

He plants a kiss on my cheek. "I love that you know that."

"You are so easily pleased," I reply with a laugh.

We go to the counter where we get our shoes and a glass of champagne, because this isn't your typical bowling alley. We then take our seats on one of the purple velvet sofas and Asher begins to input our names into the computer to start the game.

I inspect the bowling balls. They're all decorated with different famous art works, from Leonardo Da Vinci's *Mona Lisa* to Edvard Munch's *The Scream*. I recognise them all. I have Lottie and her London museum tours to thank for my art knowledge, you know.

I pick the one with the contorted face of the person screaming and hold it up for Asher. "This sums up my bowling ability."

"That bad, huh?"

"Yup."

"Well, in that case, I guess it'll be America beating England tonight because I am pretty good."

I glance up at the screen to see he's input his name as America, and mine as England. "It's like that, is it?" I say with a lift of my brows. "Bring it on."

"Oh, I plan to." He grins at me. "Ladies first."

I test out the weight of several of the bowling balls

before I decide on one with an Andy Warhol *Marilyn* picture. I get myself in position, say a little prayer I won't completely embarrass myself in front of Asher, and then bowl that baby, right down the lane. Well, when I say I bowl it right down the lane, that's how it starts out, at least. Despite me offering the ball loud, explicit instructions to stay right, it makes a bee-line for the left and rolls into the gutter, almost coming to a complete stop before it disappears next to the entirely untouched pins.

"Oh, bad luck," Asher says when I turn to face him.

"I never claimed to be good at this."

"No worries, wifey. How 'bout I give you some pointers?"

"Isn't it your turn now?" I say as I flop down onto the seat.

"You get two turns per frame." He takes me by the hand and hauls me up. "Come on, I'll show you how."

I collect another ball—this one has a painting by Gainsborough I recognise from our visit to the Tate—and Asher shows me how to hold it.

"Did you put your fingers in the holes last time?" he asks me.

"Of course I put fingers in the holes. This isn't my first rodeo, you know."

The edges of his mouth twitch. "So, you're telling me you've spent time perfecting your gutter ball?"

I nudge him in the side with my elbow. "Shut up."

"Okay, so you need to stand like this." He demonstrates and I follow suit. "No, no, no. Like this." He stands behind me and wraps his arms around me, demonstrating how to hold the ball. The warmth from his body causes my heart to thud and a pack of excited butterflies take up residence in my belly. He moves me gently into position.

"Like this?" I ask.

"Yup. Now lift the ball and aim at the middle pin," he says, his voice low and soft, like he's whispering sweet nothings into my ear rather than instructions on how to bowl a ball at a bunch of pins.

I do as he says, still hyper-aware of his manly bulk next to me.

"Now you pull your arm back and then bowl it, keeping your sights set on that middle pin." He pulls away from me, and I miss him. I actually miss him.

You have got it bad, Zara Huntington-Ross.

Doing my best to concentrate on bowling and not on how good Asher felt just now, I swing the ball behind me and then bowl it right at the middle pin. The ball goes flying down the lane and crashes with a satisfying *clunk* against the pins, knocking over all but three of them.

I leap off my spot, ecstatic that my ball not only made contact with the pins, but that it did its intended job, too. I turn to Asher, whose grin is stretched across his ridiculously handsome face. "Did you see that?"

He high-fives me. "Nice job, young Padawan."

We work our way through our turns, me with mixed results, and him with strike after strike, until it's obvious that in this particular instance America reigns supreme over England.

"Kinda like the War of Independence," he teases as we return our bowling shoes and leave the alley.

"Does that make me King George?"

"Oh, you're way too hot for King George," is his reply that has me blushing and doing metaphorical cartwheels. "What?" he asks as he takes in the look on my face.

"I don't know. It's weird to hear you say things like that."

"I get it. It's new." He slings his arm around my shoulders as we begin to walk down the street. "I'll tell you what, Zee. If I tell you you're hot every day, you'll get used to it pretty dang fast."

I snort giggle. "Only say it if you mean it."

"Oh, I mean it."

I'm doing all kinds of air punching and leaps of joy inside.

He glances at the time on his phone. "We've gotta go to our next thing."

"Is this another America versus England activity?"

"I think you'll agree with me that this one has a very clear winner, and here's a hint: it's not Uncle Sam."

We reach a Tube stop and hop onboard a train. We chat like we always do as we travel through the underground of the city, and the weirdness I've been feeling about being on an actual date with my BFF is already a distant memory.

We pop out of the Tube at Tower Hill, and hand in hand, we walk for five or so minutes until we reach the iconic Tower Bridge.

"Fancy a walk across the water?" Asher asks.

"A human impossibility."

"Not if you've got a glass skybridge. Come on."

"Seriously? I've never done that."

He grins at me. "I know. I'm your best friend, remember? I know most things about you."

We purchase our tickets and head up to the glass bridge that stretches from one end of Tower Bridge to the other. The view up here of the sun setting over the city, reflecting in the River Thames is nothing short of spectacular, and looking down at the bridge traffic and river below our feet is both thrilling and nerve wracking at the same time.

As we stand and gaze out at the view, I slide my arm

around Asher's waist. He turns his head to look at me and our gazes lock.

"Thanks for bringing me to this. I love it."

"Sometimes you've gotta be a tourist in your own city."

"I forget how amazing London is. I'm so used to it, I don't stop to smell the roses."

"I'm not sure London smells like roses, exactly. More like traffic pollution, food, and some unidentified bad aromas I try best to avoid."

I giggle. "You do understand I was using a metaphor. Don't you?"

His eyes are soft. "I do." He turns his attention from me to the view. "As I said before, you'll agree this is a clear win for England."

I watch as the glow of the sun bathes the entire city in a blanket of gold. "Definitely."

We stand side-by-side and watch the way the light changes the cityscape, our arms wrapped around one another. We point out different buildings and sights, and fall back into companionable silence. And then, without a word, he turns to me and gently cups my face in his hands, leans down, and brushes his lips against mine. I kiss him back, breathing in his delicious scent.

It feels so comfortable, so right to be here with Asher on our very first date. When he looks at me once more, I gaze up into his warm brown eyes, and I swear my heart skips a beat.

I know this is new. I know this is only our first date. But this thing between us feels big. *Huge.* And just looking in his eyes, I know he feels it, too.

Chapter Twenty-One

We stay standing together, watching the sun set on the glass bridge until my tummy begins to rumble—always so romantic.

"Sorry about that," I mumble, embarrassed.

"You're a little hungry, huh?" Asher asks with a laugh.

"I'm starving. What does a girl have to do on this date to get some food?"

He waggles his eyebrows suggestively and I bat him lightly on the arm. "Actually, I've got a place booked for nine." He consults his watch. "Which is perfect timing. Shall we go?"

"Have you got the double decker bus waiting for us or are we Tubing it?"

"That was a one-time thing. How about a black cab?"

"The bus, the Underground, and now a black cab? Asher, you really are playing loose and wild with the different transport options London has to offer."

"What can I say? I like to live dangerously."

We make our way down from the bridge and Asher

hails a cab. As we whiz through the streets, he tells me about his love of surfing.

"That is the one thing I don't like about living in London. No beach. Back in San Diego, whenever the mood struck me, I could be at the beach within thirty minutes. Here it's a major trek and you risk hypothermia the moment you step in the sea."

"It's not all bad. We've got the rain, cups of tea, and the Queen here, you know."

He lets out a low laugh. "Which are the precise reasons why I choose to live in this fine city. Particularly the tea."

"I've never known you to drink a cup of tea."

"I'm working up to it."

"Tell me more about surfing. How old were you when you learned?"

"Oh, I was just a kid. My dad and older brother would go out and I'd tag along. I'm sure I was a total pain to start with, but when I got the hang of it, we'd go out all the time."

"It was father-son bonding time."

A smile claims his face. "It was."

I think of the hand-made rack I've ordered for surfboards and smile to myself. It'll be ready soon, and I know he's going to love it.

"When Lucas, my older brother, left for college, Dad and I would go out early in the morning together. That's the perfect time to surf. Afterwards, we'd go to Marina's House of Pancakes and eat up a storm."

"Health food all the way."

"Pancakes are super good for you. Don't let anyone tell you otherwise."

"I like that you surf. Can we go to the beach one weekend soon so I can watch you do it?"

"You're already planning weekend trips for us?" he teases. "I'd love to take you away for the weekend."

We share a smile.

"You know, Zee, this may be our first date, but it feels like our thousandth."

He's voiced precisely how I feel. "In a good way?"

"In a really good way."

The black cab comes to a stop and the driver clears his throat, interrupting our moment. He tells us how much the fare is, and Asher pays as we climb out of the cab.

I look up and down the street, recognising it straight away. "We're in Notting Hill," I say in surprise.

"I thought I'd take you to my favourite place to eat." A look of uncertainty waves across his face. "If that's okay with you? I mean, I know it's not a super fancy place in Mayfair with a view or anything—"

I stop his words with a kiss. "I'm sure I'll love it, hubby."

His face morphs into a smile. "Come this way."

We walk through the door of a buzzing restaurant and immediately I'm hit by a delicious aroma of garlic and Italian herbs. Asher is greeted by name by the waiter, who looks genuinely happy to see him, shaking his hand and slapping him on the back.

"And who is this beautiful lady?" he asks as he turns to me.

"This is Zara," Asher replies, and the waiter raises his brows, his eyes widening. "So nice to finally meet you, Zara," he says to me as he takes my hand in his and kisses me a total of three times on the cheeks.

The thought that Asher has talked about me to him fills my chest with warmth.

He shoots Asher a meaningful look, and he offers me a

sheepish smile. "I am Antonio, and this is my restaurant," he says with an expansive arm gesture.

"It smells amazing in here," I tell him.

"The best Italian food in all of the city. Come, come. Sit here. I have your usual table ready for you, Asher."

Antonio leads us to a candlelit table in the window, where Asher pulls my chair out for me and we both take a seat.

"Wine?" Antonio offers.

"Do you feel like a glass?" he asks me.

"Definitely. Red?"

"We'll have a bottle of Chianti, please, Antonio, and some of your awesome garlic bread." He turns his attention to me and adds, "You are gonna die for this bread, Zee."

"If it's half as good as it smells, I bet I will."

Antonio leaves us and I turn to Asher and ask, "Your usual table? Do you bring a lot of girls here?"

He shake his head. "You're the first."

"Really? You're not just saying that?"

He reaches for my hand. "Nope. I've been saving it for, well, for you."

Those tummy butterflies from before start a Highland Fling. "Really?"

"Really."

We settle into talking, eating, sipping our wine, and enjoying one another's company. By the end of the evening, I am sold on Antonio's, and the man himself gives me a warm hug as we leave.

"You are just as beautiful and clever as Asher has been telling me," Antonio pronounces.

"Thanks a lot for giving me away," Asher replies with an embarrassed laugh.

But I'm not embarrassed. I love that he's talked with

Antonio about me, and I love that I'm the first girl he's brought here to his special restaurant.

We say goodnight to Antonio and walk slowly down the road towards his flat. It's a beautiful evening, with only a slight chill in the air, and he places his arm around my shoulder which fends off the cold.

"That place is great. I can't believe you've never told us about it before. Like when one of us has said, 'I wonder where a good Italian place is,' and you said *nothing*?"

He chuckles. "I know this is gonna sound lame, but I wanted to keep the place to myself."

"That *is* a little lame," I joke.

"Look, it was the first restaurant I went to in London when I arrived here. I was going through some stuff, and Antonio lent me his ear. I needed it at the time, and we became close. I guess he's like a dad to me. My London dad. Does that sound silly?"

"Not at all." And I know exactly what he's referring to: his wife cheating on him and his consequent fleeing to London. "Why did you bring me here tonight?" I ask.

"Because I wanted to share that part of my life with you. I want you to know the whole me, not just the fun, party guy, the guy I've been for so long."

"I want to know the whole you, Asher. So much."

"Zee," he says as he stops and turns to face me, his features losing the animation of earlier, "I was in a bad state when I got here. I was running away, I guess. I needed someone to talk to."

"You could have talked to me."

"But you see here's the thing. I couldn't talk to you. Not then."

"Why not?"

"Because I knew that if I opened up to you and told you

251

what I was going through, you'd see me in a different way. And I wanted to start fresh, with new friends, a new job, a new city, the works. I needed not to talk to you or any of our friends about what I was going through."

"I get it. You wanted to be perceived in a particular way."

His features loosen up as he smiles. "There was another reason, you know."

"What was that?"

"I thought you were pretty darn cute and there was no way I wanted to mess things up with you. And believe me, back then, I would have."

I nod, chewing on my lip. Is he going to tell me about her? Should I ask him? Is now the time he can finally open up?

He looks down at his feet and lets out a puff of air and my heart aches for him. This is so hard for him, and I want to make it better, but I've got no clue how. "And now?" I ask softly.

"Now you deserve to know the full truth. You see, the thing is, Zee, I came to London because I—" He stops speaking abruptly as he focusses on something over my shoulder, his features hardening.

"What is it, Asher?" I ask, but his eyes are transfixed on whatever it is behind me. With a hint of trepidation, I turn to see a woman standing outside his building. She's about my age, dressed in a short black dress and high heels that even I can tell make her look super-hot, with long auburn hair down her back and a frankly beautiful face.

A beautiful, *familiar* face.

"Hey, Asher," she says in an American accent with a tentative smile as she takes a couple of steps closer to us.

I gawp at her, not believing my eyes.

It's *her*.

It's the woman from the photo.

It's Asher's ex-wife.

She's here, in flesh and blood, dressed to kill and smiling at Asher as though she hadn't cheated on him with his best friend. As though she hadn't ripped his heart from his chest and stomped all over it in her killer heals. As if he hadn't run away from her to come here.

"Kristen," Asher says in a deep voice, his jaw clenched, his features tight.

She takes another tentative step closer to us, and I can see the nervousness etched on her face.

I want to pull him away, take him back to his favourite restaurant, back to the vibe we shared, the sense that we were taking a step into our new, exciting, burgeoning relationship together.

I don't.

Instead, I tighten my grip on his hand to let him know I'm here for him. "Are you okay?" I ask him in a soft voice.

He flicks his eyes to mine briefly before he returns them to his ex-wive—Kristen. "Why are you here?" he asks, his tone cold.

"I wanted to see you. I have things to say." She turns her gaze on me. "I don't know who you are but I'm guessing you're Asher's date."

"I am," I mutter.

A million thoughts are running through my head.

She's back.

Does she still love him?

Does he still love her?

Should I leave?

"Pleased to meet you," she says with an outstretched hand.

253

I blink at it, not knowing how to play this.

"Kristen." Asher's voice has a warning tone.

"What?" She says with a smile. "Don't you think your date should get to meet your *wife*, Asher?" She turns her gaze on me and waits for my reaction with a look of smug satisfaction on her face. "Because I think it's only good manners. Don't you?"

Her words don't have the effect on me she's looking for.

I flick my eyes to Asher's. He's watching me with a wary, concerned look on his face.

"Zara, I can explain," he begins.

"It's okay," I reply breathlessly, my heart hammering against my ribcage. Of all the ways for us to broach this emotional, difficult subject *this* is how it's going to happen?

"We were married, but we separated over two years ago. I wanted to tell you. Truly, I did. It was just so hard for me and I—"

"You ran away," Kristen says, her arms crossed across her chest.

I place my hand on his arm and lift my gaze to his. "It's okay," I repeat.

He studies my face for a beat, two, before he says, "You knew?" His voice is small and tight.

It's like everything stops around us.

"I...I saw a photo album in your wardrobe when I was measuring up. It fell out as I was moving some boxes. There was a picture of you and her," I gesture at Kristen, "on the cover."

He recoils from me, stepping back. "Why didn't you tell me?"

I glance at Kristen and note a look of satisfaction on her face. I reply quietly for only Asher to hear, "What was I meant to say? 'Hey, I see you've been married but you've never told me about it?' Come on, Asher. I couldn't do that."

A muscle in his face twitches. "You went through my things."

I shake my head vehemently, my eyes wide. "No. I did not. I saw the album on the floor, but I didn't open it. I promise you. I put it straight back in its box. You have my word on that." I reach for his hand, but it's balled in a fist at his side, taut with tension. "Ash, please," I say.

"He's not good with conflict," Kristen says behind me, and I'm certain I detect a note of pleasure in her voice. She's clearly been listening to every word we've said.

Asher glares at her. "Don't."

She puts her hands up in the surrender sign. "I'm just saying."

I step closer to him and place my hand on his forearm once more. His body is like an unmovable rock, his features set to hard stone. "Asher, please."

He drags his gaze from Kristen back to me. "I'm gonna have to take some time here. I'll, err, call you later."

"You want me to leave?" I ask, and my voice comes out like a scared little girl's.

A muscle twitches in his cheek. "I do."

And just like that our wonderful first date comes to a crashing, soul destroying end.

"But—"

"Please." The look on his face breaks my heart in two. Sorrow, disbelief, betrayal.

My throat tightens as panic rises in me like a hot air balloon.

This *can't* be how this goes.

But this *is* how it goes.

I let out a defeated breath. I know when I'm beaten, and

I'm well and truly beaten here. "Okay. I'll go." Tears prick my eyes and I blink them rapidly away. I glance at Kristen as I turn to leave. Her chin is high, a smirk teasing the edges of her mouth, and she looks down her nose at me. In a word, she looks victorious.

As well she might.

I've been kicked to the curb, exposed as a liar.

With a heart as heavy as a boulder, I shoot Asher one last look, but he doesn't meet my eyes.

On unsure feet, I walk away. I retrace our steps back down the street.

Alone.

Regretful.

Sorrow twisting inside.

Chapter Twenty-Two

Dear Dad
      Never have I missed you more than I do today.

What felt like the top of the world to me a mere forty-eight hours ago, now feels like the exact opposite. I messed up, Dad. Badly.

I think I've lost the man I've been waiting for, my best friend, the guy who makes my heart race with just a smile.

And I don't know how to get him back.

I wish more than anything that I could talk to you. I wish I could get your advice. I wish...I wish I'd never seen that photograph.

But I have and it's all ruined now.

I miss you.

Your Za-Za xoxo

Wallowing. I'll admit it, that's what I've been doing, pure and simple. Wallowing. It's been two full days since Asher's and my date, and it's been impossible to get him out of my mind. The look on his face when he realised I knew about his ex-wife has haunted me day and night. The way he told me to leave, the look on Kristen's face, as though she'd won.

The way Asher wouldn't meet my eyes.

Walking away from him, leaving the two of them together, was the hardest thing I've had to do since, well, since saying goodbye to my Dad.

What happened after I left? Did Kristen apologise for all that she put him through? Did he forgive her? Did he tell her he'd never stopped loving her, that I'm only a friend who he might have had feelings for but they're nothing next to his grand love for her?

Why didn't I tell him I had found out about Kristen the moment I saw that photo? If there's one thing I've learned in my thirty years it's that it's always better to be honest. If I'd just told him I'd seen it, he could have come clean about the whole thing. It would have brought us closer together as friends and laid the foundation for what was to come between us.

But I didn't. I should have, but I didn't.

I've lost him. I've lost my heart.

Sure, we've messaged each other. We were friends before any of this, so it'd be weird not to be in touch in some way or another. They haven't been deep. I apologised for not having let on that I knew. He said it was fine. He told me he hoped I'd got home okay. I said I did and thanked him for our date.

And then, nothing.

Now, it's Monday evening and I've been at ScarZar since before seven in the morning. In a totally ill-guided attempt to take my mind off Asher, I closed the shop early and spent the whole afternoon going through all the books and upcoming appointments. It's not looking pretty. I've got too much stock, too little cash flow, and too much overhead. In short, I need new interior design customers, and I need them yesterday.

But I'm not giving up. Not yet, anyway.

So, I set about rearranging the store. As I'm doing so, I put a bunch of items aside with which to design a new window display. With the size of the building, the windows aren't huge, so all I can ever put in there is one or two pieces and then accessorise them. I head out to the back room where I locate a wallpapered board and pull it out. As I look at the bright pink background covered in oversized lilies, a smile creeps across my face. I loved this when it came in and Scarlett refused to let me use it, telling me it was garish and "off point" and "you shouldn't design a room around the colour of your favourite coat." *Well, Scarlett, you are no longer here, so it's going in the window*. And I'll admit, I poke my tongue out at her in a highly mature kind of way as I haul it out of the storage cupboard and out into the shop—not metaphorically, either.

Forty-five minutes later, I've got the board in place behind a white chest of drawers, a royal blue linen chair to the side, and a swathe of white muslin hanging from the ceiling as though it were curtains. I walk outside, take a step back, and take in my handiwork. The display looks fresh, colourful, and fun, but still stylish and elegant. And Scarlett would hate it. I allow myself an especially wide smile at the thought.

I return inside and switch off the computer. Stevie is bouncing around in her pen, full of puppy energy gained from snoring softly on her bed for the last hour or so, and I know she'll be bursting to go outside and get some fresh air.

I clip on her lead and do one final glance around the shop. I look from the shelving, full of ornaments and candles and pottery, to the cushion display, and the gorgeous plush sofa I got in only weeks ago. I don't want to lose this place. I love it here. I know the business has been in a nosedive since Karina moved in around the corner, but I believe in it. I know I can make a real go of it here.

I just need a break.

I flick off the lights and lock the door. "Come on, Stevie. Let's go home." I turn to see three familiar faces appear in front of me. Tabitha, Lottie, and Kennedy. I try out a smile. I know it's feeble at best. "Hey, girls."

"Hey yourself," Kennedy says as the three of them take turns wrapping me up in a hug. "Gorgeous new window display, Zee," she says as she takes in my new window. "You're good at this styling thing."

"Of course she is. She's a qualified interior designer," Tabitha replies.

Lottie hooks her arm through mine and we begin to plod up the mews. "Come on you. We've come to take you and Stevie to the pub."

The thought of being in a room full of happy, chatting people adds a lead weight to my already heavy heart. "Thanks, but I'm not in the mood for a drink."

"So, have a lemonade," Tabitha replies with a shrug. "You're coming. No excuses."

I try a different tactic. "What about Stevie? She needs to go home. She's had a big day."

"Stevie will be just fine. She'll love it at the pub. So many people to see and smells to sniff," Lottie says as we walk around the corner and onto the high street, Stevie trotting along beside me.

"She needs her dinner," I whine. Because it definitely sounds like a whine.

"Enough with the excuses already," Kennedy complains. "We're not taking no for an answer."

"And we can order her something at the pub. Dogs like fish and chips, right?" Tabitha asks with a smile.

By now, we've reached Karina, and I find myself gazing in at their new window display. With its large bed covered in gorgeous pale yellow linens and throw pillows, to its rows upon rows of little paper butterflies hanging from the ceiling with white balls like a kid's ball pit covering the floor, it looks inviting, trendy, and achingly chic, all at the same time.

I think of my new modest display and my eyelids grow hot.

My friends notice, and they slow their pace to a stop beside me.

Lottie gives my arm a squeeze. "Your new window display looks so much better, Zee."

"Isn't that whole butterflies on strings thing been done, like, a gazillion times already?" Tabitha says with a scowl.

"Yeah, and your window is designed by *you*, not a whole team of people," Kennedy adds.

"What I want to know is how you could ever sleep with all those freaking butterflies flapping around your head?" Kennedy asks, and an unexpected giggle begins to build inside of me.

"And wouldn't you slip over on all those balls if you had to get up to pee in the night?" Tabitha asks. "You'd be like, 'wow, I need to pee,' and then you'd swing your feet onto the floor and immediately fall flat on your face in a cushion of balls." She mimes a faceplant, and my giggle bursts out of me and ends in a snort.

"Atta girl," Kennedy says with a beaming smile.

"Come on, you." Lottie pulls me along. "Let's get that drink."

Ten minutes later, we're at The Lion, a once-regular haunt for a post-work wind down for Scarlett and me, with our drinks placed on one of the wooden picnic tables, under a large tree in the outdoor beer garden.

"Have you heard from him?" Kennedy asks. There's no need to use Asher's name. We all know exactly who she's talking about.

My heavy heart reminds me it's still full to the brim with lead, no matter how amazing and kind my friends are. "We've messaged a few times but nothing of any importance. I think he needs some space right now."

"What is going on with him?" Kennedy asks. "I don't get it."

"He's probably been busy dealing with that nasty piece of work, otherwise known as his ex," Tabitha says.

"We don't know she's a nasty piece of work," I protest.

"Yes, we do," all three of my friends say with confidence.

Lottie rubs my arm. "I still can't believe she turned up like that, totally out of the blue. I mean, how rude!"

"Rude is right," Tabitha agrees. "Her timing could not have been any worse for our girl. I feel sick to my stomach as I think about it. Have you heard anything about it from your friends back home, Kennedy?"

She takes a sip of her glass of wine and places it back on the table in front of her. "Only that she's here to see him. Everyone seems to know that part, but they don't seem to know why."

"Yeah," I say as I let out a heavy breath. "That's the million pound question."

"What if she's here to get back with him?" Lottie says.

"Oh, there's no way Asher would go back to her after everything she's done. If my husband did the dirty on me with one of you, I would sooner cut off his appendage and pin it to the wall than have him back," Tabitha says, and we all believe her. Crossing Tabitha would not be a wise idea.

"Even if she has come to say sorry and ask him to come back to her, we don't know if he'll go for it," Kennedy surmises.

The thought of Asher with Kristen sends an uneasy shiver down my spine. "Can we not talk about this?" I hold up my glass of lemonade on ice. "Otherwise, I'll need something a whole lot stronger than this."

"Okay, let's change the subject then. I vote we brainstorm ideas on how to save Zara's business," Lottie offers. "At least that's something we can help with. Right?"

"Men are a total enigma," Tabitha says.

"I might be able to help," Kennedy says, and all eyes turn to her. "The rumour is that the magazine is going to be sold, so they're considering anything and everything for features. Sandra, my boss, told me on Friday that she was considering a feature on cat fashion, which is totally left field for our chic magazine."

"Cat fashion? Like dresses for cats?" Lottie questions.

"Mainly costumes, really. Apparently, it's a thing. Mermaids, astronauts, princesses. Who knew, right?"

"Why exactly are you talking about cats getting dressed up as mermaids when we're trying to work out how to help Zara save ScarZar?" Tabitha quips, ever the pragmatist. She may let loose a little too often for her own good, but she's as sharp as a tack and doesn't hold any prisoners, as Granny would say.

"It's not going to be ScarZar anymore," I reply.

Tabitha nods. "Clearly. You've got to cut 'Scarlett' out of the name right now—and your life, babe."

"Oh, that's already done," I say with a bitter laugh.

"She's dead to me," Lottie says and Tabitha and Kennedy both agree.

"Dead as a Dodo."

"Scarlett who?"

My friends are the absolute best.

"Anyway," Kennedy begins in order to refocus us, "my point is that since they're accepting features on things like cats' costumes, I bet they'll be more open to running a feature on up-and-coming local interior designer, Zara Huntington-Ross." She picks up her phone. "In fact, I'm gonna message Sandra right this minute and pitch it to her once more." She begins to tap at her phone.

Tears of gratitude well in my eyes and I wipe them away quickly with my fingertips before they get any ideas about spilling down my cheeks. "Thanks, Kennedy. You're wonderful."

She puts her phone back down on the table. "Done."

"That would be amazing exposure for Zee's new business. Ooh, I know what you can call it! It's so simple, I don't know why we hadn't thought of it before." Lottie's grin is as wide as the Channel Tunnel. "Zara," she says and she beams at us proudly.

"Honey, that name's already in use. Zara the global Spanish fashion chain, remember?" Kennedy says.

"Oh. Right. I forgot about them."

"But it's a great idea," I say to her. "I'll work on the name."

Kennedy's phone beeps and she picks it up to read the screen. Her face falls. "Sandra isn't leaping at the idea. But don't worry, babe. I'll work on her."

My little glimmer of hope has dulled. "Sure. Thanks."

"I know what. How about we upscale your online presence, babe?" Tabitha suggests. "I've got some skills in that department, and I know someone who can help."

"That's a great idea! We can all help with promoting you on social media, too. Oh, and talk to all our friends and families about how amazing you are." Lottie says. "Between Tabitha and Kennedy and me, we have got you covered."

I smile at my friends, my spirits doing their best to bounce back. "Thanks, girls. You're the best."

"And as for Asher McMillan? He loves you. That ex-wife of his is old news. You'll see," Lottie says with assuredness.

"Lottie's right," Kennedy adds. "He probably just needs time to process his ex turning up here unexpectedly."

"And me not telling him that I knew about her," I add with a slump of my shoulders. "Don't forget that part."

Tabitha leans back in her seat. "He'll come 'round, Zee. We all know he's crazy about you."

"She's right. He calls you 'wifey,' for goodness sake," Kennedy adds. "And he's your back-up guy. That's got to mean something."

Lottie slings her arm around my shoulders. "And if he doesn't remember how incredible you are, that's his loss, because we think you're amazing. Now, will someone get my girl here a proper drink? We need to celebrate Zara's new, exciting, Scarlett-free interior design business."

I laugh, shaking my head and feeling lighter than before.

I might well have lost the man I love, but I've got the best friends a girl could ever have.

Chapter Twenty-Three

Dear Dad

It's been four days since I saw Asher and I've started to get the message. He doesn't want me, and you know what? I'm okay with that. Well, not 'okay' exactly, more like I'm trying to learn to accept it. And I'll get there. I'm determined to. You raised a tenacious daughter. I was okay before him, and I'll be okay after him. As they say, it's better to have loved and lost than never have loved at all.

Onwards and upwards, as you used to say.

Love you. Miss you.

Your Za-Za xoxo

"Stevie, stay." I use my firm, *I am in control, so don't go getting any ideas* voice and hold my hand up in the gesture Dog Diva Denise taught me and Stevie watches me closely. I step tentatively back, my hand still held up in the air.

"Will she move?" Kennedy asks out of the corner of her mouth as I reach her side. "This photographer is super expensive, so we really need to get the shots."

"She's actually pretty well behaved these days. That crazy dog lady at puppy school sure sorted her out."

Thinking of puppy school brings Asher front and centre in my mind, and I quickly push thoughts of him away. Instead, I concentrate on the photoshoot. Looking at Stevie, I beam with pride. She's being such a good girl, lying on the faux fur blanket at the end of the king-sized bed that utterly dwarfs her diminutive size, her ears pricked as she gazes back at me.

"Oh, she's doing such a great job," Kennedy declares.

"I cannot thank you enough for this." I turn to face her. "It's hard to believe that only a short time ago Scarlett left and I thought my business would go under, and now I'm going to be featured in *Claudette*. If someone had told me all of this back then, I would not have believed them."

Kennedy grins at me. "Zara Huntington-Ross, owner of Za-Za Interior Design."

"It's got a certain ring to it. Doesn't it?"

"Totally. Who calls you 'Za-Za?' We all call you 'Zee.'"

"My dad."

In a kind of way, I've taken a leaf out of Emma, my sister-in-law's book. She named her activewear business after her dad, Timothy. I'm not about to call my business "Sebastian" because not only is it my dad's name, but it's my brother's name, too, and he's had more than enough attention thanks to the reality TV shows he starred in, *Dating Mr. Darcy* and *Saving Pemberley*.

No. This business is about me and me alone. So, I'm changing the name to Za-Za. Sure, it sounds a little like ScarZar, but it comes from such a different place.

It comes from love.

"Well, I think it's perfect and you know what? Scarlett

is going to be as neon green with envy as a highlighter pen when she sees this article and all these gorgeous shots."

"Thank goodness I signed the paperwork to take her out of the business yesterday."

"That girl moves fast."

"You say that like it's a bad thing," I reply with a laugh. "Asher was right. Being rid of Scarlett is the best thing to happen to me. I can start afresh, and really make a go of my new solo business. All I can say is I could kiss that client of yours who cancelled their feature in your next issue. Without them, we would not be doing this today."

"It's all worked out, and this is going to do incredible things for Za-Za."

Hope surges through me. "I hope you're right."

"I *know* I'm right."

The photographer—a French guy called Pierre who is actually wearing a black beret on a jaunty angle, feeding into every stereotype I have about not only artists but French artists at that—snaps frame after frame of Stevie and the bedroom, and I beam with pride. Stevie looks so adorably cute in the bedroom I redecorated for a client back in winter, who kindly agreed to allow us to photograph it today. If I do say so myself.

This is the penultimate stop on a full day of photographic sessions, and Stevie has been a total champion right throughout.

That puppy deserves a big, juicy bone.

First, we photographed a kitchen-slash-diner in Knightsbridge that I redesigned in the Hamptons style last year, then a country style living room with French doors that open up to a pretty garden in Maida Vale, and now this shabby chic bedroom. The final stop today is Asher's flat to take shots of a contemporary, masculine space.

I know, I know. Totally dumb move. And really, if Kennedy hadn't pleaded with me and promised to set it up with Asher herself, there's no way I would have agreed to it. But she insisted pictures of his living room would round out the magazine spread, and when she told me that Asher was out of town—probably on a romantic minibreak with Kristen in Paris, but I don't want to think about that in case it's true—I was sold on the idea.

And besides, it gives me the chance to deliver the surfboard display shelves I had made for him without having to see him in person.

Arriving at his building an hour or so later, I'm feeling a little less like it was a good idea. I do my best not to look at the spot on the footpath where he'd told me to leave on that fateful night. The spot where our blossoming love was stabbed brutally through the heart. Instead, I paste on a smile as I tuck Stevie under my arm and direct the delivery men to take the shelving unit up the stairs to his flat.

"You've got this, babe," Kennedy says as we enter the building together.

"You're positive Asher's not here?"

"I wouldn't put you through this if he were. I know how much you love him, and I know how hurt you were by it all. Let's get up there, get the shots, and then leave. Deal?"

"Deal." I bite down on my lip as I take each step with an increasingly heavy heart. When I reach Asher's floor, I pause and take a breath before I step into his flat. When I do so, I'm instantly hit by memories. Although he's only lived here for a short time, there are a few. Watching the baseball game together, wandering through the flat as we worked through design ideas, measuring up the wardrobe and finding the photograph that day.

My emotions swirl.

This is hard.

"Where d'you want this?" one of the delivery men asks me as they stand holding the shelving unit at the door.

"See the surfboards over against that wall? Over there, please."

"Right you are."

They place the unit against the wall and remove the protective plastic, I thank them as they leave. As Kennedy, Pierre, and his assistant fuss over the living room space, I put Stevie down on the floor, her lead around my wrist, and run my hand over the beautiful hand-crafted wood. It's beautifully crafted, with simple, stylised waves, evocative of the beach he so loves. Asher will absolutely love this unit, and it will display his surfboards perfectly.

When I ordered it for him, we were the best of friends, and I wanted to do something personal for him as part of his flat redesign. It was meant to be a kind of thank you for giving me his business when I needed it the most. Now that I stand here looking at it, our friendship on hold, our fledgling love story on the rocks, remorse rumbles through me.

If only I'd told him I'd found the photograph.

If only his ex-wife hadn't turned up.

If only...

I blow out a puff of air. I want nothing more than to go to him, to tell him I love him and that I'm sorry for not being up front with him about finding that photograph. I want him to open up and tell me about his marriage and what happened, to really share it with me and offer me the chance to be there for him, to listen, to support him.

And why not? Why can't I do all these things? We were friends before we became lovers. The best of friends. Our friendship counts for so much.

It's time I pulled up my big girl panties.

I need to see him.

I slip my phone out of my back pocket and bring up his name in my contacts. Before I have the chance to chicken out, I press the "call" button and lift the phone to my ear. My heart thrashes in my chest as I wait for him to reply.

The call goes straight to voicemail.

As I listen to his smooth, deep, familiar American voice telling me to leave a message, I close my eyes and steel myself to speak. The beep sounds and I don't hesitate.

"Hi. It's me," I begin, my voice trembling. "I-I want to see you. Can we meet somewhere? I want to talk to you about all this. It all feels so wrong and...and I miss you, Asher. I really, really miss you." I let out a ragged breath before I add, "So...call me. Please."

I end the call and stare out of his window at the slow moving clouds above the rows of chimneys.

What will he do when he gets the message? He said he loves me but he has history with Kristen. Deep history. Can our love compete with that?

A voice punctuates my thoughts. "Hey, Zee. Can you come over here and help?"

I snap myself out of my reverie to see Kennedy looking at me.

"Sure." I lead Stevie over to the sofa where I spot Asher's brown Padres cap with the intertwined "S D" lettering placed on the coffee table. He must have been watching a game last night. I pick it up and run my fingers over the rim. It was the moment after that game we watched together when I knew for certain that I had feelings for him.

That I wanted so much more from him than just friendship.

That I loved him.

"I want to keep zat," Pierre says, eyeing the cap in my hands. "It will go wis zee masculine bachelor vibe, no?"

"No, err, I mean, yes. Let's keep it. I'll find a spot for it." I place it over on the sofa and Stevie jumps up and instantly begins to sniff it. My heart gives a sad little squeeze. I pat her and say under my breath, "You miss him, too. Don't you?"

Stevie doesn't reply, mainly because she's a dog, but also because she's still intent on sniffing that cap, breathing in every last morsel of Asher.

"Yeah, you do," I mumble.

"Hey, Zee? Do you want these surfboards put in the rack?" Kennedy asks.

"I'll help."

"Don't worry. We've got it. Right, Dwayne?"

Dwayne is Pierre's assistant, and in his perfectly tailored purple suit and highly shined patent leather shoes he looks like he'd rather do anything other than pick up a surfboard.

"Zara's stronger than me. Ask her. I'll take the puppy." Pierre whisks Stevie's lead from my wrist and sits down next to her on the sofa.

"Thanks a lot, Dwayne," Kennedy mutters, throwing him a look.

"What? I've just had a mani. Carlos would kill me if I chipped a nail," Dwayne explains.

"That would obviously be a disaster," Kennedy quips, but her sarcastic tone is lost on him.

"I know, right?" is his reply.

Kennedy rolls her eyes at me. "Aren't assistants meant to assist?"

"Clearly surfboards are outside of his job description," I tell her.

Together, we tilt the boards on their sides and slot each one into the shelving unit. Standing back to get a full view, we agree it looks perfect in a very Southern California, beachy way.

"His heart will melt when he sees this," Kennedy says. "You know that. Don't you?"

"I think his heart is otherwise occupied these days."

"You don't know that."

"I guess not."

She rubs my arm. "I'm so sorry you're going through this."

"That makes two of us."

"Love sucks."

I blow out a breath of air. "It sure does."

Pierre calls us over to the living room, and I set about preparing the rest of the room to be photographed. Once again, Stevie does an amazing job lying where she's told and looking adorable, and before long we've got the shot.

"Zat is a wrap!" Pierre announces with a flourish, and just like that, we're packing up and readying to leave.

That's when I hear a key in the lock.

With my heart in my mouth, I turn to see the door pushed open, expecting to see Asher standing in the doorway—and wishing I could escape through a window.

Instead, a woman in a dark green, slim-fitting pants suit and horn-rimmed glasses walks into the flat. She's accompanied by a man in a navy suit, and they smile at me as they walk inside. They're followed by more people, all similarly dressed in conservative, well-cut suits, and they begin to wander around the flat, looking at the furniture and the paintings, pointing things out to one another, and talking quietly.

"What's going on?" I ask Kennedy.

"I have no idea," she replies in such a way that suggests to me that she actually does have an idea.

I arch my eyebrows. "Kennedy?"

"Look, you seemed so heartbroken, Zee, and I know how much you love him."

"What did you do," I ask, aghast.

She screws up her face.

"Kennedy?"

"I called him and told him you were here. You seem so heartbroken, Zee, and I know he loves you, even if his ex has turned up and thrown a wife-sized banner in the works."

"You called *Asher*?" I breathe, my heart thudding so loudly in my ears I can barely hear my own voice.

"Don't hate me."

"But-but you said he was out of town."

"I meant he wasn't in the Notting Hill part of town."

"Town is not Notting Hill. Town is London. *All* of London."

She flicks her wrist. "Details," she replies before her face creases into a smile. "I think he might be about to turn up to see you."

"You do?" I breathe.

"But who these people are and what they're doing here, I have no idea. Shall I go ask?"

I open my mouth to reply, but she's already wandered over to the woman in the green pants suit and begun talking with her.

And that's when I see him.

Asher.

My belly does all kinds of crazy flips as I watch him scan the room. My desire to flee mounts. I eye the window. We're too far up.

I shouldn't be here.

I need to leave.

I glance back at him.

Too late, his eyes land on mine, and a surge of electricity makes my limbs tremble.

The living room now has at least twenty people crowded into it, and I stand rooted to the spot as he makes his way through the assembled group towards me.

Is he going to tell me to leave once more? Is he angry?

I shouldn't be here.

He comes to a stop and I try not to notice how good he looks. In his navy suit and crisp, white open-neck shirt, his dark, intense brown eyes bore into me. "Hey," he murmurs.

"H-hi." I try to swallow down the lump in my throat. Fail.

"I hope you don't mind me turning up here after your shoot."

"It's your flat so, you know."

"It's good to see you. I...I brought some people with me."

I crack a small smile. "Just a few of your closest friends?"

"Colleagues and clients, actually. I thought they might like to see the work of London's most exciting up-and-coming interior designer."

"You brought them here to see me?" I ask in wonderment.

"Well, you and your work. I figured the new ScarZar, or whatever you're calling it now—and I hope the name cuts your former business partner right out—could do with some new clients. All of the people in this room are looking for an interior designer."

Utterly stupefied, I scan the crowd. "All of them?" I croak, my voice irritatingly breathless.

"All of them," he confirms, and as I flick my eyes back to him he's smiling, his features soft and loving. "Asher, I don't know what to say."

"Why don't you go talk to them about what you do. I'm gonna go make myself useful."

"Okay." I pause before I add, "Thank you for doing this for me. I...I don't know whether I deserve it."

"Just go talk to them, 'kay? We can talk later."

I nod at him, my mind sprinting from A to Z and everything that lies between. Does this mean he's forgiven me for not mentioning I knew about his wife? Does it mean we're back to being friends?

Could it even mean he wants something more from me?

But then I remember Kristen, and come crashing back to Earth with a sickening *thud*.

He shoots me his Asher grin that leaves me weak at the knees, before he turns on his heel and begins laying things out on the kitchen bench: wine glasses, cheeses, some packets of crisps.

I blink at him. He's catering to these people now? He *planned* this?

"Excuse me, miss? Are you Zara?"

Reluctantly, I tear my eyes from Asher and turn to see a balding middle-aged man with bushy eyebrows and a pleasant, open face. He's holding Stevie in his arms. "Yes, I am. I see you've met my dog."

"She is just as sweet as Asher said she would be," he says as Stevie does what she always does: tries to lick his earlobes.

I blink at him. Asher told this man abut Stevie?

"Can I talk to you about my flat?" he asks. "I've got no idea how to decorate it and I want to make it feel like home now that my divorce has finally come through. I need a fresh start, you know?"

My lips curve into a smile as warmth spreads down my limbs. "Sure, I can help you with that. Can you tell me more about it?"

I spend the next hour and a half talking with prospective clients as Stevie bounces around the place, basking in people's attention. My eyes keep finding Asher, and he spends his time offering people snacks and topping up their wine glasses, and the feeling in the room is one of positivity, congeniality, and possibility.

By the time the last person leaves, Kennedy, Asher, Stevie and I collapse in the much-admired living room, exhausted.

"Asher, you are a genius bringing all those people here straight after the shoot," Kennedy declares. "How many new clients did you get, Zee?"

"I've got twelve appointments in the next two weeks, plus that guy Sanjay is coming into the shop at midday tomorrow to check out some upholstery to recover his living room suite. Apparently, he wants to redo one of his 'wings.'"

"Sanjay is seriously loaded," Asher explains. "Super rich investment banker."

"The kind of client you want, babe," Kennedy tells me. "I say we raise our glasses to a totally successful day. A photoshoot for next month's magazine, and a bunch of new clients for Za-Za."

"Za-Za?" Asher questions.

"That's the new name for my business. I've cut the Scarlett element."

He smiles at me. "Good for you. Why Za-Za?"

"It's what my dad used to call me."

His eyes lock onto mine. "I love that."

I smile shyly at him. "Yeah. Me too."

"Actually, you know what? I'm gonna let you two chill together." Kennedy rises to her feet.

"It's fine," I protest.

"No, no. I just remembered I've got a thing I need to get to. It's super important." She shoots me an encouraging look before she breezes out of the room. A moment later, she reappears briefly and tells us, "Bye, you two," and then disappears out of the flat all within about twelve seconds.

Asher and I are left alone in his living room, Stevie snoring lightly on the mat on the floor.

"So," I begin, not quite sure what to say.

"So," he echoes.

We fall into an awkward silence before he says, "I love the surfboard rack. Did you have it custom made?"

From my spot on the sofa, I look over at it against the wall. In the soft evening light it's positively glowing. "I did. It's got waves on it to remind you of the beach back home."

"Where?" he asks as he rises to his feet and strides over to it. "I haven't had a chance to look closely at it yet."

I follow him. "There," I say, pointing at the pattern. "I had the guy carve them in, but I came up with the design."

He turns to me. "It's awesome."

"I'm glad you like it."

"Like it? I love it."

I see the intensity lying behind his eyes. In a rush of gratitude, I blurt out, "You did so much for me today and I'm so grateful to you. Thank you. I know things have been weird between us lately, and I totally owe you a huge apology for not having come clean about knowing you were married. It was so dumb of me and I'm so, so sorry. I really hope you can—"

He stops my words with his warm, soft mouth pressed

against mine, and my eyes ping open in surprise. He's kissing me? He's kissing me! It takes me a moment to fully realise what's happening, but when I do, I kiss him right back, looping my hands behind his waist as he pulls me closer to him with his strong, muscular arms. As our kiss deepens, my head spins with love, excitement—and confusion. It's a potent cocktail, and one that has us locked together for a dizzyingly long time.

Eventually, we pull apart and catch our breath.

I'm the first to speak. "Does this mean...?"

"It means I love you, Zee. With all my heart, I love you."

A delicious heat radiates through my chest. He loves me. Asher loves me! I'm ecstatic. Ecstatic and still confused. "But what about Kristen? She wanted you back, didn't she? Are you two...?"

"What? No! That was never in the cards."

"But you sent me away so the two of you could be alone." I try to keep the hurt from my voice.

"I sent you away because I was hurt, and I needed to find out what she was doing here. I didn't know she was planning on turning up, and I certainly didn't invite her. We're over, Zee. Done. She wanted a different outcome, but I told her no."

"She wanted you back."

"It was never gonna happen. Not with her. She's ancient history to me. I've been over her for a long time now, and finally, she's signed our divorce papers."

"You're divorced now?"

"Yup. It's official."

"Congratulations?" I say and he lets out a soft laugh.

"It was a long time coming, and I'm happy to have drawn a final line under it. And there's something else," he says as he gives me a squeeze, "I've fallen in love with this girl, and I'm totally crazy about her."

"You are?"

"Oh, yeah."

Cartwheels, jumping for joy, punching the air. I'm doing it all right now in my head. This feels *amazing*!

"I love you," I murmur as I bunch his shirt in my fist and pull him to me for another kiss.

Some time, and a whole lot of totally hot snogging on his new bachelor pad sofa later, I contentedly drape my legs across his lap, our fingers laced together. Stevie is still sleeping soundly on the floor, exhausted from all the attention earlier.

"I owe you an apology, Zee," Asher begins. "I kept what happened with Kristen to myself, when I should have told you about it a long time ago."

"I get it. You were hurt. You needed time."

"At first, I did. You're right. But being here in a new city meant I had time to process things, and I realised I was better off without her. When she left me for my friend Dylan I was hurt badly, so I packed up and left San Diego."

"That must have been terrible for you."

"Your best friend sneaking around behind your back with your wife? Yeah," he replies with a chortle. "But you know what, Zee? In the end, I realised she'd done us both a favour. We weren't right for each other, no matter how hard I'd tried to make it work."

"How long were you married?'

"Not even a year. She was my college sweetheart. At the time, a bunch of our friends were getting hitched. It made sense for us to do it, too. It was a mistake."

"And then you came here to London."

He gives my hand a squeeze. "The best decision I ever made."

"Is that so?"

"Definitely. I got to start fresh without the daily reminders of what had happened. No one here knew anything about my life in San Diego. Plus, I met this incredibly gorgeous girl who wormed her way into my heart."

"Really? What was her name?" I tease.

"Caroline. Or was it Carolyn?" he replies with a cheeky grin, winning a bat on his arm from me.

"You're hilarious, hubby."

"You know it. *Wifey.*" He loads the last word with layers of meaning as his eyes lock with mine, and my belly goes flip-flop.

But I'm getting ahead of myself here. Sure, I can absolutely see us married to one another someday. Perhaps with a batch of kids, a couple of dogs, and that chicken coop in tow. Who knows?

But for now, I'm content just being with Asher. I'm content exploring our love, seeing where it takes us. Together.

Epilogue

"Look at her in this shot. Isn't she the cutest?" I point at the full-page photograph, my heart melting at the look on Stevie's face. She's alert and intelligent looking, and like she's gazing out at the viewer, challenging them not to adore her.

"You do realise you've said that about every single photo of her. Don't you?" Asher asks with a grin, his arm slung around my shoulders as we sit on the emerald green sofa in my newly revamped shop, Za-Za.

I giggle as I pat a sleeping Stevie, snuggled up at my side, warm and soft. "What can I say? I'm totally right."

He kisses me good and long and replies, "We should probably get the lipstick off of our faces. Your guests will be here in less than two minutes. We can hardly have the woman of the hour with smeared makeup at the launch of her new store."

"But I love kissing you so much."

"I promise we can do a lot more of it after everyone has gone."

"I'm gonna hold you to that, hubby."

Right on cue, there's a knock at the door that grows and grows until it sounds like a pack of ogres, baying to get in.

"That'll be my quiet and unassuming friends," I say as I leap to my feet and pull the door open. "Hi, girls."

"Zee, OMG! This is *so* exciting!" Lottie says as she pulls me in for a hug and I get a lungful of her perfume.

"Look at the state of your face!" Tabitha declares as she and Kennedy peer at me.

"Far too much snogging. Clearly," Kennedy says. "Asher, you need to try your best to keep your lips off of our girl tonight."

"I'm making no promises," he replies.

Tabitha regards Kennedy in surprise. "I didn't know Americans said 'snogging.'"

"This American is a Londoner now," she replies with a grin, and then her face drops. "Although I've not exactly been doing a whole lot of snogging, myself. Or *any* snogging, for that matter."

"You'll want to fix that. Stat," Tabitha replies.

"Charlie Cavendish is coming to the launch tonight," I lead and watch for her reaction.

"Why would I care about Charlie Cavendish?" she replies.

"Because maybe you don't really hate him? Maybe what you really want to do is rip his shirt off and run your fingers over his hard abs while you kiss his face off?" Tabitha suggests with a sweet and—utterly fake—innocent smile. She knows she's winding her up.

Kennedy scoffs. "I assure you I do not. And anyway, tonight is about Zee, not about snogging Charlie Cavendish. Which I'm not going to do. *Ever.*"

All four of us nod and smile at her, Asher included.

"What?" Kennedy asks, her eyes wide. When all we do

is continue to smirk at her, she snaps, "Go get yourself cleaned up, Zara. And you, too, Asher. No one wants a boyfriend with a patchy red face at her new shop unveiling."

"Yes, ma'am," he replies as he throws me a wink and saunters towards the back of the shop.

"Babe, this place looks amazing," Lottie declares as she grips my arm.

Asher and I spent hours and hours at the weekend hanging paper cottonwool clouds from the ceiling and pasting embossed white wallpaper on boards to stand behind white chairs with pretty pale blue cushions. We'd collected driftwood and shells while on our first ever mini-break as a couple when we went to Cornwall a few weeks ago. While we were there, I got to watch Asher surf for the very first time. I even gave it a shot. Let's just say he was hot and I was definitely not. But getting to see him with his wetsuit rolled down to expose his taut, muscular body after his surf made the humiliation of falling off my board in totally flat water absolutely worth it.

And I'm still smiling.

"Looking around, I feel like I've spent the day at the beach, and now I'm relaxing in my coastal chic home as my wetsuit dries on the line outside," Lottie declares.

"You get all that from some fluffy clouds on strings?" Tabitha asks with a laugh. "Seriously, though, Zee. It does look amazing in here."

I beam at them. "Thanks, girls."

I leave my friends to chat as I head out the back to fix my makeup. Asher is nowhere to be seen, so I flick open my compact and wipe the smudged lipstick away with my fingertips before I reapply a fresh layer.

I re-enter the shop and do a last-minute check. I had the

caterer deliver a bunch of what Asher tells me are California beach snacks. I've got mini tacos, mini açai bowls, as well as corn chips with guacamole and tropical fruit cups. We're serving margaritas, beer, and kombucha to drink, and Asher's acting as the cute California barman.

The ring of the bell over the door alerts me to the arrival of guests. I turn to see my family walking in. Emma immediately greets her good friend, Kennedy with my brother, Sebastian, who throws a smile my way and mouths, "Give me two minutes." I beam back at him as Mum and Granny greet me with hugs and kisses.

"Why is everything white, Zara," Granny questions, her preferred *I've sucked a bitter lemon* look on her face.

"It's a style statement, Mummy," Mum explains. "Isn't that right, darling?"

"It's coastal chic," I reply.

"I don't care what sort of statement it's making, it needs colour and you certainly don't want those dirty bits of driftwood in here. You of all people should know that, Zara. You went to that furniture and curtain making college."

"It's called interior design school, Granny, and the driftwood is part of the scheme."

"Well I think it's terribly odd."

"Shh, Mummy. This is Zara's big moment. If she wants dirty bits of driftwood in here, then we need to let her," my mum says.

Asher appears at my side and takes my hand in his, saving me from having to defend my design again. "Good evening, ladies. You're both looking wonderful," he says, and Mum immediately giggles like a teenage girl. Even Granny cracks a smile.

Such is my boyfriend's effect on women.

My boyfriend. Wow, I love saying that.

"We needed to get a little dressed up for our darling Zara. It's not every day your daughter launches a new business." She places her hand on my forearm and adds, "I love that you called it Za-Za, sweetie. Your dad would have been so very proud to see what you've made of yourself."

"He wouldn't have liked dirty bits of driftwood," Granny sniffs.

"Mummy," Mum warns.

"Your mother is right, Zara. Your father would be proud of you," Granny confirms, her chin raised as she fights back the emotion the mention of my dad inevitably ensues in her.

"Wasn't that article in Kennedy's magazine amazing?" Asher says. "Zara's booked out until about the year 2035 right now. Aren't you, wifey?"

Both my mother's and my granny's eyebrows lift to the ceiling at his nickname for me.

I take a mental note to get him to cease and desist on the "wifey" front when we're with my family. The last thing I want is for them to go planning a wedding right now.

I sneak a look at Asher. Well, not the *last* thing...

"Do you have a lot of bookings, Zara?" Mum questions.

"Not quite to 2035, but I am booked up," I reply with a laugh.

Truth be told, I've got too many clients to manage these days. Asher's ploy to invite his work colleagues and clients to his flat that day began to pay off almost immediately, and six weeks later when the feature in *Claudette* came out, I became inundated with enquiries. So much so I could really do with employing another designer.

But I'm enjoying being a solo operator too much for that just yet.

"That awful Scarlett must be spitting tacks at your

success," Granny says with a wicked smile that lights up her face. "Good riddance to her, I say."

"She can spit all she likes. She'll never have the success our Zara has because she's too focused on herself," Mum says, and I have to agree with her. Scarlett was very upset when she found out about the magazine article, even going so far as to pay me a visit at the shop and exclaim that she wanted to come back and I needed to change the name back to ScarZar and wouldn't it be just lovely if we could put all that silly business behind us now and get back to being friends?

My reply was a sweet thank you but no thank you. I've learnt my lesson with Scarlett. She turned red and stormed out of the place, back to her junior designer's job at Karina where apparently she has to dust the shelves every day and re-plump cushions after customers have sat on them.

I'm not sure it's exactly the career move she was looking for when she abandoned ScarZar, but as the saying goes, you make your bed and you must lie in it—which is especially relevant for a decorator.

Asher brushes a kiss against my cheek. "I'll go serve some drinks to people, shall I?"

"I'll be right over to help."

He gives my hand a squeeze. "Stay and talk. Enjoy your moment. You deserve this." He shoots Mum and Granny another smile before he excuses himself.

Mum leans closer to me. "I like this one, darling."

I glance over at Asher. He's pouring out some drinks from a margarita pitcher. Tabitha is laughing at something he's said, and his broad grin renders his face achingly handsome. "I like him, too."

"Why did he call you 'wifey,'" Granny asks. "Give me your left hand."

"We're not engaged, if that's what you're thinking," I reply.

Mum beams at me. "But you might be, darling. Someday soon."

"We're not going to have another American in the family, are we?" Granny grumps.

"Granny, we've only just started dating. It's early days yet."

"But you told us he was your back stop boy."

I giggle and it ends in a snort. "Back-up guy, Granny. A back stop is the chain link fence behind home plate in baseball."

Asher's love of baseball is clearly rubbing off on me if I know *that* level of detail about the game.

"It's all Dutch to me, darling. Just get on with it. If you love him, marry him," she says. "You do love him, don't you?"

A grin claims my face as a delicious warmth spreads through me. "I do, Granny."

Mum claps her hands together in glee. "You can get married and then make me a grandchild."

I give a surprised laugh and my eyes find Asher once more. Although it's only been seven weeks and six days since our very first date that ended in such disaster, I know Asher's the man I want to spend my life with. We may be taking it slow right now, learning about one another, exploring this new relationship of ours, but my heart has already well and truly made its mind up. And as the saying goes, the heart wants what the heart wants.

And my heart wants Asher.

People have begun to arrive, and the place is filling up. I circulate, saying hello and chatting to clients and family and friends alike. Even though the shop is small, we've managed to jam in a decent number of people, all of them wishing me well, all of them happy to be here for me and to support my new venture.

I spot Victoria and her goth daughter, Chloe, by the window display and go over to greet them. "I'm so pleased you made it. How do you like your newly decorated flat, Chloe?"

Chloe gives me a disinterested shrug. "S'okay."

Victoria rolls her eyes. "She loves it, Zara. You did a marvellous job." She leans in towards me and says quietly, "And I love that gorgeous lamp you gave me as an apology."

"It was the least I could do after what happened with Stevie."

"Well, I certainly appreciated the gesture. Tell me, are you available to have a look at my house? My dining room could do with some updating and the pool room is a disaster."

"Of course. I'm pretty busy right now, but as a valued customer, I'll do my best to fit you in."

"Marvellous."

I feel a hand tapping my arm and turn to see an elderly woman grinning up at me.

"Muscles Mavis! I'm so glad you came." I lean down to give her a quick hug. Mavis has got into the habit of stopping by the shop every Tuesday lunchtime to say hello. I think she's hoping I might decide to follow someone and enlist her services again. So far I've not needed to do so, but she is ever hopeful. And I like having her around.

"Thank you so much for inviting me," she says. She glances around the room. "Which one's your fella, then?"

"I'll be sure to introduce you. He's dying to meet you."

"Is he now? Well, as long as he treats you right, he's all right by me."

I beam at her. "You're wonderful, Mavis. You being here means a lot to me. Thank you for coming."

She waves her hand in the air. "Oh, don't you go getting all emotional and whatnot on me now."

I laugh. "It's a big day for me."

"That it is. Enjoy it."

"Hello, my young sister all grown up."

I turn to see Sebastian, his wife Emma, and their adorable toddler Darcy grinning at me.

"I'm so glad you came," I say as I hug them all and bop Darcy on the nose. She giggles before she buries her head in her mum's shoulder.

"We wouldn't miss it for the world. The shop looks so beautiful," Emma says. "We think you're nothing short of amazing the way you've picked yourself up and landed square on your feet. You sure have got some snap in your garters, girl."

I giggle. "Some what in my what?"

"Oh, it's an old Texas saying meaning you're totally capable. I like to keep my home state lingo going now that I live here."

"Emma's right about your garters, even if it's a very strange expression to me," Sebastian says with a chuckle. "I always thought you would do great things, and here you are, showing us that you really are quite something."

I beam at the compliment. Sebastian and I have always had a close relationship, particularly after our dad passed away, but he's never been one to see me as anything but his younger sister. He'd always tease me about being a tearaway or a party girl, saying I never took anything too seriously, always looking for a good time.

He was right. But not anymore. Sure, I still have fun,

but I've matured. I've grown up. And I've found my purpose in life.

"I always figured you thought I was an eternal kid who was only interested in having fun," I quip in good humour.

"Oh, I thought that, too," he replies, and we both laugh.

I put my hand on my little niece's back. "Darcy? Do you want to see Stevie? I know she's dying to see you."

"Puppy?" she questions as her attention snaps back to me, her big brown eyes wide as saucers.

"Yes, puppy. She's out the back in her pen because there are so many people here tonight, but I know she would love some pats from her special friend."

"Me wanna see puppy," she tells her mum.

"Well, in that case, we'd better go see her," Emma replies.

I lead Emma and Darcy to the back room where Stevie bounces around in excitement that someone is finally paying her attention.

"Gentle hands when you pet her, honey," Emma instructs as she watches Darcy with Stevie inside her pen. She straightens up and says to me, "I love the new name, Zara. You're honouring your dad, and I think that's so special."

My chest expands. "I guess that's something we've got in common."

She wraps her arm around my shoulder and gives me a squeeze. "It sure is."

"Here you are." Asher arrives at the entry, his bulk filling the room. "You've got a speech to give."

"My speech. Right." I ask Darcy, "Is it okay with you if I pick Stevie up?"

"Stevie puppy," she replies, and I take it as a yes.

With Stevie cradled in my arms, we make our way back

into the shop where Asher tinkles a spoon against a wine glass for me to get everyone's attention. With all eyes on me, I begin the speech I've rehearsed in front of Asher—and the mirror—a bunch of times in the last couple of weeks.

"Stevie and I say welcome to our little coastal chic world," I begin, holding Stevie up for everyone to see. "It is so great to have you all here, and I cannot tell you how deeply touched I am by your love and support of me and my new solo venture. When my business partner decided to move to other pastures, I was left with a choice: close up shop quite literally, or fight on. Stevie and I decided to fight on. At least that's what I thought she meant by racing wildly around the shop as I balanced the books."

People burst into laughter and applause, and I hear Asher whooping as Kennedy calls out, "You go, girl!"

"Why coastal chic? Well, I met a guy just over two years ago, and we became the best of friends. Although he's a partner in a top London law firm these days, at heart he's a California surfer guy, a bit of beach bum, really. This space is my gift to him, to remind him of home, but to make sure he stays right here with me in olde London town." I find Asher in the crowd and we share a smile.

"I'm not going anywhere," he replies, and there's a ripple of laughter and applause that rolls around the room.

I take a deep breath and look down at Stevie before I launch into the next part of my speech. She gazes back up at me as though she knows I'm about to tear up. "You know, there's someone missing tonight. Someone important to me. Someone who believed in me. I wish with all my heart he could have been here tonight because—" my voice cracks, and I press my lips together to try to stem any errant tears that might decide to break free. I try again with, "He," only for my voice to waver. Something catches my attention out of the corner of my eye, and I glance over and see Asher, watching me with soft eyes.

"You got this," he mouths.

Bolstered, I flash him my smile and have another try. "Anyone who knows me knows I'm a total daddy's girl. It's true." I shrug with a watery smile. "But hey, I've made my peace with it. Tonight, at the launch of Za-Za, the nickname my dad always used for me, I hope he's proud of me. Proud of the woman I've become, just as I am always proud to call him my dad." I take a deep breath and my lips curve into a smile. "I'm now the sole proprietor of Za-Za Interior Design, and I am so excited about where this new chapter of my life is about to take me. Oh, and Stevie, too. We can't forget her." I grin at Stevie and she bangs her tail against me.

There's a 'whoop' from my group of friends, and I shoot them a quick smile.

I raise my eyes to the little paper clouds hanging from the ceiling. "Dad, I wish you could be here tonight. I love you and I miss you. This one's for you." Even though I feared it would happen, tears roll down my cheeks and I wipe them quickly away as everyone applauds and Mum rushes over to me and gives me a tight hug, squashing Stevie between us.

"Well said, darling," she breathes into my ear. "Your dad would have been so very proud of you."

"Thanks, Mum."

The party continues for some time, and then, when most people have left, just Asher, Kennedy, Lottie, Tabitha, and Stevie—who's passed out on my lap after all the excitement—remain. We sit on the floor together, eating the leftovers, sipping our drinks, and talking. I'm leaning up against

Asher, feeling the reassuring warmth of his strong, firm body behind me.

"Look at you," Lottie says to me with a grin. "You're the sole proprietor of Za-Za, a shop that's already a huge success story. And what's more, you've got your own love story, too."

I smile up at Asher. "Yeah, life isn't too shabby right now."

"Babe, you make shabby look chic," Tabitha says.

Kennedy questions, "Is that a pun?"

"A very good one, I think," she replies.

"Well, I for one am super happy for you two," Kennedy says. "Now, if you could only weave your magic and sort our lives out, that'd be awesome."

"No problem. We can do that, right?" I ask Asher.

"What do you want, girls? Profitable businesses, good friends, or a hot guy like me?" He waggles his eyebrows playfully.

I shove him in the arm. "You can't call yourself a hot guy. That's for us to decide."

"She's right," Tabitha agrees. "Only we girls can decide who's hot and who's not."

"Totally," Kennedy and Lottie agree.

"But yeah, I definitely want all of that," Kennedy says with a wistful look in her eyes. "Although I've got the good friends already. You guys are the best and you've made my move to London so easy."

"I'm glad Emma gave you to us," I reply. "I guess there's only so much time you can spend watching her and my brother get all lovey-dovey with one another." I shiver at the thought. "They do way too much of that."

Tabitha arches an eyebrow. "And you two don't?"

I giggle as Asher plants a kiss on the top of my head.

"You're just gonna have to get used to this, sorry. Love

will do that." Asher says and I beam at him. My boyfriend. My love.

"I've gotta go," Kennedy says as she hops up to her feet. "Gorgeous evening and well done, Zee."

"I should go, too," Lottie says, and she shoots Tabitha a look.

"Oh, yes. Me, too," she agrees.

We all rise to our feet and say goodbye with hugs and I love yous, as though we're not going to see one another for a year.

With the shop empty but for me and Asher, we begin the clean up. As I collect empty glasses from the table, I feel a pair of hands circle my waist. I turn around to see Asher smiling down at me. He plants a kiss on my cheek and says, "Do you know how proud I am of you?"

"Very?" I chance with a grin.

His laugh is low and sexy and it rolls right through me. "I got you something to commemorate the occasion." He reaches inside his jacket pocket and pulls out a black box the size of his hand, tied up with a hot pink ribbon. "Open it."

I pull the ribbon off and open up the box. I gaze at what's inside, my heart doing all sorts of squeezes. "Asher, it's gorgeous," I gush. Carefully, I pull the glass perfume bottle out of its velvet bed and inspect it. Like the one he gave me for my birthday all those months ago, this bottle is beautiful. It's striped with black, the silver stopper ornate and delicate. "Is this...?" I ask, thinking of my Pinterest board and the exact same antique Murano glass perfume bottle I've been coveting for so long.

"It is."

"But how? It must have cost a fortune."

He shrugs, his eyes dancing. "You're worth it. Plus, you

wouldn't let me invest in this place, so I had to do *something* with my money."

I beam at him, my heart full to the brim with love and contentedness.

We started out as the best of friends, and here we find ourselves as lovers. Falling in love with your best friend, your client, and your back-up guy may not be the wisest thing to do, but for us it's the perfect ending to the perfect story.

And I wouldn't have had it any other way.

Dear Dad,

Things have worked out pretty well for your little girl. I've got a successful business, a great group of friends, and I'm in love with the most wonderful man.

So please don't worry about me, Dad. I'm in good hands.

Miss you. Love you.

Yours always,

Za-Za xoxo

THE END

Acknowledgments

This book has been so much fun to write. I loved Zara as a character in the *Love Manor* books, and I always planned to write her story, right from the moment she popped out from behind a tree in *Dating Mr. Darcy*. She's strong and knows herself, and I hope I stayed true to her character in this book.

I always say there's a little part of me in each and every character I write, and Zara is no exception. Like Zara, I didn't take life too seriously in my 20's, I found turning 30 quite tricky, and I didn't fall for the man who would become my husband until I hit the big 3-0, too. Also like Zara, I lost my much-loved dad too young. Although I didn't write to him like she does, I still miss him every day and often find myself thinking how much he would love that I became a writer.

Not only that, I realised when reading through this story that I'd inadvertently put my dog, Dizzy, in this book. Although she's not a Jack Russell, she's so like Stevie! From the ear licking (and nibbling) to the perpetually happy mood, to the deep connection she and Zara share, she's my darling Dizz through and through.

I have the best readers! They email me, review my work, chat to me on social media. They tell me what they love about my books, end even when they've spotted a typo that's somehow managed to make its way through the editing process. Thank you all, you're the best. I hope I keep writing books you can continue to enjoy.

As always, I have my critique partner to thank for helping me make this book what it is. Thank you, Jackie Rutherford for all your kindness, support, and notes. After a lot of books, we've become quite a team, you and I, and I so value our friendship and working relationship.

Thanks also to Kim McCann and Julie Crengle for your proof reading skills.

My family is always so supportive of me, even if I can get a little obsessed with all things books. So thank you, my husband and son, for putting up with me, giving me ideas, and always being there for me.

About the Author

Kate O'Keeffe is a *USA TODAY* bestselling and award-winning author who writes exactly what she loves to read: laugh-out-loud romantic comedies with swoon-worthy heroes and gorgeous feel-good happily ever afters. She lives and loves in beautiful Hawke's Bay, New Zealand with her family and two scruffy but loveable dogs.

When she's not penning her latest story, Kate can be found hiking up hills (slowly), traveling to different countries around the globe, and eating chocolate. A lot of it.

Made in the USA
Middletown, DE
18 December 2022